Praying for
Your Second Chance

Prayers
from Numbers
and Deuteronomy

BOOKS BY ELMER TOWNS

Knowing God Through Fasting

Praying the Psalms

Praying the Proverbs, Song of Solomon, and Ecclesiastes

Praying the Book of Job

Praying the Book of Revelation

Praying the Gospels

Praying the Book of Acts and the General Epistles

Praying Paul's Letters

Praying the New Testament

Praying Genesis

Praying Your Way Out of Bondage:
Prayers From Exodus and Leviticus

Praying for Your Second Chance:
Prayers From Numbers and Deuteronomy

AVAILABLE FROM DESTINY IMAGE PUBLISHERS
www.destinyimage.com

PRAYING FOR
YOUR SECOND CHANCE

PRAYERS
FROM NUMBERS
AND DEUTERONOMY

Book Eleven in *Praying the Scriptures* Series

Elmer L. Towns

DESTINY IMAGE® PUBLISHERS, INC.
P.O. Box 310, Shippensburg, PA 17257-0310

"Speaking to the Purposes of God for This Generation and for the Generations to Come."

This book and all other Destiny Image, Revival Press, Mercy Place, Fresh Bread, Destiny Image Fiction, and Treasure House books are available at Christian bookstores and distributors worldwide.

For a U.S. bookstore nearest you, call **1-800-722-6774.**

For more information on foreign distributors, call **717-532-3040.**

Or reach us on the Internet: **www.destinyimage.com.**

ISBN 10: 0-7684-2760-6

ISBN 13: 978-0-7684-2760-8

For Worldwide Distribution, Printed in the U.S.A.

1 2 3 4 5 6 7 8 9 10 11 / 13 12 11 10 09

CONTENTS

PRAYERS FROM NUMBERS

Preface

The Story of Writing the Book of Numbers

Date: 1490 B.C. ~ Place: Foot of Sinai

A wet overcast covered the Sinai desert; everything was muddy-slick. Everyone stayed in their tents, only those who had duties went outside. Yet the rain didn't pour, it was a misty atmosphere rain.

The flap to Moses' tent was propped up and Moses sat under it dry and protected. He was feverously writing at his table.

"Are you writing another book?" his brother Aaron asked as he came in out of the rain.

"I have to," Moses told his brother, "God is urging me to write." Moses wrote their goings out according to their journeys by the commandment of the Lord (see Num. 33:2).

Moses said, "I've been keeping track of the days we've been here at the foot of Sinai." Moses kept track of the months by the lunation of the moon. Moses, like all people of that day, counted time by observing a new moon.

Aaron, the older brother of Moses, answered, "It seems we've been here forever, the people are ready to travel to the Promised Land."

Moses laughed; he knew time moves slowly for impatient people, and the people of Israel had waited all their lives to go home to the Promised Land. But not that much time had elapsed. It was only a year and two weeks since they had left Egypt. The people had been camping at the foot of Sinai for 10½ months.

Moses told Aaron, "It's only been a month since we set up the Tabernacle for the people to worship God." Moses knew if the people depended on word of mouth, the story of the Exodus and journey to the Promised Land would not be very accurate. People's feelings would temper the truth—that's why he kept an accurate record.

In the last 30 days Moses had written the Book of Leviticus; a book containing the words of God. God was doing many things among His people, and Moses was making a record. God was speaking audibly, and Moses was writing down accurately what God was saying for future generations. Accurate worship and obedience of future generations depended on Moses' accurate record.

The original title of the book was "In the Wilderness," the first words of the book (see Num. 1:1). Later the Greek name *Numbers* was used in the Latin Vulgate, and was adopted by English versions as well. Numbers gets its name from the fact that the children of Israel were numbered (a census) at the beginning and the end of the book (see Num. 1:3-54 and 26:1-63).

The people were numbered to indicate who was truly an Israelite. (The mixed multitude was not included.) The early church numbered its people to determine who was really a follower of Jesus Christ (Acts 2:41,47; 4:4; 5:14; 6:1,7). Today are you numbered among those who truly follow the Lord?

The Book of Numbers picks up the narrative story that ended in Exodus. In First Corinthians Paul describes the wilderness wanderings and says, "Now these things became our examples" (see 1 Cor. 10:6 NKJV). The word *example* is *tupos*, a type that is a divine foreshadow of things to come. The failure of rebellious Israelites to enter the Promised Land could be a picture of the faithless organized church of today failing to possess the heavenly things promised by Christ.

When Paul describes "The goodness and severity of God" (Rom. 11:22), he summarizes the theme of Numbers. God is severe by allowing all the nation, 20 years of age and older, to die in the desert because of their rebellion and unbelief. God is good because He takes the children under 20 years of age and under into the Promised Land.

As you pray your way through the Book of Numbers, determine you will not make the mistake that Israel made. My prayer is that Numbers will motivate you to follow God with all your heart.

Also in this volume you will find *Praying for Your Second Chance: Prayers from Numbers and Deuteronomy.* When all the adults, age 20 or over, refused to enter the Promised Land, God punished them. They all died and were buried in the sand. But those who were 20 years and younger were given a second chance. God gave them the opportunity to enter the land of Canaan. Technically, the Book of Deuteronomy is a series of sermons preached to the next generation. When they had a second chance to enter the Promised Land, Moses preached to get them spiritually ready to cross Jordan.

Did you know that our Lord is the God of the second chance? He will forgive every sin (1 John 1:7) and give us another opportunity to obey Him. Have you ever messed things up? Have you ever disappointed the Lord? If so, God will give you a second chance to serve Him. Maybe not in the same way, or at the same place, and maybe He will not use you as greatly as He might have the first time. The issue is not the second opportunity that you will have; the issue is God. Have you re-attached yourself to His purpose for your life? If you've gotten off the path, go back to the place where you left God's path. Repent. Confess your sin (see 1 John 1:9). God can use you again, *pray for your second chance.*

Elmer Towns
Written from my home
at the foot of the Blue Ridge Mountains

Numbers 1

THE ISRAELITES ARE COUNTED

The Lord spoke to Moses in the Tabernacle in the desert of Sinai on the
first day of the second month, in the second year after they left
the land of Egypt.

"Count the entire group of the people of Israel. List the name of each
man with his clan and with his family group. You and Aaron
must count all males who are 20 years old or older. They will
serve in the army of Israel. List them by their divisions."

Lord, thank You for speaking audibly to Moses
To reveal the truth of the Book of Numbers.

Today, You do not speak audibly to Your children
To tell them what they should know or how to live.

Lord, I will read and study Your words in the Scriptures,
Because that's how You speak to me today.

Everything I need to know to live a holy life
Is contained in the pages of Scripture.
I will search for Your plan for my life in the Bible.

Amen.

"One man from each tribe is to be the chief of his family group. He will
be organized with you as a counselor. These are the names of
the men who will help stand with you:

From the tribe of Reuben—Elizur, the son of Sheduer;

From the tribe of Simeon—Shelumiel, the son of Zurishaddai;

From the tribe of Judah—Nahshon, the son of Amminadab;

From the tribe of Issachar—Nethanel, the son of Zuar;

From the tribe of Zebulun—Eliab, the son of Helon;

From the sons of Joseph:

From the half-tribe of Ephraim—Elishama, the son of Ammihud;

From the half-tribe of Manasseh—Gamaliel, the son of Pedahzur;

From the tribe of Benjamin—Abidan, the son of Gideoni;

From the tribe of Dan—Ahiezer, the son of Ammishaddai;

From the tribe of Asher—Pagiel, the son of Ocran;

From the tribe of Gad—Eliasaph, the son of Deuel;

From the tribe of Naphtali—Ahira, the son of Enan."

All these men were summoned from the community to be rulers or administrators of the tribes of their forefathers. They were chiefs of the clans of Israel. Moses and Aaron set aside these men who had been hand-picked. Then Moses and Aaron gathered the whole community together. This was on the first day of the second month. The people registered themselves (literally according to the births) with their clans and with their family groups. All the men who were 20 years old or older were listed by name. Moses did exactly what the Lord commanded. Moses listed or counted the people while they were in the desert of Sinai.

The tribe of Reuben was counted first. Reuben was the first son who was born to Israel. All males 20 years old or older who were able to serve in the army were listed. They were each listed by name with their clans and with their family groups. The tribe of Reuben totaled 46,500 men.

The tribe of Simeon was counted. They listed all the males 20 years old or older who were able to serve in the army. Each of them were listed by name with their clans and with their family groups. The tribe of Simeon totaled 59,300 men.

The tribe of Gad was counted. They listed all the males 20 years old or older who were able to serve in the army. Each of them were listed by name with their clans and with their family groups. The tribe of Gad totaled 45,650 men.

The tribe of Judah was counted. They listed all the males 20 years old or older who were able to serve in the army. Each of them were listed by name with their clans and with their family groups. The tribe of Judah totaled 74,600 men.

The tribe of Issachar was counted. They listed all the males 20 years old or older who were able to serve in the army. Each of them were listed by name with their clans and with their family groups. The tribe of Issachar totaled 54,400 men.

The tribe of Zebulun was counted. They listed all the males 20 years old or older who were able to serve in the army. Each of them were listed by name with their clans and with their family groups. The tribe of Zebulun totaled 57,400 men.

The half-tribe of Ephraim was counted. (Ephraim was a son of Joseph.) They listed all the males 20 years old or older who were able to serve in the army. Each of them were listed by name with their clans and with their family groups. The half-tribe of Ephraim totaled 40,500 men.

The half-tribe of Manasseh was counted. They listed all the males 20 years old or older who were able to serve in the army. Each of them were listed by name with their clans and with their family groups. The half-tribe of Manasseh totaled 32,200 men.

The tribe of Benjamin was counted. They listed all the males 20 years old or older who were able to serve in the army. Each of them were listed by name with their clans and with their family groups. The tribe of Benjamin totaled 35,400 men.

The tribe of Dan was counted. They listed all the males 20 years old or older who were able to serve in the army. Each of them were listed by name with their clans and with their family groups. The tribe of Dan totaled 62,700 men.

The tribe of Asher was counted. They listed all the males 20 years old or older who were able to serve in the army. Each of them were listed by name with their clans and with their family groups. The tribe of Asher totaled 41,500 men.

The tribe of Naphtali was counted. They listed all the males 20 years old or older who were able to serve in the army. Each of them were listed by name with their clans and with their family groups. The tribe of Naphtali totaled 53,400 men.

Moses, Aaron, and the 12 rulers of Israel counted all these men. There was one chief from each of the family groups. Every Israelite 20 years or older who was able to serve in the Israelite army was counted. Each man was listed with his family group. The total number of all the men counted was 603,550 (it is estimated that the entire nation of Israel, including all the women and children, was about 3 million people).

The ancestral tribe of Levi was not listed with the others. (They had a registry of their own, which was separate. The first census reported 22,270; and the second census gave 23,000. However, they counted all the males from 1 month old and up.)

The Lord had told Moses: "Do *not* count the tribe of Levi or include them in the census with the other Israelites. Instead, appoint the Levites over the Holy Tent of the Covenant. They must take care of it and everything that goes with it. They must carry the Holy Tent and everything with it wherever it goes. They must take care of it and make their camp around it. Any time the Holy Tent is moved, the Levites must take it down. Any time it is set up, the Levites must do it. If anyone else goes near the Holy Tent, then that person will be put to death!"

Lord, those who serve You in ministry must be peaceful,
Not men of vengeance, war, and shedding blood.

Lord, those who serve You must try to "save" others, not kill them.
They must keep their hearts pure to worship You.

Lord, help me keep my heart pure from anger or retaliation
As I live in a world of lawlessness, crime, and murder.

Lord, help me give myself to worship as did the Levites,
May I serve You in purity of conscience.

Amen.

"The Israelites will make their camps (pitch their tents) in separate divisions, each man near his family flag. But the Levites must make their camp around the Holy Tent of the Covenant. Then I will not punish the Israelite people. And the Levites must guard the Holy Tent of the Covenant. They are in charge of it."

So, the Israelites did everything exactly as the Lord commanded Moses.

Numbers 1

THE STORY OF MOSES DISCOVERING THE JOY OF WRITTEN WORDS

Date: 1490 B.C. ~ Place: Foot of Sinai

Moses sat in his tent at his desk, his feet propped up with hands behind his head, he was thinking about the books he was writing. The people wanted to get on their journey to the Promised Land, but they had to wait while he wrote.

"Moses writes a book that no one will read," one man said.

Several told Moses that he was wasting his time, "Who will read his books?" They explained he was the only one who could read and write.

"I will teach all the Levites to read" was Moses' simple answer. He explained that there would be priests who would be teaching—priests who would instruct the people in the law of God. "They must read and know the Book of God before they can live it."

Moses knew one day the Levitical family would be divided into priests who sing the Psalms, priests who teach the people, priests who copy the Law (the Massuretics), and the ministry priests who sacrifice for the people. Then in an afterthought, Moses thought of those priests who would do the janitorial work of cleaning the temple and the armed priests who would guard and police the tent of God.

Moses' eyes were shut, but he wasn't sleeping—he was thinking about the future of reading. He dreamed of a day when all Israel would be able to read his books—or better, they could read God's actual words. He saw in his mind Rabbis teaching young boys to read the Hebrew language he was perfecting.

Back in Mesopotamia people used sticks to make impressions on clay, he thought how crude and imperfect their writing. When the clay hardened, all they had was a picture of a man plowing with animals in a field. Moses realized how imperfect pictures were to communicate. "How old was the man?" and "What type of animals did he use?" and "What was he planting?" "What was he thinking?"

Moses realized that his Hebrew words on leather could describe the seeds, the kinds of animals, and the age of the man. His words could tell a reader what the man was thinking. His words could communicate if the farmer was happy, and if it was his field, or if the man was a disgruntled slave planting for his hated master. "Words communicate life, while pictures only command attention," Moses smiled to himself.

Moses was writing words that could be decoded by the brain of the reader; these words were images that represented sounds and a combination of sounds represented a meaning. When a reader saw the words of Moses written on leather, they could instantly recall pronunciation and the meaning of that word.

Even before Moses finished writing one of his books, he enjoyed re-reading what he wrote. His favorite recollection was the story of creation in the Book of Genesis. When he re-read how God created the world, Moses blocked out the presence of other people around him. Like daydreaming or thinking about past events, Moses entered into a hypnotic-like state because the story on the scroll captured him. Reading was almost like sitting alone in a cave and reliving creation.

"I've stumbled onto an incredible discovery that could change the world." This scroll had power; words sprang off the page, and living people walked in front of his eyes. The words were the dynamic of the moment, for they captivated Moses' thoughts; and best of all, words forced Moses to think on God.

Moses walked to the door of his tent to see hundreds of people walking to do a task, or buying and selling, or preparing meals, or just talking.

Closing his eyes, Moses imagined every one of them reading the words of God. He thought, "When everyone reads God's words, it will be like living in Heaven."

Sometimes Moses re-read his scrolls to discover some new truth about God, truth he had not seen when originally writing God's words. Sometimes his heart jumped for joy when he learned new things about God. Moses wanted the people to share the same discovery process that he experienced from reading God's Word. He thought, "If every Israelite could read and enjoy God's Word, they could be a nation of priests who would not sin. They would enjoy worshiping God and serving Him."

The more Moses thought about the bookishness of books, the wordiness of words, and readishness of reading, the more he realized he was examining the relationship between a believer and God. As a child of God got lost reading in the world of books, the more he was describing a person's connection to God.

When the reader's mind melts into the story he's reading, he becomes asynchronous with the author, the two becoming one in experience. Moses, the author, and the reader would become one—the reader blocking out everything else so the "cave" effect can happen any time reader and book came together.

Moses walked back into his tent to gaze at the three long, silver, tube-like containers of Genesis, Exodus, and Leviticus. He absentmindedly tapped on the hard silver with his fingernails and said, "These books will change the world because they will transform individuals. It's not these books that will change people; it's the message of these books. When they read these books, they will experience the life of God and God will change the world through transformed individuals."

Moses re-read the beginning of Exodus and revisited his confrontation with Pharaoh and the ten plagues on Egypt. He was glad that he kept an accurate recall, for he had already forgotten some details. Again Moses vicariously identified with the victory of the Exodus and even greater, the victory over demon-inspired religions of Egypt. Then Moses thought, "If I am encouraged with God's past victories, think how future generations will be encouraged when they read these stories."

Moses walked across the tent to where he slept. The rug was there and a pillow for his head. He was tired. After all, Moses was 82 years old and he needed some rest in the middle of the day. So he lay on the pallet and propped his head on a gigantic fluffy pillow. Moses unrolled the scroll of Exodus, read a few sentences, and was asleep.

Moses snored loudly so the people in the next tent knew he was sleeping. What they didn't know was Moses had the Book of Exodus stretched across his stomach. Thus, Moses began an age-long tradition of going to sleep when reading a book.

My Time to Pray

Lord, thank You for those who taught me to read,
And thank You for teachers who taught me to write.
I read and write with such ease,
I forget how hard it was for Moses to learn both.

Lord, thank You for inspiring Moses and all the others
Who wrote the Old and New Testament Books of Scripture.

Without them I wouldn't know the contents of Christianity,
Nor would I know how to serve and worship You.

Lord, ideas and words come from Your eternal mind,
You know and understand all things in Heaven and earth.

Lord, Jesus, You are the Word who was in the beginning,
You teach us to read and communicate words, because You are the Word,

Thank You for my Bible, because without it

I wouldn't have accurate understanding of who You are,
And what You did in the ages past.

Amen.

Numbers 2

THE ARRANGEMENT OF THE TRIBES

The Lord said to Moses and Aaron: "The Israelites should make their camps around the Meeting Tent. But they should not camp too close to it (probably no closer than a quarter mile, 2,000 cubits [see Joshua 3:4]). Each person should camp under the flag or banner of his family group. The camp of Judah will be on the east side, where the sun rises. They will camp by three divisions there under their flag. The ruler of Judah is Nahshon, the son of Amminadab." There was a total of 74,600 men in Judah's division.

Next is the tribe of Zebulun. The ruler of Zebulun is Eliab, the son of Helon. There was a total of 57,400 men in Zebulun's division.

There was a grand total of 186,400 men in the section of Judah (including Issachar and Zebulun). They will be in their three divisions. They will be the first group to march into battle.

The three sections of the camp of Reuben will be south of the Holy Tent. They will camp under their flag. The ruler of the people of Reuben is Elizur, the son of Shedeur. There was a total of 46,500 men in Reuben's division.

The tribe of Simeon will camp next to them. The ruler of the people of Simeon is Shelumiel, the son of Zurishaddai. There was a total of 59,300 men in Simeon's division.

Next is the tribe of Gad. The ruler of the people of Gad is Eliasaph, the son of Reuel. There was a total of 45,650 men in Gad's division.

There was a grand total of 151,450 men in the section of Reuben (including Simeon and Gad). They will be in their three divisions. They will be the second section to march into battle.

When the Levites move the Meeting Tent, they will be in the center of the camps. Each person will be with his division flag. The 12 tribes will move out in the same order as they camp.

The three divisions of the camp of Ephraim will be on the west side. They will camp under their flag. The ruler of the people of Ephraim is Elishama, the son of Ammihud. There was a total of 40,500 men in Ephraim's division.

The tribe of Manasseh will camp next to them. The ruler of the people of Manasseh is Gamaliel, the son of Pedahzur. There was a total of 32,200 men in Manasseh's division.

The tribe of Benjamin will camp next to them. The ruler of the people of Benjamin is Abidan, the son of Gideoni. There was a total of 35,400 men in Benjamin's division.

There was a grand total of 108,100 men in the section of Ephraim (including Ephraim and Manasseh). They will be in their three divisions. They will be the third section to march into battle.

The three divisions of the camp of Dan will be on the north side. They will camp under their flag. The ruler of the people of Dan is Ahiezer, the son of Ammishaddai. There was a total of 62,700 men in Dan's division.

The tribe of Asher will camp next to them. The ruler of the people of Asher is Pagiel, the son of Ocran. There was a total of 41,500 men in Asher's division.

The tribe of Naphtali will camp next to them. The ruler of the people of Naphtali is Ahira, the son of Enan. There was a total of 53,400 men in Naphtali's division.

There was a grand total of 157,600 men in the section of Dan (including Asher and Naphtali). They will be the last to march into battle.

The four camps will all travel under their own flags. These are the
Israelites who were counted by family groups. The total number
of Israelites in the camps, counted by divisions, was 603,550 (if
all the men of the fighting force of Israel were standing in close
ranks, it would occupy 12 square miles).

Moses did not count the Levites among the other people of Israel. This
is what the Lord had commanded. So, the Israelites obeyed
everything that the Lord commanded Moses. They camped
under their flags. Each person traveled with his clan and family
group.

*Lord, I know You do all things decently and in order (see 1 Cor.
14:40).*
*There were approximately 3 million people in the wilder-
ness.*

Your common sense demanded them to travel and live in order.

Lord, it would take 100 square miles for them to camp
So You guided them where to camp around the Tabernacle.

You provided them daily manna to eat; the harvest
Must have been overwhelming.

So I now understand how You feed all Your children
Worldwide spiritually every day.

Lord, it took 12 million gallons of water each day to satisfy
Their daily needs. Now, I understand
How you satisfy the thirst of Your children worldwide.

PRAYING FOR YOUR SECOND CHANCE

Lord, the counting of the children of Israel reminds me
That You do not overlook one of Your children.

Amen.

Numbers 3

THE SONS OF AARON

At the time when the Lord spoke to Moses on Mount Sinai, this was the family history of Aaron and Moses: These are the names of Aaron's four sons: Nadab (the firstborn), Abihu, Eleazar, and Ithamar. Those were the names of Aaron's sons. Moses anointed them to serve as priests. But Nadab and Abihu died when they sinned in the presence of the Lord; when they made an offering in the presence of the Lord in the desert of Sinai, but they used unauthorized fire. Neither Nadab nor Abihu had any sons. So, Eleazar and Ithamar served as priests during the lifetime of their father, Aaron.

The Duties of the Levites

The Lord said to Moses: "Bring the tribe of Levi to Aaron the high priest, and anoint them in his presence so that they may help him. They will help Aaron perform his duties and support the obligations of the whole nation of Israel at the Tabernacle. They will do the work of the Holy Tent. The Levites must take care of everything connected with the Tabernacle. They must serve the people of Israel by doing the work of God in the Holy Tent. Those serving the Levites will help Aaron and his sons (these were teaching-Levites, copying-Levites [scribes], janitor-Levites, police-Levites, etc.) Ordain Aaron and his sons to serve as priests. Anyone else who comes near the holy things must be put to death!"

The Lord also said to Moses: "Listen, I am choosing the Levites from among all the Israelites. The Levites will take the place of each of the firstborn Israelites that opened the womb. (Firstborn sons were considered to be the favored ones. The firstborn sons received a double portion of the inheritance [see Deut. 21:17], the father's blessing [see Gen. 27], and special treatment [see Gen. 43:33].) The Levites will be Mine.

"Each firstborn child is Mine. When you were in Egypt, I killed all the firstborn Egyptian children in the land of Egypt. I set apart for Myself every firstborn of Israel to be Mine, including animals and human beings. They all belong to Me! I am the Lord."

Lord, You want Your children to have a good memory,
   Because You want us to remember what You did in the past.

Lord, I remember when You saved me, thank You.
   I remember many things You've done for me.
   Thank You for all the lessons You've taught me.

Lord, You punished Nadab and Abihu for forgetting Your instruction,
   May I never forget Your commandments,
   Both positive and negative.

Lord, it was a great miracle that delivered Israel
   From Egypt, through the Red Sea.
   I will remember Exodus, just as You wanted Israel to remember it.

Amen.

The Levites Are Counted

Again, the Lord spoke to Moses in the desert of Sinai: "Count the
Levites by family groups and by clans. Count every male 1
month old or older." So, Moses obeyed the Lord's command and
counted them all.

These are the sons of Levi: Their names were Gershon, Kohath, and
Merari. The names of the Gershonite clans were: Libni and
Shimei. The Kohathite clans were: Amram, Izehar, Hebron, and
Uzziel. The Merarite clans were: Mahli and Mushi. These were
the clans that belonged to the Levites, by their family groups.

The clans of Libni and Shimei belonged to Gershon. These were the
clans of the Gershonites. They had a total of 7,500 males (1
month or older). The clans of the Gershonites camped on the
west side, behind the Holy Tent. The ruler of the Gershonite
family groups was Eliasaph, the son of Lael. In the Meeting Tent,
the Gershonites were responsible for taking care of these things:
the Holy Tent, its covering, the curtain at the entrance to the
Tabernacle, the curtains in the courtyard, the curtain at the entry
to the courtyard around the Holy Tent and the altar, and the
ropes. They must do all the work connected with these things to
take down the Tabernacle and set it up.

The clans of Amram, Izehar, Hebron, and Uzziel were all the Kohathite
clans. They had a total of 8,600 males (1 month or older). They
were responsible for taking care of the sanctuary. The Kohathite
clans camped south of the Holy Tent. The family-group ruler of
the Kohathite clans was Elizaphan, the son of Uzziel. They were
responsible for the Ark of the Covenant, the Table of Show
Bread, the Lampstand, the Brazen Altar, the utensils of the sanctuary which the priests used, the veil that separated the Holy of
Holies, and all the work connected with taking down and setting up the Tabernacle.

The main ruler of the Levites was Eleazar, the son of Aaron, the high priest. Eleazar supervised all those Levites who were responsible for the sanctuary.

The clans of Mahli and Mushi belonged to Merari. They were the Merarite clans. They had a total of 6,200 males (1 month or older). The family-group ruler of the Merari clans was Zuriel, the son of Abihail. They camped on the north side of the Tabernacle. The Merarites were responsible for the covering and frame of the Holy Tent, the braces, the posts, the bases and all of its equipment, to do all of the work connected with setting up and taking down these things. They were also responsible for the posts in the courtyard which surrounded the Holy Tent and their bases, their tent pegs, and their ropes.

Moses, Aaron, and Aaron's sons camped on the east side of the Tabernacle. They were located in front of the Meeting Tent, where the sun rises. They were responsible for the sanctuary. They did this on behalf of the Israelites. Anyone else who came near the sanctuary was to be put to death! Moses and Aaron counted all the Levite men by their clans, as the Lord commanded. There was a total of 22,000 males 1 month or older. (Note: This number was rounded.)

Lord, just as the Tabernacle was in the center of the camp,
And Your presence was in the Tabernacle,

So I want Your presence in the center of my life;
May others see You living in me.

Lord, You choose to live in the center of all believers,
When they rebelled, You withdrew Your presence.

So Lord, I worship You and yield to Your will,
Come live in the center of my life.

Lord, at the end You will occupy the center of Heaven.
"Behold, in the midst of the throne...and in
The midst of the elders, stood a lamb" (Rev. 5:6).

Amen.

The Lord said to Moses, "Count all the firstborn Israelite males (1 month old or older), writing their names on the list. Take the Levites for Me instead of all the firstborn sons of Israel. Take the animals of the Levites instead of the firstborn animals from the sons of Israel. I am the Lord."

So Moses did as the Lord commanded. The count of all the firstborn sons of the Israelites was 22,273. The Lord also said to Moses: "Take the Levites instead of all the firstborn sons of the Israelites, and dedicate them to Me. And take the animals of the Levites instead of the animals of the other Israelites and dedicate them to Me. And, these were redeemed. So collect two ounces (literally, "5 shekels") of silver for each of the sons. Give the money ("silver") to Aaron and his sons as a payment for the Israelites who were redeemed."

So Moses collected the redemption money from those who were redeemed by the Levites. Moses collected 35 pounds of silver, using the standard set by the sanctuary. Thus Moses obeyed the command of the Lord, giving the redemption money to Aaron and his sons.

Numbers 4

THE DUTIES OF KOHATH'S SONS

The Lord spoke to Moses and Aaron: "Count the Kohathites among the Levites. Count them by clans and by family groups. Count the men from 30 to 50 years old. (A priest began ministry at age 30, but age 25 was set here, probably because they had an apprenticeship of five years to learn exactly what to do.) They will all ministers in the Tabernacle. They are responsible for the holy things in the Meeting Tent. When the Israelites move, Aaron and his sons must go into the Holy Tent and take down the inner veil which separates the Holy Place from the Most Holy Place (see Exod. 36:35). Then they must cover the Ark of the Covenant with it. They must cover this covering with the outer covering protecting the Tabernacle. Then they must spread the solid blue cloth over that. And they must insert the poles for carrying."

Lord, You had a reason to command a man to begin serving
    In the Tabernacle when he was 30 years old

Just as You waited for Jesus to be 30 years old
    Before He began His life ministry.

Lord, You want people to serve You in wisdom
    You want them to learn from childhood and adolescence
    The important lessons that come from experience.

Lord, You have said, "Not a novice," (1 Tim. 3:6),
    Lest he be lifted up with pride.

41

Because You don't want selfishness in ministry.
    You also want a minister who knows what to do.

Lord, may I grow in spiritual maturity as did Christ,
    So I can serve You effectively.

Amen.

"Then they must spread a blue cloth over the Table of Show Bread. They must put the dishes, the spoons, the bowls, and the jars for drink offerings on the table. They must always leave the bread on the table. Then they must put a red yarn cloth over all of these things. They must cover everything with a covering of leather. Then they must insert the poles in place.

"They must cover the Lampstand (Menorah) that gives light, covering its bowls, its wick-trimmers, and trays with a blue cloth. They must cover all the containers for the olive oil used in the lamps. Then they must wrap everything inside a covering of leather. They must put all these things on a frame for carrying them.

"They must spread a blue cloth over the Altar of Incense. Then they must cover it with a covering of leather. They must insert its poles in place.

"They must gather everything used for serving in the sanctuary. They must wrap everything in a blue cloth, and cover them with a leather covering. They must carry these things on a frame.

"They must remove the ashes from the Brazen Altar, then spread a purple cloth over it. Then they must gather all the things used for serving—the fire pans, the meat hooks, the shovels, and the pans; putting all these on the Brazen Altar. Then, they must spread a covering of leather over it. Then they must insert the carrying poles in the rings on the altar. (The sacred fire was to be kept burning, even during a complex move.) When the camp is ready to move—after Aaron and his sons have finished covering the sanctuary and all the holy things—then the Kohathites may go in and carry away everything. But they are not to touch any holy things, otherwise, they will die! It is the job of the Kohathites to carry the furniture and their instruments that are in the Tabernacle.

"Eleazar, the son of Aaron, the high priest will be responsible for the Holy Tent, being responsible for everything in it: the olive oil for the lamp, the sweet-smelling incense, the continual food offering, and the olive oil used to anoint priests—everything in the sanctuary and its containers."

The Lord spoke to Moses and Aaron: "Don't let the clan group of the Kohathites be destroyed from among the Levites. Do this for the Kohathites. Then they may go near the Holy of Holies and not die! Aaron and his sons must go in and tell each Kohathite man what to do and what to carry. The Kohathites must not enter the Holy of Holies and look at the holy things—even for a moment. (These Levites were not to witness the dismantling of the sanctuary.) If they do, then they will die!"

The Duties of Gershon's Sons

And the Lord spoke to Moses: "Count the Gershonites by their clans and by their family groups. Count the men from 30 to 50 years old. Everyone has a job to do in the Tabernacle. This is what the Gershonite clans must do and what they must carry—the pieces of cloth of the Tabernacle. They must also carry its covering and the covering made from leather on top of it. And they must carry the curtains for the entrance to the Tabernacle. (These items were heavy; two wagons pulled by oxen were required to move them.

The Merarites were charged with moving even heavier things—the whole framework of the Tabernacle [see Num. 4:31-33]. They were given four wagons and the oxen needed to pull them [see Num. 7:7].) They must carry the curtains that go around the courtyard. They must carry the curtain for the entry point, or gate, to the courtyard, along with the ropes and all the equipment used with the curtains. Aaron and his sons will supervise what the sons of the Gershonites do and what they carry. Ithamar, the son of Aaron, the high priest will direct their work."

The Duties of Merari's Sons

"Count the sons of Merari by their clans and by their family groups, from 30 to 50 years old. Everyone has a job to do at the Tabernacle. Their job is to carry the frame of the Holy Tent, its cross-bars, its posts, and its bases. They must also carry the posts that go around the courtyard, their bases, their tent pegs, and their ropes. They must carry everything that is used with the poles around the courtyard. Tell each man exactly what to carry. Ithamar, the son of Aaron, the high priest will direct their work."

The Sons of the Kohathites Are Counted

Moses, Aaron, and the administrators of the community counted the sons of the Kohathites by their clans and by their family groups—from 30 to 50 years old—everyone had a job to do for the work at the Tabernacle. The clans had a total of 2,750 men. Moses and Aaron counted them, just as the Lord had commanded through Moses.

Also, the Gershonites were counted by their clans and by their family groups—from 30 to 50 years old—everyone was given a job to do for the work at the Tabernacle. There were 2,630 men. Moses and Aaron counted them, just as the Lord had commanded.

Also, the men in the clans and the family groups of the Merarites were counted—from 30 to 50 years old—everyone was given a job to do for the work at the Tabernacle. The clans had a total of 3,200 men. Moses and Aaron counted them, just as the Lord had commended.

Moses, Aaron, and the administrators of Israel counted all the Levites by their clans and by their family groups—from 30 to 50 years old—everyone was given a job to do for the work at the Tabernacle; also they carried it from place to place. The total number of these men was 8,580. Each man was counted, just as the Lord had commanded through Moses. Each man was told his work, and what to carry. This occurred just as the Lord had commanded through Moses.

Numbers 5

KEEP THE CAMP PURE

And the Lord spoke to Moses: "Command the Israelites to send away anyone with leprosy. Send away anyone who emits body fluid. And send away anyone who has touched a corpse. Send them away from the camp whether they are men or women so they do not contaminate the camps. I am living among you." So, the Israelites obeyed and sent those people outside the camp, just as the Lord had told Moses.

Lord, a new believer must learn Your requirements,
As soon as he or she begins following You.

Followers must be pure inwardly and outwardly.
So You make them separate themselves
From all sin and filthiness of daily life.

Lord, You make Your followers separate themselves
To protect them from physical contamination
And inward filthy attitudes and actions.

Just as You commanded Israel to separate unclean people,
Today all Your followers must separate themselves
From all influence that will harm them.

Amen.

Restore to Others for Wrongdoings

The Lord spoke to Moses: "Tell the Israelites: when a man or woman
does something wrong to another person or is committing a sin
against Me, that one is guilty. He must confess his sin. And he
must fully pay for the wrong he has done. Then he must add 20
percent to his sacrifice, and give it to the person he wronged.
However, if the victim is dead, and does not have any close relatives to receive the payment, then the one who sinned owes Me.
That person must pay the priest, and the priest must sacrifice a
male sheep to clear him of any guilt. And every offering which
they bring to the priest, will belong to the priest. No one is
forced to give these holy gifts. However, if someone does give
them, they belong to the priest."

How to Treat an Unfaithful Wife

Then the Lord told Moses to speak to the Israelites, "If a man's wife
might be unfaithful to him, and she might have had sex with
another man, however her sin has been kept hidden from the
eyes of her husband (perhaps no one saw it, and she was not
caught in the act), yet her husband has strong suspicions
whether she did sin or not, the husband should then take his
wife to the priest, along with an offering for her. This offering
should be two quarts of barley flour. He must not pour olive oil
or incense on it, because this is a food offering for jealousy. It is
to find out if she is guilty. The priest will bring in the woman
and make her stand in the presence of the Lord. He will take
some holy water in a clay jar. Then he will put some dirt from
the floor of the Holy Tent into the water. The priest will make
the woman stand in My presence. Then he will loosen her hair
(uncovering her head was a sign of her being deprived of the
protection of her husband). Then he will hand her the food

offering for jealousy. And he will hold the bitter water that could bring a curse upon her. Then the priest will give an oath. He will ask, 'Has another man had sex with you? Have you been unfaithful to your husband?' If you have not done this, then this bitter water will *not* hurt you. But, if you *were* unfaithful to your husband, and you *did* have sex with another man who is not your husband, then, the priest will cause her to take the oath that will bring a curse upon her. He will say to the woman, 'If you are guilty, the Lord will bring a curse upon you among the people. Your belly will swell up, and you will not be able to have a baby! This water will bring the curse, and you won't be able to have a baby!' The woman must say, 'I completely agree' ('So be it!' literally, 'Amen! Amen!' that is, she states she is totally innocent). The priest should write these curses on a scroll (or, it could have been upon a wooden tablet). Then he should wash off the ink of the words into the bitter water. Then he will make the woman drink the bitter water that could bring the curse. When she does, it might make her sick. Then the priest will take the food offering for jealousy from the woman's hand. And he will present it in My presence. Then he will bring it to the altar. Then the priest will take a handful of the food offering, and he will burn it on the altar as incense. After that, he will make the woman drink the water. He will make her drink it to discover whether she is pure sexually or not. He will know if she has sinned against her husband. When the bitter water goes into her, it *will* cause a curse. And her belly will swell up. And she will not be able to have a baby. The woman will become accursed among her people. But, if the woman did *not* sin, and she is sexually pure, then she is innocent. She *will* be able to have a baby."

Lord, You demand that both man and woman be pure,
    You want them to be faithful to their spouses.

If anyone sins sexually, they don't need a priest,
> *They stand before Jesus Christ who is our High Priest.*

Today no test determines if any have sinned.
> *Jesus, You know the truth of all actions and all intentions*
> *of all people.*

Forgive any who have given into the temptation,
> *Whether they sin with their mind or their bodies*
> *Cleanse us and accept us back into fellowship.*

Lord, help us to live sexually pure.
> *Give us strength against temptation*
> *So we can live wholesome lives to glorify You.*

Amen.

Numbers 6

THE VOW OF A NAZIRITE

And the Lord told Moses: "Speak to the Israelites: If a man or woman wants to make a special vow to Me, this person becomes a Nazirite." (A Nazirite took sacred vows to Yahweh which were usually temporary, self-imposed discipline such as abstaining from wine, not cutting their hair, or not touching a dead body and/or unclean food. The word *Nazirite* comes from the root *Nazar* which means "to vow," a person who makes a special vow to God. Christ was not a Nazirite, but He was called a Nazarene because He was from a village called Nazareth [see Matt. 2:23]. The people of Nazareth were probably very dedicated people, hence, that's why the city was called "people of the vow." These people probably were very zealous to keep the law, which was a good environment for the Son of God to grow to maturity. Some "Nazirites for life" found in the Bible were: Samson [see Judg. 13:5,7; 16:17] Samuel [see 1 Sam. 1:11], and John the Baptizer [see Luke 1:15]. The men of Acts 21:23-26 had probably taken a temporary Nazirite vow, and Paul paid their expenses.)

"During his vow, he must not drink wine or beer. He must not drink strong drink, nor even grape juice, or eat grapes or raisins. While he is a Nazirite, he must not eat *anything* that comes from the grapevine, he must not even eat the seeds or skins. (A sour drink could be made from the kernels of unripe grapes. And, cakes could be made from the husks.) During the time that he vowed to be consecrated to God, he must not cut his hair. He must be holy for God until his vow is over. He must let his hair grow long. During his special time of separation, he must not go near a corpse. Even if his own father, mother, brother, or sister dies, he must *not* touch them. This would make him 'unclean.' He must still keep his special promise to God. While he is a Nazirite, he is holy to Me."

Lord, vowing the Nazirite vow of the Old Testament
  Is similar to vowing a fast today.

It means I am making a commitment to You, Lord,
  So You will answer my prayer that I seek.

Lord, I know I cannot bargain with You, So that
  You answer a prayer because I keep my vow.
  That is good works, and we cannot bargain with You.
  You answer our prayers because of Your grace.

Lord, I fast to know You more intimately and completely,
  When I abide in You, You answer my request.

Lord, when I vow a fast, give me strength.
  May I be strong enough to discipline myself
  So I can bring glory to You and worship You.

Amen.

"If he is next to someone who dies very suddenly, his hair has been made unclean. So, after seven days, he must shave his head to be 'clean.' Then, on the eighth day, he must bring two doves or two young pigeons to the priest who will meet him at the entrance to the Tabernacle. The priest will offer one bird as a sin offering, and offer the other bird as a whole burnt offering. This will atone for sins. That same day, he will again vow to let his hair grow out for Me. He must give himself to Me for another special length of time. He must bring a male lamb that is 1 year old as a penalty offering. The days of his former vow do not count, he must begin his vow again. That is because he became 'unclean' during his first time of a vow.

"This is the teaching for the Nazirite. When the time of the first vow is completed he must go to the entrance of the Tabernacle. (When this limited vow was accomplished, he would cut his hair, and bring it to the Brazen Altar for a ceremony that releases him from his vow.) He will give his offerings to Me there. He must offer a 1-year-old male lamb as a whole burnt offering, with no physical defects. He must also offer a 1-year-old female lamb with no physical defects as a sin offering. And he must bring a male sheep with no physical defects for a peace offering. He must also bring the food offerings and drink offerings that go with them. And he must bring a basket of bread that has been made without yeast. These loaves are made with flour mixed with olive oil, and wafers made without yeast spread with olive oil. The priest will offer these things in My presence at the entrance of the Tabernacle. Then the priest must shave off the Nazirite's hair that he grew for the vow. The priest will put that hair onto the fire that is under the sacrifice of the peace offering. After the priest has shaved off the hair of the Nazarite, the priest will put a boiled shoulder from the ram into the Nazirite's hands, and from the basket the priest will also give him a loaf and a wafer, both made without yeast. Then the priest will present them in My presence as an offering. They are holy; they belong to the priest. Also he must present the breast (or, "brisket") of the wave offering as well as the thigh of the offering that is raised to me. After that ceremony, the Nazirite may drink wine. This is the teaching for the Nazirite vow. If a person makes such a promise, then he must give all of these gifts to Me. If he vowed to do more, then he must keep that vow. That is also the teaching about the Nazirite vow."

Lord, teach me how to end my fast
Or complete a promise I vow to You.

I will pray for strength to be faithful,
Knowing I can do all things through Christ who strength-
ens me.

I will be humble, knowing it was not my strength,
But it was Christ working through me.

I will glorify You for Your strength.
It is not I, but Christ who lives in me.

Amen.

The Lord spoke to Moses: "Tell Aaron and his sons how to bless the Israelites. Say to them:

'May the Lord bless you and keep you.
May the Lord cause His face to shine upon you.

May He have mercy on you.
And may the Lord watch over you and give you peace.'

So, that is the way Aaron and his sons will place My name upon the Israelites. And I will bless them."

Lord, bless me and keep me close to You,
Shine Your face into my life,
And may others see Christ in me.

Lord, have mercy upon me and be gracious to me.
Watch over me, and lift up Your face to me;
Give me Your peace as I follow You.

Amen.

Numbers 7

The Leaders Make an Offering

When Moses finished setting up the Holy Tent one month after completion of the Tabernacle, he anointed it and dedicated it, as well as all of the objects inside it, including the Brazen Altar and everything that was used in sacrifice. Then the rulers of Israel gave their voluntary offerings. These were the heads of the family groups and rulers of each tribe—the men who were in charge of counting the people. (It was about six weeks after receiving the Law until they departed from Mount Sinai.) They brought six covered wagons and 12 oxen to the presence of the Lord. Each ruler donated an ox. Each pair of the rulers donated a covered cart. They contributed these things in front of the Holy Tent. Then the Lord spoke to Moses: "Accept these gifts from the rulers. Use them in the work of the Meeting Tent. Give them to the Levites; they need them to move the Tabernacle." So, Moses accepted the carts and the oxen and gave them to the Levites. He gave two carts and four oxen to the Gershonites for their work to help move the Tabernacle. Then Moses gave four carts and eight oxen to the Merarites to help them move the Tabernacle. And he put Ithamar, the son of Aaron the high priest, in charge.

Moses did not give any oxen or carts to the Kohathites because they carried the holy things on their shoulders.

Then the rulers presented the dedication offering of the altar on the same day that it was anointed. The rulers presented their offering in front of the altar. The Lord had already told Moses, "Each day (it took an entire day to properly receive the gifts and register them—a total of 12 days) one ruler must bring his donation. The gifts will dedicate the altar (referring collectively to the Brazen Altar and the Altar of Burning Incense) to Me."

On the first day, Nahshon, the son of Amminadab, presented his gift from the tribe of Judah. He brought one silver dish that weighed about 3¼ pounds and one silver bowl that weighed about 1¾ pounds. Both the dish and the bowl were filled with flour mixed with olive oil. This was for a food offering. He also brought one golden spoon that weighed about 4 ounces, filled with incense. He also brought one young bull, one male sheep, and one male lamb that was a year old. These were for a whole burnt offering. He also brought one male goat for a sin offering. He also brought two oxen, five rams, five male goats, and five male lambs that were a year old. All of these were for the peace offering sacrifice.

On each successive day, each ruler of the remaining 11 tribes brought the same offering to God. On the second day, Nethanel, the ruler of the tribe of Issachar, brought his offering. On the third day, Eliob, the ruler of the tribe of Zebulon, brought his offering. On the fourth day, Elizur, the ruler of the tribe of Reuben, brought his offering. On the fifth day, Shelumiel, the ruler of the tribe of Simeon, brought his gift. On the sixth day, Eliasaph, the ruler of the tribe of Gad, brought his gift. On the seventh day, Elishama, the ruler of the tribe of Ephraim, brought his gift. On the eighth day, Gamaliel, the ruler of the tribe of Manasseh, brought his offering. On the ninth day, Abidan, the ruler of the tribe of Benjamin, brought his offering. On the tenth day, Ahiezer, the ruler of the tribe of Dan, brought his offering. On the eleventh day, Pagiel, the ruler of the tribe of Asher, brought his offering. On the twelfth day, Ahira, the ruler of the tribe of Naphtali, brought his offering.

Lord, the leaders brought their gifts to You in front of
All the people as an example of generosity.
May I be a generous example to all.

Also, they brought offerings of all the various sacrifices
That they should make for their sins.

Lord, I too ask You to forgive my sins
So I may be accepted in Your fellowship.

Lord, help me be a good example to all who follow me,
May they see godliness in me,
And may they want to follow You.

Amen.

So, this was the dedication offering on the day that Moses set aside the altar for its use. And the rulers of Israel brought their gifts—12 silver dishes, 12 silver bowls, and 12 golden spoons. Each silver dish weighed about 3¼ pounds. And each bowl weighed about 1¾ pounds. All the silver dishes and silver bowls totaled about 60 pounds. The 12 golden spoons which were filled with incense weighed 4 ounces each. Together, the golden spoons weighed about 3 pounds. The total numbers of animals for the whole burnt offering were: 12 bulls, 12 rams, and 12 male lambs that were a year old. There was also a food offering where 12 male goats were sacrificed as a sin offering. The total numbers of animals for the peace offering sacrifice were: 24 bulls, 60 rams, 60 male goats, and 60 male lambs, a year old apiece. These were all after Moses had anointed them.

Then Moses went into the Tabernacle to speak with the Lord. (This incident marks the beginning of a new pattern of communication between God and Moses, which was to occur again and again over the next 40 years or so. Compare Exodus 25:20-22. Moses, as the mediator, was now among the people of Israel, not up above them on the peak of a mountain, far away.) He heard the Lord speaking to him from between the two golden angels above the mercy seat which is on top of the Ark of the Covenant. And the Lord spoke to him there.

Lord, Moses went into Your presence to speak with You,
  May I be just as committed to seek Your presence,

So I can speak to You in prayer and intercession,
  And hear You speaking to me through Your Word
  And fellowshipping with You in communion and meditation.

Lord, I commit myself to daily seek Your face,
  So I can live my life according to Your plan.

  Amen.

Numbers 8

AARON LIGHTS THE LAMPS

And the Lord told Moses to tell Aaron, "Put the eight lamps where they can light the area in front of the Menorah." (There were no windows in the Tabernacle, the Lampstand was the *only* source of light inside the sanctuary.) Aaron put the lamps so that they lighted the area in front of the Menorah. (Aaron first lit the middle lamp from the Brazen Altar fire, and then he lit the other lamps from each other. Thus, all inner parts of the Tabernacle were well illuminated.) Aaron obeyed the command which the Lord gave Moses. The Menorah was made of hammered gold, from its base to its flowers. It was sculptured exactly the way that the Lord had shown to Moses.

Lord, spiritual light begins at the Brazen Altar fire where
Blood was spilt to atone for our sins.

When we sing, "There's power in the blood," we mean
There is illumination power in the atonement.

The entire inner sanctuary where You dwelt had light.
Lord, I come into Your presence to worship You,
Help me see Your work in my life.

Lord, I receive light to see how I should live when
I enter the sanctuary of Your presence.

Jesus, You are the light of the world, shining in darkness.
Shine some light in my darkness.
I need better eyes to see how to live.

Amen.

The Levites Are Cleansed

The Lord spoke to instruct Moses: "Take the Levites (this was probably *not* done on a single day in one ceremony) away from the other Israelites and make them ceremonially clean. Sprinkle cleansing water on them (undoubtedly taken from the bronze laver in the sanctuary). Have them shave their bodies and wash their clothes. Then they will make atonement for themselves. They must take a young bull and the food offering that goes with it—flour mixed with olive oil. Then take a second young bull for a sin offering. Bring the Levites to the front of the Tabernacle and gather all the Israelites (that is, a select portion of the nation, probably the representative firstborn sons). Bring the Levites into the presence of the Lord. Then the Israelites (the chiefs of the 12 tribes) should put their hands on the Levites to ordain them into ministry. Aaron will present a wave offering for the Levites in My presence. They will be like an offering presented from the Israelites to Me. Then the Levites can truly serve Me.

"The Levites will put their hands on the heads of the bulls. One bull will be a sin offering to Me, the other bull will be a whole burnt offering to Me. This will make atonement for the sins of the Levites. Cause the Levites to stand in front of Aaron and his sons. Then present the Levites as a wave offering to Me. In this way, you will set apart the Levites from the other Israelites. They will be Mine." (The Levites were exempt from military service or secular work. Instead, the Levites were completely devoted to the security of, the maintenance of, and the support of the Tabernacle.)

"So, make the Levites pure, and present them as a wave offering to Me. Then they may serve Me at the Tabernacle. The Levites will be given completely to Me from among the Israelites. I have taken them for Myself instead of taking every firstborn son of every

Israelite woman. Every firstborn male in Israel—man or animal—belongs to Me! I took the life of every firstborn in the land of Egypt. So now, I reserve the firstborn for Myself. I have chosen the Levites as gifts to Aaron and his sons to serve on behalf of all the Israelites. The ministry of the Levites will build a hedge as a protective shield. Then no disaster or plague will strike the sons of Israel when they come and worship in the sanctuary." So, Moses, Aaron, and all the Israelites obeyed God. And the Levites did exactly what the Lord had commanded to Moses.

The Levites made atonement for themselves and washed their clothes. Then Aaron presented them as a wave offering to the Lord. Aaron also made atonement for them, to prepare them for ministry.

After that, the Levites came to the Tabernacle to do their task, as directed by Aaron and his sons. They did with the Levites what the Lord had commanded Moses.

Then the Lord spoke to Moses, "Command every Levite man who is 25 years old or older to come to the Tabernacle. Each one has a ministry to do in the work of the Tabernacle.

"Each Levite must retire from his job at the age of 50, not to work anymore. He may help his fellow Levites to stand guard at the Meeting Tent. But he must *not* offer sacrifices himself. This is the way you are to supervise the Levites as they do their jobs."

Lord, everyone has a talent (1 Cor. 7:7, 1 Pet. 4:10), so
  You expect us to use our talent to serve You.
  Help me be faithful with the gifts You've given me.

Lord, all of us have an ability that You want us to use
  In our service to You.
  I will do the best I can with the talent You've given me.

Lord, give me strength and wisdom to do the best I can,
With the talents and gifts You've given me.

Amen.

Numbers 9

OBSERVE THE PASSOVER MEAL

Then the Lord spoke to Moses in the desert of Sinai in the first month of the second year after the Israelites left the land of Egypt, and said, "Tell the Israelites to celebrate the Passover holidays (see Exod. 12). It recounted their deliverance from Egypt. This festival at the base of Mount Sinai was kept on the exact day of what had occurred only 12 months before. It was the first anniversary of the Exodus. (This event occurred prior to the census of Numbers 1:1ff. The next recorded celebration of the Passover occurred in the Promised Land, at the set time each year—the fourteenth day of this month.) They should celebrate at twilight and obey all its rules and regulations." So, Moses told the Israelites to celebrate the Passover, and so they did.

However, some of the people could *not* celebrate the Passover on that day because they were ceremonially unclean because they had touched a corpse. So, they (Mishael and Elizaphan who had recently buried their cousins Nadab and Abihu) went to Moses and Aaron and said, "We are unclean because we touched a corpse! Why are we prevented from offering gifts in the presence of the Lord? Why can't we join the other Israelites?"

Moses said to them, "Wait, I will find out what the Lord says about you." Moses was able to go straight to God to receive God's revelation.

Then the Lord spoke to Moses: "Tell this to the Israelites: 'If you or your descendants might become unclean because of touching a corpse, or someone might be away on a trip during the Passover festival, you can still celebrate the Lord's Passover. However, you must celebrate it at twilight on the fourteenth day of the second month. Eat the Passover lamb with bitter herbs and bread made without yeast. Do not leave any until the next morning. Don't break any of its bones. Follow all the rules whenever you celebrate the Passover.'"

Lord, thank You for grace written in the law
For times when we physically can't keep the law.
Thank You for Your mercy and patience.

Lord, I will keep Your commandments as best I can,
Considering my ability and conditions.

Lord, forgive me when I sin, and be gracious to me
When I am unable to do the things You want done.

Amen.

"Anyone who is clean and is not away on a trip must eat the Passover. If he doesn't, he must be separated from his people. Why? Because, he did not give an offering to Me at the set time. He must carry that guilt. A resident foreigner (later, this term came to mean a proselyte; a Jewish convert) living among you may celebrate the Passover, but he must follow all the rules. (Circumcision was an indispensable condition of participating in the Passover Feast.) You must have the same rules for foreigners as you have for yourselves."

The Fiery Cloud

On the day that the Tabernacle was set up, God's cloud covered it from dusk until dawn. The cloud above the Holy Tent looked like fire. The cloud stayed above the Holy Tent (it looked like fire at night). Whenever the cloud moved from its position over the Holy Tent, the Israelites moved. Wherever the cloud stopped was where the Israelites camped. (There were no less than 42 spots that we know of where they stopped to camp during the next 40 years.)

Lord, the Shekinah cloud was Your presence with Israel,
Thank You for guiding them with Your presence.

Lord, I want Your presence in my life.
I know You live in my heart since I was saved,
May I feel Your presence for the rest of my life.

Amen.

So, the Israelites moved at the Lord's command, and they camped where He stopped. While the cloud stayed over the Holy Tent, they stayed at that place. Sometimes the cloud stayed over the Tabernacle for a long time, so the Israelites obeyed the Lord and did *not* move out. Sometimes the cloud was over the Holy Tent only a few days. Upon the Lord's command, the people camped. And at His command, they moved out. Sometimes the cloud stayed only from dusk until dawn. Whenever the cloud lifted the next morning, the people moved on. Whenever the cloud lifted, whether day or night, the people moved out.

The cloud might stay over the Holy Tent for two days, or one month, or longer. As long as it stayed put, the people would camp. But whenever the cloud lifted, they moved.

At the Lord's command the people camped, and at His command, they moved. They obeyed the Lord's order that He commanded through Moses.

Lord, I live in a world darkened by sin and lawlessness,
Light my path so I will know where to walk,
And I will not lose my way.

Lord, Your light is always there. When I sin or wander from the
light,
It's hard to see the light, even though
You're just as bright as You've always been.
I will stay close to the light so I'll not get hurt.

Lord, teach me to begin walking, when the light moves ahead
And teach me to not run ahead of Your lighted path.
I can sleep unafraid in the light
And I can pray and read Scripture;

It feels safe in the light; I can see danger,
Also, the light is warm and cozy.

Amen.

Numbers 9

THE STORY OF THE NATION MOVING ACROSS THE DESERT

Date: 1490 B.C. ~ Place: Foot of Mount Sinai

Israel waited in the shadow of Mount Sinai for 11 months. They arrived in the spring after celebrating Passover in Egypt. They lived at the foot of Sinai through the blistering heat of summer, while they enjoyed the cooler fall, and through the long winter shadows.

Israel arrived as escaped slaves from Egypt—an unorganized mob. It was at Sinai they became a civilized nation. Isn't a civilized people one who lives under law, communicates with one another by a common language they speak and write, seeks the good of each individual and the good of the nation, and worships the Supreme Being, whom they obey and serve?

The very sight of Israel's camp reflected order and purpose. At the center was the sacred tent—the Tabernacle—and an ominous, brooding cloud that hovered over it. That was the cloud of glory, called the Shekinah cloud. God's presence descended into the Tabernacle in that cloud.

The priest and serving Levites camped immediately around the Tabernacle, like an inner circle to protect the sacred tent, as though God who has all power needed protection. Then three tribes each camped on a side of the Tabernacle, three to the north, three to the east, three to the south, and three to the west.

What a marvelous spectacle when the cloud lifted up from the Tabernacle! The priest sounded with the ten silver trumpets for everyone to get ready to march. Then there was a second sight when Israel began moving out. Up front was the Ark of the Covenant—the symbolic presence of God among His people. The Ark of the Covenant with its mercy seat was first—the physical place God sat among His people. At later times it went "three days journey in front of the people to seek out a place of rest."

When the people moved out, Judah went first—this would be the tribe of David and eventually the tribe from which Jesus would come. Next moved out the tribes of Issachar and Zebulon, then followed the sons of Gershon and Merari with six wagons carrying the heavier parts of the Tabernacle (see Num. 7:1-9).

Next came the tribes of Reuben, Simeon, and Gad, then a long winding line of Kohathites carrying on their shoulders the vessels of worship. Last came the remaining six tribes; Ephraim led three and Dan led the final three.

My Time to Pray

Lord, the church is a mighty thing that You lead,
  You have set a time for each of us to march,
  And set a time for each of us to rest.

Lord, it takes a lot of coordination for You to get
  All Your people to march at the same time.
  Each one following the person in front of us,
  All of us following You our Leader.

Lord, help me to fix my place in this huge parade,
  Help me to not lag to bother those behind,
  Help me not run ahead to bump into those in front.

I want to learn to walk at the pace You taught me,
  And to carry the burdens You have for me.
  Help me to fit comfortably into Your joyful procession.

Amen.

Numbers 10

SILVER TRUMPETS

The Lord spoke to Moses: "Make two trumpets of hammered silver, and use them to summon the people and to begin marching. When they blow both trumpets, the entire community must gather themselves in front of you at the entrance to the Tabernacle. If only one trumpet is blown, then the rulers of the tribes must gather themselves in front of you. And when you blow the trumpets once, the group camping on the east should move out. When you blow them again, the group camping on the south should move out. Whenever you want to gather the congregation, blow the trumpets; however, use different trumpet sounds for signaling different things. The trumpets should be blown by Aaron's sons, the priests.

"You must blow the trumpets when you are fighting an enemy who attacks you in your land. The Lord your God will remember you and will save you from your enemies.

"Also, blow the trumpets at happy times such as during your festivals and at new moon festivals. Blow them over your whole burnt offerings and over your peace offering sacrifices. They will help you remember that I am the Lord your God."

The Israelites Leave Sinai

God's cloud lifted up from the Tabernacle of the Covenant on the twentieth day of the second month of the second year (about 38 years transpired between Numbers 10:11 and Numbers 20:13, counting the year before they started their journeys and the year when they were poised to invade Canaan). So, the Israelites moved from the Sinai desert until the cloud stopped in the desert of Paran. This was their first time to move, and they did it at the command of the Lord through Moses.

Lord, just as Israel followed You by following Moses,
Remind me that You lead through those
Preachers who give me the Word of God.

I will faithfully follow human preachers as long as
They follow You and point me to You.

Lord, human preachers are not always right,
Because they turn away from Your Scriptures
Or they refuse to preach Your Scriptures.

I will learn the Scriptures so I'll know
When they are true to You and Your Word.
Lord, I'll be faithful to Your Word, God.

Amen.

The divisions from the camp of Judah moved first under their flag.
Nahshon, the son of Amminadab, was the commander.
Nethanel, the son of Zuar, was the commander of the tribe of Issachar. Eliab, the son of Helon, was the commander of the sons of Zebulun.

Then the Holy Tent was taken down. The Gershonites and the Merarites, who carried it, moved next.

Then the divisions came from the camp of Reuben under their flag.
Elizur, the son of Shedeur, was their commander. Shelumiel, the son of Zurishaddai, was the commander over the division of the

tribe of Simeon. Eliasaph, the son of Deuel, was the commander over the division of the sons of Gad.

Then the Kohathites came, carrying the holy things of the sanctuary. The Holy Tent was to be set up before they arrived.

Next, the divisions from the camp of the sons of Ephraim came under their flag. Elishama, the son of Ammihud, was their commander. Gamaliel, the son of Pedahzur, was the commander over the sons of Manasseh. Abidan, the son of Gideoni, was commander over the division of the sons of Benjamin. The last ones were the rear guard for all the tribes. These were the divisions from the sons of Dan under their flag. Ahiezer, the son of Ammishaddai, was their commander. Pagiel, the son of Ocran, was the commander over the division of the sons of Asher. Ahira, the son of Enan, was the commander over the division of the sons of Naphtali. This was the order that the Israelite divisions marched when they moved out.

Hobab was the son of Reuel the Midianite. Reuel, who is also called Jethro, was Moses' father-in-law. Moses said to Hobab his brother-in-law, "We are moving to the land God promised to give us. Come with us. We will be good to you, because the Lord has promised good things to Israel."

But Hobab answered Moses, "No, I will not go. I will go back to my own land and to my relatives."

But Moses said, "Please don't leave us. You know where we can camp in the desert. You can be our guide. (Literally, 'our eyes.' Hobab was an experienced nomad; he could point out precisely where water, fuel, and pastures could be found.) If you come with us, then we will share with you all the good things that the Lord gives us."

So, they left the mountain of the Lord. The Ark of the Covenant went in
front of the people. (Normally, the Ark of the Covenant stayed in
the center of the army, however Joshua 3:3-6 shows that sometimes the Ark of the Covenant preceded the people.) They
looked for a place to camp after three days' journey. And the
Shekinah cloud of the Lord was over them during the day when
they left their campground. When the Ark of the Covenant left
the camp, Moses prayed,

"Rise up, O Lord who is always present!
Scatter Your enemies!
Make those who hate You run from You!"

And when the Ark of the Covenant was set down, Moses said,

"Return, O Lord who is always present,
To the thousands and thousands of people of Israel."

Lord, Israel knew You were with them when they saw the cloud,
Today, I know You are with me everywhere,
Because You promised it in the Word of God.

By faith I will trust You to be with me
To protect, guide, and cause me to grow in grace.

Lord, thank You for Your promise in the Word of God,
For without it I would be left to my own resources.

Amen.

Numbers 10

THE STORY OF AN INVITATION TO HOBAB

Date 1490 B.C. ~ Place: Marching Through the Wilderness

From time to time, members from different nomadic tribes came to visit Moses, and to see the "spectacle." Hobab, son of Reuel, Moses' father-in-law, was such a one from a nomadic tribe. Hobab was a man of the land; he knew the water wells, the pastures, springs of water, and shortest routes through mountain ranges. Moses asked his brother-in-law:

"Please do not leave, inasmuch as you know how we are to camp in the wilderness." Moses asked, "Be our eyes" (Num. 10:31). Moses was asking his brother-in-law to guide Israel to the Promised Land.

The request was only natural to anyone traveling through an unknown, hostile territory. But wasn't it a question of doubt? Hadn't God promised to lead His people by a pillar of fire at night and a cloud by day? Does Moses now doubt God's direction by asking a human guide to lead him?

But there's another problem. The Lord wanted His people to be separate from the nations of the earth. Their eating habits were different, their clothes were different, even the cut of their beards was different. Also, God didn't want His people intermarrying with other nations, for foreign wives would lead God's people into idolatry. Is Moses compromising their separation from heathen nations?

Moses promises his brother-in-law, "Whatever good the Lord will do to us, the same we will do to you." (Num. 10:32).

The request by Moses seemed logical. God's people didn't know what was on the other side of each foreboding mountain, nor did they know what emergencies they would meet, nor what enemies may lurk in the next ravine.

Anything seemed better than reliance on a cloud that was not a man. Moses didn't want to cut himself off from those who knew the land; yet God had a better plan, because God knew the dangers better than any man. God knew the best campgrounds for a night or for a year. God would personally lead them step by step to the land He promised.

My Time to Pray

Lord, You speak to me through others, and You lead me
Through humans who are just like me.

But You want me to look to You first and last,
You want me to look to You always,
Especially before I look to others for help.

Lord, teach me to rely on You and You alone,
Then to accept Your help from others
And to follow those whom You send to lead me.

Amen.

Numbers 10

THE STORY OF FOLLOWING
THE GLORY CLOUD

Date: 1490 B.C. ~ Place: Leaving Mount Sinai

...the cloud was taken up from above the tabernacle of the Testimony. And the children of Israel set out from the Wilderness of Sinai on their journeys...And the cloud of the Lord was above them by day...So it was, whenever the ark set out, that Moses said: "Rise up, O Lord! Let Your enemies be scattered..." (Numbers 10:11-12, 34-35).

For a year and a half, Israel camped at the foot of Sinai. During that time, God laid out the laws and values by which they were to organize themselves into a nation. This included the social laws so they could live together in peace, with a maximum amount of liberty for all. God told them principles of how to worship Him with sacrifices, and what offerings they must bring to Him at the Tabernacle. God gave them laws concerning the religious, social, moral, business, and judicial areas of their lives. *Thank You, Lord, for showing me how to live.*

When Israel left Egypt, they were a mob of freed prisoners, with no discipline, no national respect, and no national purpose. During their stay at Sinai they organized themselves into an army; now they were ready to march.

The Shekinah glory cloud lifted from the Tabernacle. The silver trumpet sounded. Everyone broke camp and got ready to leave Sinai.

Then the cloud lifted and they marched. They followed the cloud, which was the same as following God Himself. Wouldn't it be easy for you to follow God if you could see the cloud out front every day? *O Lord, lead me.*

What an awesome sight—approximately 3 million people on the move at the same time! Before them was the Shekinah leading the way. Moses didn't know what path to take, so he asked his brother-in-law, "Please do not leave...You can be our eyes" (Num. 10:31). It's always good to have someone show us the way because they know the way. *Lord, give me people in my life to show me the way.* The desert had many dangers: poisonous water, predators, snakes, and hostile nomadic tribes. But the Israelites shouldn't have worried. All they had to do was look up. The protective cloud was there by day; it was a pillar of fire at night. They remembered how the Red Sea opened up and the cloud led them through on dry land. So now all they had to do was follow the cloud. *Lord, I'll go where You lead.*

The cloud and the mercy seat marched together in front of Israel. Both were symbols of God's presence. The cloud symbolizes God's leadership of His people, as well as God's protection. Remember, when Pharaoh and the Egyptian army were poised to attack Israel from the rear, the cloud moved to the back of the multitude. The Egyptians got lost in the thick darkness of the cloud and couldn't attack. You need God's presence to protect you from your enemies. *Lord, protect my backside when I can't protect myself.*

The cloud set upon the Ark of the Covenant, symbolizing God sitting on His throne, which was the mercy seat. That's where the high priest came on the Day of Atonement to sprinkle the blood of a sacrificial animal. The Ark was at the heart of worship, for worship always is grounded in forgiveness of sins. As the average Israelite saw the Ark being carried before them, they were reminded of their duty to worship. Notice the reciprocal relationship. When we feel the presence of God, it stimulates us to worship. At other times in our life, we begin worshiping, and it attracts God's presence. Which must come first? There is no rule; either will work. *O God, I need Your presence.*

As they daily marched toward their destiny—the Promised Land—their future was intertwined with worship. Each day and each step they progressively unshackled their former chains of Egypt. The prison doors were open, and they were marching toward freedom, but they couldn't be completely free until they entered the land of Canaan. Since the Ark was leading them, their worship was the key to their destiny. It's the same with you. Your daily worship of God invites His presence with you in your daily march. Perhaps you haven't experienced His symbolic cloud leading your life because you haven't been worshiping. Put God to the test. Put worship at the center of your life, and you'll experience His glory filling your life. *Come Lord as I worship.*

As the Israelites marched through the wilderness, they won battle after battle. First they defeated the Egyptian army—a symbol of the world. Then at Horeb, they defeated Amalek, a symbol of the flesh. Israel's military power was not in their army, nor was it in the armaments they picked up on the beach of the Red Sea from drowned Egyptian soldiers. No! Israel's military strength was in the cloud and the Ark. Israel's strength was in God Himself. Doesn't that say something to you about how to be strong? Let God fight your battle; be strong in the Lord. If you're following the cloud, you don't have to worry about the enemy, just look up to make sure you're close to the cloud. If the cloud is over you, go peacefully about your daily activity. *Lord, I see You up ahead, wait for me.*

What is the secret of your victory? Close relationship to the cloud and blood on the mercy seat. And how is your relationship to God established and maintained? Through worship! When you look up to see the cloud, worship. *Lord, protect me.*

So, at the heart of your daily walk with God, you must worship. When you struggle with evil principalities and powers, you must worship. For a beacon to guide you to your personal destiny, you must worship. The central focus of your church's life and your personal life is worship. Are you willing to allow worship its place in your life? *Lord, I worship You.*

PRAYING FOR YOUR SECOND CHANCE

Lord, keep me from looking down in discouragement,
  May I look up to see You,
  Leading me by Your symbolic presence.

Lord, may the cloud remind me to worship You
  And follow You without complaint.
  Get glory out of my obedience today.

  Amen.

Numbers 11

THE PEOPLE MURMURED

The people complained to the Lord about their troubles. When the Lord
heard them, He became angry. Fire from the Lord burned
among the people, devouring the edge of the camp. So, the people cried out to Moses. He prayed to the Lord, and the fire was
stopped. So, that spot was called Taberah. The people named it
Taberah because the Lord's fire had burned among them.

Lord, give me a good memory so I won't forget
The places and times I disobeyed You.

Help me remember my disobedience and the consequences
I suffered because I disobeyed You.

Lord, may my memory keep me from future consequences,
May I always obey You from now on.

Amen.

Some troublemakers (Hebrew: "the riff-raff") among them wanted better
food. Soon all the Israelites began grumbling too. They cried
out, "We want meat! We remember the fish in Egypt that we ate
for free. We also had cucumbers, watermelons, leeks, onions,
and garlic. But now, our soul withers away, we never see anything except this manna!"

The manna was like small, coriander seeds. It looked like resin gum.
The people went out to collect it, then ground it up in hand
mills, or crushed it between stones. They cooked it in a pot and

made it into cakes. It tasted like bread baked with olive oil. When the dew fell on the camp each night, so did the manna.

Moses heard all the people—every tribe—crying out (an organized, public demonstration of discontent). Each person stood at the entrance of his tent to complain. The Lord became very angry, and Moses was also upset. Moses asked the Lord, "Why have You brought me, Your servant, this trouble? Why haven't I found favor in Your sight? Why did You make *me* responsible for all these people? I am *not* the father of all these people. I did not give birth to them. Why do You make *me* carry them to the land that You promised to our ancestors? Must I carry them in my arms as a nurse carries a baby? Where can I get meat for all these people? They continue to complain to me, 'We want meat to eat!' I cannot take care of all these people *alone*! It is too much for me! If You are going to continue doing this to me, then kill me quickly! If I have found some grace in Your eyes, put me to death! Then I won't have any more troubles!"

Seventy Leaders Selected

The Lord said to Moses, "Bring Me seventy of the elders (older men) of Israel. Pick men whom you know are wise among the people. Bring them to the Meeting Tent. Have them line up there with you. I will come down and speak with you there. I will take some of the Spirit that is in you, and will give it to them. They will help you take care of the people. Then you will not have to take care of them alone.

"Tell the people: 'Make yourselves holy. Tomorrow you will eat meat. The Lord has heard your cry: "We want meat! We were better off in Egypt!" So now, I will give you meat to eat. You will not eat it for just one day, two days, five days, ten days, or even twenty days. No, you will eat that meat for a whole month. You will eat it until it comes out your noses! You will *hate* it. That is because you have rejected *Me*. I am here among you, but you have cried out in My presence. You said: "Why did we ever leave Egypt?"'"

Moses said, "O Lord, there are 600,000 men in this camp, and yet You say: 'I will give them enough meat to eat for one month?!' If we killed all the flocks and the livestock, that would not be enough to feed all the people. If we caught all the fish in the sea, even that would not be enough to feed them!"

But the Lord answered Moses, "Do you think that I am weak? Is anything too difficult for Me to do? You will see that I can do what I say!"

Lord, many times I doubt Your ability to do things,
  Just as Moses didn't believe You could feed the multitude.

Yet, You brought quail to feed almost 3 million people,
  This was exceedingly above and beyond what the people expected.

Lord, give me faith to trust You for great answers by faith,
  Take away my unbelieving heart,
  I believe, help then my unbelief.

Amen.

So, Moses went out to the people. He told them what the Lord had said. Moses gathered together 70 of the elders of the people. He had them stand in a semi-circle near the front of the tent.

Then the Lord came down in the cloud and spoke to Moses. The Lord took some of the Spirit that was on Moses, and put it on the 70 individual elders. With the Spirit in them, they prophesied, but just that one time. (They never did it again. Their proper function was *governing*, not prophesying.)

Two men named Eldad and Medad were also listed as "elders." However, they had *not* gone to the Tent. They stayed in the camp. Nevertheless, the Spirit also rested upon them. So, they prophesied within the camp. A young man ran to Moses and said, "Eldad and Medad are prophesying in the camp!"

Joshua, the son of Nun, said, "Moses, my master, stop them!" (When Joshua was a young boy, he had been Moses' assistant.) But Moses answered, "Are you afraid for me? I wish all of the Lord's people could prophesy. I wish the Lord would give His Spirit to all of the people." Then Moses and the elders of Israel returned to the camp.

The Lord Sends Birds

The Lord sent a strong wind from the sea (the southeast wind blew from the Eastern Gulf of the Red Sea), blowing quail into the area all around the camp. The quail flew about 3 feet off the ground. Quail were everywhere for one day's walk in any direction!

The people went out and gathered quail all that day, that night, and the next day. Each one gathered at least 60 bushels of birds. (It was more than enough food for a month.) Then the birds were spread all around the camp. (They were probably salted to dry for future use.)

But the Lord became very angry, giving the people a terrible sickness. (The stomachs of the Israelites were accustomed to manna [a light food]; they were not prepared for such a rapid change of diet, that is, heavy meals of quail meat.) They got sick while the meat was still in their mouths, because of gluttony. So, the people named that place *Kibroth-Hattaavah* ("graves of gluttony"), because they buried those who wanted food that was different from the manna. From Kibroth-Hattaavah, the people went to stay at Hazeroth.

Lord, help me be careful for the things for which I pray,
Sometimes You answer our prayers
But, the results we seek actually harm us.

I will pray for things You promise in Your Word,
So that I pray in Your perfect will.

Lord, You are very gracious to us, and You are wise,
May I never doubt Your promises.

Amen.

Numbers 11

THE STORY OF ISRAEL COMPLAINING ABOUT NO MEAT

Date: 1490 B.C. ~ Place: Marching Through the Wilderness

The evening meal had been enjoyable. A wife baked bread cakes out of the manna, which tastes like coriander seeds. The cakes rose in the oven and with a little berry preserves, the meal was delightful. But her husband complained, "Why doesn't God give us meat instead of bread?"

Another wife had ground the manna so it was fine like corn meal; a little milk was added after it was boiled and the evening meal was as tasty as oatmeal. Her husband also complained, "I miss my meat."

As the evening sky turned black, several men gathered around the burning embers of a dying fire. They compared their evening meals, and all began to complain, "Oh, for some meat that we could get our teeth into!"

They remembered the delicate fish their Egyptian slave masters gave them. Then they reminisced about the wonderful spices of Egypt, leeks, onions, and garlic. "Oh, I wish I could go back," one man wished.

"Me too," a second complained, "I'd give up this sandy freedom of the desert for the food of Egypt."

The men complained about the manna, complained about the sand, complained about God's guidance. These rabble-rousers upset everyone else they talked to the next day. Before long, there was a tidal wave of discontent against Moses and manna, the provided food. "Day after day, nothing to eat but this manna." They complained even louder, "We're sick and tired of manna."

A hungry man shouldn't complain about the feast God provides. While manna was not meat and potatoes, it kept them and their families from starving. When people yearned for the exotic foods of their slavery, they forgot the sting of the whip and their burdens in the hot sun. When they complained about the food God gave them, they complained about God Himself.

It doesn't take long for a bitter man to infect his family, and before you know it, his whole tribe is complaining. Then a few nights later, it seemed every man stood in his tent door, complaining to his neighbor about the "lousy manna" they had for dinner.

Moses became discouraged when he heard the people complaining about their food. He went into the Tabernacle to talk to God about the problem.

Moses said, "Why did You give me this terrible burden and these complaining people? All they do is criticize everything."

The Lord Listened

Moses continued, "Am I their father that I should carry them in my arms? Am I to nurse them like babies? Where am I supposed to get meat for them?"

Then the Lord got extremely angry at the people of Israel. God had delivered them from slavery, given them the gold and silver of Egypt, protected them as they walked through the Red Sea, defeated the Amalekites, and given them manna to eat, rather than let them starve. No wonder God was angry. Rather than trust God, they complained about the quality of their meals, like students are never satisfied to eat in the cafeteria.

God told Moses, "I will come talk with you at the Tabernacle door. Get seventy men to serve with you, they will help you bear the burden of the people."

Then God told Moses, "Tell the people to sanctify themselves, tomorrow I will give them meat to eat. I have heard their whining and fussing. I will give them meat—not one day, or two days, not one week or two weeks; but I give you enough meat for one month. Tell them they'll have enough meat to stuff themselves, gag themselves, and make them sick."

Moses couldn't believe his old ears—a month of meat—that was unbelievable. Moses looked out over the thousands of tents and hundreds of thousands of fires in the night. "A month of meat?" He doubted to himself.

Moses told God, "Israel has over 600,000 foot soldiers, plus women and children. If we slaughtered all our milk cattle and oxen who pull our wagons, that wouldn't be enough to feed the people." As Moses bowed his head before the presence of God, he peeked quickly into the thick cloud of black smoke to ask,

"How can You do that God?"

God answered, "Do I not have enough power to do what I want?"

So Moses bowed to the omnipotent promise of God. He would wait to see what God would do.

The 70 elders gathered with Moses at the Tabernacle. He stationed them to stand a few feet from one another around the Tabernacle. Then the glory cloud came down and filled the Tabernacle with God's presence. God took the same Spirit that was upon Moses and put it on the 70 men so that each one prophesied. Even though that is the only time it happened, the Spirit indeed did rest on them.

Two of the 70 had not joined Moses at the Tabernacle. They too received the Spirit and they also prophesied. A young man ran to tell Moses that Eldad and Medad were prophesying in the camp.

"Make them stop," Joshua, Moses' assistant, came to tell Moses what the two men were doing.

"Don't be jealous," Moses told Joshua, "I wish every man in the camp were prophesying."

The Lord sent a strong wind toward the East, blowing quail from the Red Sea marshes toward the wilderness. Soon the sky was dark with flying quail—meat from Heaven. The quail were flying 3 or 4 feet above the ground.

Men ran out from their tents into the desert. With their walking sticks, they knocked the quail out of the sky. And they didn't stop at one or two, nor did they stop at a basketful, which was a day's allotment of manna. Men began selfishly making piles of quail; each man had dozens and dozens of quail. It had been so long since they had meat, their emptiness drove them to excess; they kept knocking quail out of the sky as long as any flew in their direction.

The women sprang into action, picking feathers, draining blood, and cutting out the innards; they spread their loot out over the desert. Three million people had many more than 3 million quail.

God in Heaven was saying, "Moses didn't think there was enough meat for 3 million people, but there is no limit to my power." When Moses was thinking of slaughtering the animals he could see, God saw the millions of wildlife in the swamps and marshes of the Red Sea. God used His wind to sweep several million quail over the children of Israel, more than they could kill and eat.

But God had become angry with the complainers of Israel. It wasn't just their complaints and ungrateful spirits. When they prayed for meat, it was a prayer of unbelief. Their prayer was fueled by lust and driven by unbelief—they disbelieved the very nature of God Himself.

That night as they were lustfully gorging themselves with their prizes, the Lord's anger blazed against them. A severe plague broke out among the people. Many died and were buried there at the place that became known as *Kibroth-Hattaavah*, "the graves of craving."

My Time to Pray

Lord, help me learn how to pray to You properly,
And to always pray for the right things in life.
Not as Israel wrongly prayed for meat.

I shouldn't pray for everything I want,
> *Because some things I want are not Your will.*
> *Some things I want are opposite to Your will.*

Lord, help me to learn Your mind and to know Your plan on earth,
> *I want to pray for Thy will to be done in my life.*
> *I want You to be glorified in my life.*

Amen.

Numbers 12

MIRIAM IS PUNISHED

Miriam and Aaron began to criticize Moses, who had married a Cushite woman (probably an ethnic slur). Whoever she was, Miriam was simply jealous of this non-Jewish wife. However, this was only a pretext; the real issue was whether Moses had the authority given to him by God or not.

They said to themselves, "Is Moses the *only* one whom the Lord speaks through? Doesn't He also speak through *us*?" The Lord heard their complaints. Now Moses was a very humble man, perhaps the least proud person on earth.

So, the Lord suddenly spoke to Moses, Aaron, and Miriam, saying, "All three of you, come to the Meeting Tent *now!*" So the three of them went.

The Lord came down in the pillar of cloud, and stopped at the entrance to the tent. He called Aaron and Miriam to come near. Then He said, "Listen to My words: If there is a true prophet to whom I speak, I, the Lord, will show Myself to him in visions and speak to him with a dream. But, my servant Moses I trust to lead all of My people. I speak face to face with him and I speak clearly, not with hidden meanings. He has even seen My form (somehow God manifested Himself in such a way as to be recognizable to mortal eyes). You should be afraid to speak against My servant Moses."

The Lord was very angry with them, and His anger burned against them, but He left. The cloud lifted from the tent, and when Aaron turned toward Miriam, he saw her white with leprosy!

Lord, thank You for Your grace and patience,
You immediately judged Miriam for her sin.

If You judged my sin immediately, I'd never make it

For I have a sin nature that's prone to sin,
And I have an ego that's hard to control.

Lord, thank You for Your grace and patience with my sin.

I claim the forgiveness of Jesus from the cross
The blood of the Lord Jesus Christ cleanses from all sin.
(See 1 John 1:7.)

That's the only basis for my Christian walk.

Amen.

Aaron begged Moses, "Please, my master, forgive us for sinning so foolishly! Miriam is like a dead woman! I beg you, don't let her be like a baby that is born with half of its flesh eaten away!"

So Moses cried out to the Lord, "O God, please heal her—please!"

The Lord answered Moses, "If her father had surely spit in her face, then she would have been humiliated. So, put her outside the camp for seven days (as a public example of God's displeasure). After that, she may come back."

So, Miriam was isolated outside the camp for seven days. But the people did not move on until she came back in. After that, the people left Hazeroth and camped in the desert of Paran.

Lord, it is so easy to complain, even Aaron and Miriam,
Leaders in Israel, fell into the trap of complaining.

Miriam Is Punished

But You never allow any sin to go unpunished,
Even when leaders give in to selfish criticism,
Even for a seemingly small sin like criticizing.

Lord, keep my heart's desire pure and straightforward.

Keep me from comparing myself to others.
May I be filled with the fruit of the Spirit.
May I glorify You with my words.

Amen.

Numbers 12

THE STORY OF MIRIAM AND AARON COMPLAINING ABOUT MOSES' NEW WIFE

Date: 1490 B.C. plus ~ Place: Marching Through the Wilderness

Not much is known about it and not much is said about it, but Moses' wife Zipporah had died. Moses the leader wanted the people to focus on God. In his humility, Moses didn't want undue pity and concern.

So Zipporah was buried quietly and privately. Many of the Israelites didn't know about her death and were not informed of her burial. Like others who died as the nation marched through the wilderness, the procession stopped for awhile, Zipporah was buried, and the procession moved on to follow the cloud leading them through the wilderness.

Moses didn't even write of Zipporah's death in the books he was writing to record the journey of God's people from Egypt to the Promised Land. Again, the meekness of Moses kept him from writing of his wife's death, lest the personal life of Moses take away from the story of God and how He led His people.

Many women came to help set up and take down Moses' tent. They scurried about to make life in the desert as easy as possible for an old man over 80 years of age.

One woman did more to help Moses then all the other ladies. She seemed to know exactly what Moses wanted, and when she prepared a meal it was the best Moses ever ate, or at least that's what he told her.

This woman was a foreigner from Ethiopia, delivered with Israel out of Egypt. She chose against Egypt and chose to follow Jehovah, the God of the Jews. And she became a proselyte who worshiped Jehovah with all her heart, perhaps she worshiped more vigorously than all of the more reserved Jewish women. And this woman demonstrated her faith by practical service. She served Moses as devotedly as she served Jehovah.

After Moses' grieving was over, his old eyes began to notice this striking black woman scurrying about his tent. Everything Moses lost in Zipporah, he found in this woman from the Cush people of Ethiopia. Those who say love is sweeter the second time around don't know what they are saying. The second time love comes more quickly because there's not much time left. The second time, two people jump past crazy youthful love into mature love, without the showy emotional expressions.

Love came quickly to Moses and this unnamed Ethiopian woman. When Aaron and Miriam, Moses' brother and sister, were invited to the marriage, they went without realizing what was going on. They hadn't been asked to approve the new bride.

A little later Miriam and Aaron compared notes and found that both disagreed with Moses' choice of a second wife. Miriam was the most vocal:

"She's black...she's not from one of the twelve tribes." Miriam complained the new wife didn't understand their Jewish ways, even though she deeply worshiped Jehovah.

Aaron complained that Moses hadn't asked him about marrying the girl, "After all, I'm his brother, we've talked about everything." Then Aaron added, "I'm the high priest and I have the Urim and Thummim; people come to me to find the will of God. Moses should have come to me to determine if this woman was God's will for his life."

The more Aaron and Miriam talked, the more they found reason to disagree with Moses' decision and the more they disagreed with Moses himself.

Both Miriam and Aaron thought that Moses was making more decisions unilaterally. They thought Moses was not asking them, nor was he asking the elders, nor was he telling the multitude what he was doing.

"God speaks to us," Miriam told her brother, "Moses thinks he's the only one who hears God's voice."

Miriam forgot God hears everything we hear, so God heard the complaints of Miriam and Aaron, and God was angry with what He heard. God called Moses, Aaron, and Miriam and told them,

"Go immediately to the Tabernacle."

When the three arrived at the Tabernacle, the glory cloud descended over the entire tent and God spoke to the three of them. God said,

"I communicate with prophets with visions and dreams. But that's not how I communicate with Moses. I have given to Moses the task of leading my entire nation. I speak with Moses face to face, I don't speak to him with vague sentences, but I speak to Moses directly."

The Lord told Miriam and Aaron they should have not criticized Moses. That was it—God abruptly rebuked them and He left. As the cloud began to rise from over the Tabernacle, Aaron and Moses thought that was the end of the situation. God had rebuked them and left.

But as the cloud left, both Moses and Aaron saw their sister turn white. She was white with leprosy. God had a sense of humor. Miriam complained about the black-skin woman, so God turned her white.

Aaron knew he had sinned. He was the first to speak, "Please don't punish me for our foolish speech. Please forgive me. Miriam is like a stillborn baby, already dead."

Aaron realized the cause of leprosy, and that it meant Miriam's premature death. The skin rots and falls from the bones. The victim was ostracized and isolated, with no warmth of human contact. It meant rotting skin until death.

Moses, the one against whom Miriam sinned, cried out, "Heal her, O Lord." Moses fell to the ground to beg God to heal his sister.

Miriam was excommunicated from normal life as was required by the law of God. Seven days of isolation was required to determine if she was healed. After that time, it was determined that Miriam was healed. The entire nation waited in Hazeroth, until Miriam's healing was verified, then they left for Paran.

My Time to Pray

Lord, help me realize criticism is a sin against You,
Help me look for the good in all people,
And keep me from wrongly criticizing others.

Lord, if I would spend my time praising You
I wouldn't have time to criticize others.

Forgive my sin of criticism and complaining,
And give me a new passion to worship You.

Amen.

Numbers 13

THE TWELVE SPIES

And the Lord spoke to Moses (the original idea came from the Israelites themselves [see Deut. 1:22] because of their lack of faith in God, nevertheless God permitted it): "Send some men to explore the land of Canaan for you. I have given that land to the Israelites. Send one leader from each ancestral tribe." So Moses obeyed the Lord's command and sent the 12 Israelite leaders (spies) out from the desert of Paran. These were their names:

From the tribe of Reuben—Shammua, the son of Zaccur;

From the tribe of Simeon—Shaphat, the son of Hori;

From the tribe of Judah—Caleb, the son of Jephunneh;

From the tribe of Issachar—Igal, the son of Joseph;

From the tribe of Ephraim—Hoshea (Joshua), the son of Nun;

From the tribe of Benjamin—Palti, the son of Raphu;

From the tribe of Zebulon—Gaddiel, the son of Sodi;

From the tribe of Manasseh (a half-tribe of Joseph)—Gaddi, the son of Susi;

From the tribe of Dan—Ammiel, the son of Gemalli;

From the tribe of Asher—Sethur, the son of Michael;

From the tribe of Nephtali—Nahbi, the son of Vophsi;

From the tribe of Gad—Geuel, the son of Machi.

These were the names of the men whom Moses sent to explore, or "spy on," the land.

Lord, sometimes we should just go where You lead us,
We should not demand information about the future
We should just trust You.

Lord, sometimes when we demand to see the path where You lead
And we want to know about tomorrow
We are not trusting You.

Lord, sometimes we humans doubt Your leadership,
We want more information before we follow,
We are afraid to trust You.

Lord, forgive me when I try to negotiate my future,
Instead of following Your clear leading.
Teach me to trust You.

Amen.

Moses sent them to explore the land of Canaan, and said, "Go up this way through southern Canaan (literally, 'into the desert Negev') and then go up into the hill country. See what the land is like. Are the people who live there strong or weak? Does the land have a few people or many people? What kind of land are they living in? Is it good, or is it bad? What about the towns where they live? Do these towns have fortress walls? Or, are they open camps? What is the soil like? Is it fertile or poor? Are there trees there or not? Do your best to try to get some of the fruit from that land." It was the season when grapes were starting to get ripe (July or August).

So, they went up and explored the land thoroughly. They went from the desert of Zin (the southern extremity of Palestine) all the way to

Rehob by Lebo-Hamath (the northern gateway to Palestine). They went up through the southern area and came to Hebron, where the tribes of Ahiman, Sheshai, and Talmai lived. They were the descendants of Anak. (The Anakites were men of great stature, so large that they scared people.) They came to the Valley of Eshcol, where they cut off a branch from a grapevine. It had one bunch of grapes on it, and was so heavy they carried the branch on a pole between two men. They also obtained some pomegranates and some figs. (The Valley of Eshcol means "cluster," because the Israelites cut off the big cluster of grapes there.)

They explored the land for 40 days, and then returned to the Israelite camp.

Lord, Israel wanted to "walk by sight," not "by faith,"
　　And they saw what You had promised them.
　　Why didn't they trust You?

Even when they "walked by sight" and saw Your promise,
　　They refused to believe You'd give them
　　What You had promised them.

Lord, teach me to "walk by faith" not "by sight"
　　So I can enjoy fellowship with You
　　And glorify You with my implicit obedience.

　　　　Amen.

Conflicting Reports

The 12 spies traveled and returned to Moses, Aaron, and the whole group of Israelites at Kadesh, in the desert of Paran. The men gave a report to the entire community, and showed everyone the fruit from the land. They told Moses, "We went to the land where you sent us. It surely is a land where abundant food grows! It is flowing with milk and honey. Here is some of the fruit that comes from it!

"But the people who live in that land are powerful and fierce. Their cities are fortresses protected by big walls; they are huge! We even saw some Anakites (giants) there. The Amalekites live in the southern area, and the Hittites, the Jebusites, and the Amorites live in the hills. The Canaanites (those of the Phoenician race) live from the Mediterranean sea to the Jordan River."

Then, Caleb told the people in the presence of Moses to be calm, saying, "We should certainly go up and capture the land, because we surely have the power to do it!"

But the other men who had gone up to Canaan with him said, "We are *not* able to attack those people! They are stronger than we are!" So, those other men gave a discouraging report to the Israelites about the land that they had explored. They said, "The land that we passed through to spy on is dangerous—it would eat us up! The people we saw there are very tall. We saw the Nephilim people (giants) there. The Anakites come from the Nephilim people. We felt like grasshoppers. (Literally, 'We were like grasshoppers in our own eyes.') And, we looked like grasshoppers to them."

Lord, unbelief looks at the obstacle and enemies,
And cries out in unbelief, "It can't be done!"

Faith looks at Your promises and Your almighty hand,
And cries, "It will be done!"

Lord, may I not look at where You're leading me,
And draw back in unbelief.

May I walk forward in strong faith to do Your will,
Because You have always kept Your promises.

Amen.

Numbers 13

THE STORY OF CALEB'S FAITHFULNESS

Date: 1490 B.C. ~ Place Kadesh-Barnea

Caleb's name meant *"a dog,"* but don't think of him as an irritating dog that barks at night, or sniffs constantly. Rather, think of Caleb like man's best friend, a faithful dog. Caleb was faithful to the leadership of Joshua and Moses, he was faithful to the Lord, and most of all he was faithful to himself.

Even when all Israel wanted to stone him because he disagreed with the report of the ten spies, Caleb was completely faithful to the Lord. Again, think of a dog; anything his master tells him to do, a dog will attempt to do. That was Caleb. God, his Master, had told him to go search out the land; and he did so faithfully, and brought back a faithful report.

Twelve spies were sent to the land, Joshua and Caleb among them. Ten came back and all agreed, "It is a land that floweth with milk and honey, but it was full of giants, their cities had high walls, and Israel was not able to capture the land." Caleb, along with Joshua, had a different opinion. Both dared to stand against the ten, and ultimately against all Israel. Caleb said:

"Let us go up, we are able to possess the land."

It was then that the people took up stones to stone the two.

Notice the Bible says, "Caleb...follows Me wholeheartedly" (Num. 14:24 NIV). He wasn't driven by God to go into battle, nor did he rebel and have to be punished. He was willing to die for the Lord in conquering the land because God had told them he would give the land to Israel.

It is said that before a man actually dies in battle, he has to die to self-will, self-pleasure, and a selfish life. He has to die before he dies, and Caleb did that. In the same way a child of God today must take up the cross of Christ and be co-crucified with Christ, then that person is able to serve Christ in a better and more fruitful way. And the martyr for Jesus Christ must be willing to die, long before he or she dies for Him.

Again, "follows Me wholeheartedly." That means he did not join with the murmuring multitude to complain about the food, or the conditions, or the lack of water. That meant he did not doubt the leadership of the Shekinah fire, nor did he hold back when God said move forward. He did not follow the Lord by continual stops and starts, rather Caleb followed the Lord with his whole heart.

God made a promise to Caleb, "Him will I bring into the land." When every male over 20 years died, only Caleb and Joshua lived to go into the Promised Land. The ten unfaithful spies died under a plague, and didn't enter the land. Those who believed the report of the spies also died and didn't enter the land.

Caleb was willing to give his life for the Lord his Master, and therefore Christ his Lord ultimately gave His life for Caleb and all those like Caleb who follow him.

They all died (see Num. 14:37-38), that is everyone died except Joshua and Caleb. One day when they entered the land, someone would point out that the older ones, "all died," then they would point to Caleb and say, "except that man who faithfully followed the Lord."

"But because my servant Caleb has a different spirit and follows Me wholeheartedly, I will bring him into the land he went to, and his descendants will inherit it" (Num. 14:24 NIV).

Numbers 14

THE PEOPLE REBEL AT KADESH-BARNEA

During that night, the whole community began crying out loud and weeping. They complained against Moses and Aaron, saying, "We should have died in the land of Egypt! Or, we should have died in this desert! (They were not thankful to God for all His miracles of deliverance or provision. These foolish people had completely forgotten what abject slavery was really like. So, God granted their wish to die in the desert.) Why is the Lord bringing us to this land—so we will be killed by swords?! Our wives and little children will be captured! We would be better off going back to Egypt!"

Lord, they should have been careful about their words
That they wanted to die in the desert,
Because that's exactly what happened.

Lord, teach me to be careful with my intense prayer
Or my idle requests to You,
Because You may give me what I ask.

Lord, guide my mouth when I pray to You,
So that You give me what I should have,

Not the things I request that are out of Your will.

Lord, I will pray in the Holy Spirit,
So that my requests are in Your will.

Amen.

They said to each other, "Let us appoint a new leader and go back to Egypt!"

Then Moses and Aaron laid face down on the ground in prayer in front of the whole congregation of the Israelites who had gathered there.

Joshua and Caleb were among those who had explored the land. Joshua and Caleb tore their clothes and said to the entire gathering of the Israelites: "The land which we passed through to explore is a very, very good land! Since the Lord is pleased with us, He will lead us into the land and will give it to us! It is a land that produces abundant food. Only, do not rebel against the Lord! Do not be afraid of the people of that land! We will chew them up! They have no protection, and the Lord is with us! So, do not be afraid of them!"

Then the entire community talked about killing Joshua and Caleb by stoning them.

But, the glory of the Lord suddenly appeared to all of them at the Meeting Tent. And the Lord said to Moses, "How long will these people provoke Me? How long will it be before they trust in Me? What about all the miracles that I have done among them? I will send a terrible sickness among them. (It was a warning which was suspended because of the intercession of Moses.) I will disown them! And, I will make you, Moses, into a great nation. It will be stronger than they ever were!"

Then Moses said to the Lord, "No! The Egyptians will hear! They know You brought up these people out of Egypt by Your great power. Then the Egyptians will tell this to those who live in this land. They have already heard about You, O Lord. They know that You are among Your people. And they know that You were seen face to face. They know You are the *Lord!* They know that Your cloud column stays over Your people. They know that You lead Your people by that cloud during the day and with a fire column at night. The nations have heard about Your fame. If You put Your people to death all at one time, then the nations will talk! And here is what they will say:

"'The Lord was not able to bring these people into the land that He promised them. So, He killed them in the desert.'

So please show Your strength now, O my Lord! Be what You have said originally. You said: 'The Lord does not become angry quickly. The Lord has great mercy. The Lord forgives sin and rebellion. However, the Lord will not let guilty people get away with sinning; they *will* be punished! When parents sin, He will also punish their children. He will punish their grandchildren, great-grandchildren, and great-great-grandchildren.'" Show Your great mercy! Please forgive the sin of this people! You have tolerated them since the time they left Egypt until now."

Lord, Moses had a difficult job when interceding to You.
He had to change Your mind so You
Wouldn't destroy Your people Israel.

Moses didn't just plead Your mercy or goodness
(which is a good basis to pray)

But Moses based his request on the promises
That You made Your people.

Moses also reminded You what the heathen would say
If You destroyed Your people in the desert.

Lord, Moses interceded and You listened to Him.
He had the prayer-ability to touch Your heart.

Lord, I want that ability in my prayer so I can get answers;
Teach me how to find Your heart in prayer.

Amen.

The Lord answered, "I forgive them, just as you have requested. But as surely as I live, as surely as My splendor fills the entire earth, I vow that they will never see that land. All those men saw My splendor. They saw the miracles that I did in Egypt and in the desert, but they have disobeyed Me and they put Me to the test ten times (a Hebrew idiom which means "very frequently")! *None* of them will see the land that I promised to their ancestors! No one who provoked Me will see that land! However, My servant Caleb has a different spirit within him (Joshua was the constant assistant to Moses and his eventual successor; there was therefore no need to mention Joshua here). He follows Me completely. So, I will bring him into the land where he has already gone. And his descendents will own some of that land. The Amalekites and the Canaanites are living in the valleys. So, tomorrow leave here and turn back. Follow the desert road toward the Red Sea."

Then the Lord spoke to Moses and Aaron: "How long must I tolerate this evil community who are constantly complaining against Me? I have heard the grumblings that these Israelites are directing toward Me. So tell them, 'This is what the Lord says: "I heard what you said! As surely as I live, I will do these things to you! You will die in this desert! Every one of you who is 20 years old or older and who was officially counted will die! Why? Because You complained against Me—the Lord! None of you will enter the land that I vowed for you to live there...with the exception of Caleb and Joshua! You said that your children would be captured, but I will bring them into that land. And they will enjoy what you rejected! As for you, your carcasses will rot in this desert! Your sons must be shepherds here in the desert for 40 more years! They must suffer because of your unbelief until your carcasses have rotted in the desert! You must suffer for your own sins for 40 years. This means one year for each of the 40 days that you explored the land. You will come to think of Me as your enemy. I am the *Lord*. I have spoken! I will certainly do these things to this whole evil community! They have come together against Me. So, they will all die together here in this desert!'"'"

Lord, our sin can delay Your plan for us
    But it will not cancel Your plans.

Lord, teach me to persist in prayer for answers
    So that I find Your perfect plan for my life.

Lord, when sin delays what You want to do for me,
    Teach me patience to wait for Your perfect will.

Amen.

Because the men whom Moses had sent to explore the land returned and spread their complaints against God to the whole community, giving a false, discouraging report about the land of Canaan, God punished them. Therefore, the Lord killed those ten men with a terrible sickness in His presence, because they had given such a false, misleading report about the land. Out of those 12 men who went to explore the land, only two did not die, Joshua the son of Nun, and Caleb the son of Jephunneh.

All the Israelites were very sad when Moses told these things to them. They wept. Early the next morning, they started to go toward the high hill country. They admitted, "We have sinned! Look, we're here! We will go wherever the Lord tells us to go!"

But Moses said, "Why are you still violating the Lord's command? You will *not* succeed! Do *not* go up! The Lord is *not* with you! You will be defeated by your enemies! The Amalekites and the

Canaanites will face you, and they will kill you with their swords. Why? Because you have already turned away from the Lord; you are not following Him anymore. The Lord will *not* be with you!"

Nevertheless, they were stubborn. They went on up to the high hill country of the Lord, but Moses and the Ark of the Covenant did not leave the middle of the camp.

Then the Amalekites and the Canaanites who lived in those mountains came down and they attacked the Israelites. They beat the Israelites back all the way to Hormah.

Lord, those rebellious Jews tried to go where You commanded

But they did it at the wrong time in the wrong way.
They did it without Your presence.

Lord, I want to know Your perfect will for my life,
And I want to do it in a perfect way,
Help me walk with You perfectly.

Lord, help me remember that a good act on a second day

Does not cover up my rebellion on the first day.
Help me obey You instantly and completely.

Amen.

Numbers 14

THE STORY OF UNBELIEF
AT KADESH-BARNEA

Date: 1490 B.C. ~ Place: Kadesh-Barnea

A t last the people of Israel reached Kadesh-Barnea on the very border of the land God promised to them. From Kadesh-Barnea they could see the low green foot hills of the Promised Land, unlike the desert where they had lived for a year and a half. Four hundred miles of hard desert travel was almost over. Green hills ahead.

But these people had complained many times before, and had doubted God many times before. Would they once more doubt God and complain about His provision for them?

Seeing the green hills on the horizon, you'd think the people of Israel would run toward rest and comfort. Think of what they'd give up when they reached the visible green hills. No longer would they daily eat manna, but they'd have barley and wheat. No longer would they drink water from hot desert pools, but they'd drink from cool mountain brooks and streams. No longer would they pack up to move their possessions from place to place. No longer would they set up a nightly watch to protect them from desert raiders. When they reached the Promised Land every man would sit under his fig tree and enjoy his own home.

But once a person rebels against God, it's hard to be obedient. Their unbelief wanted proof that their doubts were real. Moses reminded them 40 years later, "And every one of you came near to me and said, 'Let us send men before us, and let them search out the land for us, and bring back word to us of the way by which we should go up, and of the cities into which we shall come'" (Deut. 1:22). They wanted proof that the land of milk and honey was really as sweet as promised. But they were not questioning the promise; they were doubting God Himself who gave the promise.

So God agreed and told Moses, "Send men to spy..." (Num. 13:2). Hadn't God promised to give them the land? Hadn't God promised to be with them? When we walk by human sight, we are left to human ways. When we walk by faith, we enjoy God's guidance and God's protection.

They sent 12 spies, one from each tribe. The 12 men saw what God promised, "We came to a land...surely it floweth with milk and honey." To prove their point they brought grapes so abundant, it took two men to carry the load.

But ten spies reported the enemy was strong, they lived in cities behind huge walls, and they were physically huge. The ten spies groveled in fear, "We were grasshoppers in their sight" (see Num. 13:33).

The last two spies—Joshua and Caleb—disagreed with the ten. The two optimistically said, "If the Lord delights in us, then He will bring us into this land and give it to us" (Num. 14:8).

The ten spies looked at the promises of God through difficulties, while the two saw what God could do, so the difficulties were no problem. Here was the fatal mistake. Unbelief only sees the difficulties in life, while faith looks into the heart of God and knows He can overcome difficulties. The ten spies, along with all Israel who believed their pessimism, lost the Promised Land because of their unbelief. It was not the strength of their foes that defeated them, for they never fought one battle in the Promised Land; they were defeated by their own unbelief.

Lord, may my heart of unbelief never defeat me.

Unbelief was their first sin; complaining about God was their second sin. They murmured against Moses, "If only we had died in the land of Egypt!" (Num. 14:2).

Their third sin was forgetfulness. They said, "Let us select a leader and return to Egypt" (Num. 14:4). They forgot the sting of the whip and the long torturous work days. And many people today choose the vicious taskmaster of addictive sin that squeezes the very life from their bodies, rather than choosing freedom in Christ.

This was the bitterest hour for Moses. He had loved the Jews, and he had sacrificed his position in Egypt for them. Their continued existence was because of his intercession for them. He had led them from one miracle to another. Yet they wanted to fire him and give his authority to "another" leader.

But the greatness of Moses is seen in the house of greatest disappointment. He fell on his face before the Lord. As his life task of leading Israel into the Promised Land crumbles before his eyes, the thunderstorm of unbelief destroys the vision of a land flowing with milk and honey.

They were within days of picking fresh grapes in the valley of Eschol. They could see shade trees everywhere. Their life dream was crashing to the ground, yet Moses' face was toward the ground—praying. Have you been there before? Have you rushed into God's presence when you couldn't go anywhere else?

Joshua and Caleb rose to the occasion. They pleaded with the ten spies and the multitude, "Only do not rebel against the Lord, nor fear the people of the land, for they are our bread; their protection has departed from them, and the Lord is with us. Do not fear them" (Num. 14:9).

But the congregation didn't just reject Joshua and Caleb, they wanted to stone them. What an evil response to men who speak for God.

Temptations come to reveal the evil in the heart. Did you see the difference? Temptation revealed the ten spies trusted in themselves. The multitude believed the spies. Temptation made the multitude pull their robes of self-protection around themselves.

Temptation brought out the best of Joshua and Caleb. When tempted, they trusted in God and they claimed the power of God to defeat their enemies.

While Joshua and Caleb were pleading with the multitude, Moses was on his face, pleading with Jehovah. God wanted to destroy the multitude on the spot. But Moses interceded, "Now if You kill these people as one man, then the nations which have heard of Your fame will speak, saying, 'Because the Lord was not able to bring this people to the land...therefore He killed them in the wilderness'" (Num. 14:15-16). So Moses asked, "Pardon the iniquity of this people, I pray, according to the greatness of Your mercy..." (Num. 14:19).

Then God first gave a reason for the terrible judgment on the people, "Because all these men who have seen My glory and the signs which I did in Egypt and in the wilderness, and have put Me to the test now these ten times...they certainly shall not see the land of which I swore to their fathers..." (Num. 14:22-23).

But what was the terrible judgment? "The carcasses of you who have complained against Me shall fall in this wilderness, all of you who were numbered..." (Num. 14:29). Their outburst of unbelief was actually rebellion against God. They refused to enter the land, so God will allow them to die in the wilderness. Until they die, their bed will be sand, their meals will be sand, their daily vision will be the hot burning sand. And finally, their graves will be sand.

This is a picture of those who refuse to believe God and follow God. Their bed is sin, their food is sin, their vision each day is sin, and in sin will they be buried.

All that night the people mourned greatly. They didn't cry because of their sin. They wept because their outward pleasures were taken away. How many times have we wept under the punishment of God because our pleasures are taken away, rather than weeping because we've disobeyed God and we chose sin over God's plan for our lives?

The following day we see fake repentance and obedience without faith. The following day they "repented" and they tried to enter the Promised Land by self-reliance and bravado courage. They went to battle, "Then the Amalekites and the Canaanites who dwelt in that mountain came down and attacked them, and drove them back as far as Hormah" (Num. 14:45).

Israel tried to do the right thing in the wrong way and on the wrong day. Yesterday was their day of faith and obedience. Today was a day late to do God's will. Today revealed their murmuring and rebellion. They were defeated because they sinned.

They were defeated because God was not with them. "Neither the ark of the covenant of the Lord nor Moses departed from the camp" (Num. 14:44). Remember, when you go into battle, make sure God's presence and God's man go with you.

My Time to Pray

Lord, help me always keep Your time in my life.
Israel didn't enter when You commanded them to go,
They disobeyed and lost everything they worked for.

May I always obey Your command to go,
And may I obey when You tell me to go.
Lord, help me obey Your will today in Your way,
So that tomorrow I will look back on today
And know I have obeyed You in faith.

Lord, when I always do Your will on the day You command,

Then I'll praise You for my tomorrows and past obedience
And yesterday will be my foundation for today.

May I please You and do Your will today

So that all my yesterdays will be foundation for tomorrow.

Amen.

Numbers 15

RULES ABOUT OFFERINGS

And the Lord told Moses to speak to the people and tell them: "You will enter a land which I am giving you as your home. There you will give the Lord offerings made by fire. These may be from the herd or the flock, and the smell will be pleasing to the Lord. These offerings may be whole burnt offerings or sacrifices for special vows, or they may be offerings which are voluntary gifts to Me. Or they may be festival offerings.

"The one who brings his offering must also give a food offering to Me. It should be 2 quarts of flour mixed with 1 quart of olive oil. Each time you offer a lamb as a whole burnt offering or as a sacrifice, you must also prepare 1 quart of wine as a drink offering. If you are offering a male sheep, you must also prepare a food offering. It should be 4 quarts of flour mixed with 1¼ quarts of olive oil. In addition, prepare 1¼ quarts of wine, as a drink offering to Me. The smell of it will be pleasing to Me. Sacrifice a young bull. This might be as a whole burnt offering or a peace offering or for a special vow to Me. Bring a food offering with the young bull of 6 quarts of flour mixed with 2 quarts of olive oil. Also, bring 2 quarts of wine as a drink offering made by fire. And, its smell will be pleasing to Me.

"All who are natural-born Israelites must perform these things, and the smell of their offerings by fire will be pleasing to Me. If foreign proselytes live with you now or in the future, they must offer offerings by fire, the smell will be pleasing to Me. But they must do it the same way you do. The law is the same for you as it is for the foreigners among you. It will be a law from now on for your generations. The teachings of the Torah and the rules are the same for you and for the foreigners who live among you."

Lord, help me remember the nature of a sacrifice.
A sacrifice is giving up something I need,
Or something I use, or something I enjoy.

Lord, when I sacrifice something to You, it's a choice
To put You and Your work first,
And put me and my plans second.

Lord, Israel was asked to show their faith and love to You,
By sacrificing their animals and crops to You.

Quite a sacrifice for those living in an agricultural society;
They gave You necessities, not luxuries.
May I be willing to sacrifice my necessities,
To demonstrate my faith and love to You.

Amen.

Then the Lord told Moses to tell the Israelites, "You are going to another land. I am taking you there. Before you eat food there, offer up part of it to Me as a raised offering. You must raise up a loaf of bread from the first harvest of your grain, as a present from the threshing floor. From now on, offer the first part of your dough to Me as a raised offering.

"Now what if you forget to obey any of these commands which I the Lord gave to Moses? These are the Lord's commands given to you through Moses. They began on the day when I gave them to you, and they will continue from now on for your children. Nevertheless, if you forget to obey one of these commands, or the community might not remember a command, then the whole community must offer a young bull as a whole burnt offering. The smell of it will be pleasing to Me. By law, you must also give a food offering and a drink offering along with it. Also, you must bring a young goat as a sin-offering."

Lord, I know that You have the attributes of personhood,
That You see, handle, hear, taste, and smell.

While You have these abilities to communicate with Your world,

You don't have physical eyes, hands, ears, mouth, or nose.
These are called anthropomorphisms so we humans
Can better understand You and Your ways.

Lord, You have the ability to smell the things of earth
And You enjoy the smell of good things.

I'm glad You are pleased with the smell of cooking meat
For those were the sacrifices of Your people

As they showed their devotion to You in the Old Testament.

Lord, I sacrifice my life to live for You (Rom. 12:1);
Be pleased with my devotion to You
And use me for Your glory.

Amen.

"The priest will atone for sin for all the Israelites. They will be forgiven, if they did not know that they were sinning. Therefore, they must bring gifts to Me for the wrong that they did. They must bring an offering by fire and a sin offering. Also, all of the foreigners who live among them will be forgiven because it was done in ignorance.

"If a person might sin without meaning to do it, he must bring a year-old female goat for a sin-offering. The priest will cancel the sin of the person who sinned in My presence. He will be forgiven. The same instruction applies to everyone who sins without meaning to do so—whether they are natural-born Israelites or they are foreigners who live among you.

"Anyone who sins on purpose (intentionally) is blaspheming Me. That person must be separated from his people; the same is done for anyone born among you or for a foreigner. Why? Because that person has turned against My word and broken My command. That individual must surely be separated from the others because He is guilty."

Lord, this passage reminds me how much You hate sin,
Especially when Your followers sin willfully.

Lord, I will do my best to obey Your commandments
And not sin as I live on this earth.

Lord, I don't know everything, so I sin unintentionally
Forgive me of all my sins of ignorance.

Help me to learn what I must do and give me strength
To please You and live above sin.

Amen.

Punishment of the Sabbath-Breaker

While the Israelites were still in the desert, they found a man who was collecting wood on the Sabbath day. Those who caught him brought him to Moses and Aaron and he stood before all the people. They put the man under guard, because it had not yet been declared what should be done to such an individual. Then the Lord said to Moses, "This man must surely die! All the people must kill him by throwing stones at him outside the camp."

So, the entire community took that man outside the camp, and killed him by throwing stones at him, just as the Lord had commanded Moses.

And the Lord told Moses to tell the Israelites, "Sew for yourselves tassels on the corners or hem of your clothes. Put a blue thread in each one of these tassels of the corners. Wear them from now on. They will remind you to practice all of My commands. This will keep you from following what your flesh desires or what your eye wishes for. That way you will remember and obey all of My commands. Then You will be a holy people for Me. I am the Lord, your God. I brought you out of the land of Egypt to be your God. I am the Lord, your God."

Numbers 16

THE REBELLION OF KORAH

Korah (a cousin of Moses), Dathan, Abiram, and On turned against
Moses. Korah was the son of Izhar, the son of Kohath, who was
the son of Levi. Dathan and Abiram were brothers, the sons of
Eliab. And On was the son of Peleth. Dathan, Abiram, and On
were from the tribe of Reuben. (Perhaps these Reubenites were
trying to assert the birthrights of Reuben, Jacob's firstborn son.)
These four men gathered 250 other Israelite men who were well-
known leaders chosen by the Jewish community. They challenged the authority of Moses. They assembled as a group
against Moses and Aaron and said, "You two men are not more
important than the whole group! *All* the people are holy, and
the Lord is among them. Why do you put yourselves above the
whole congregation?"

When Moses heard this, he laid down on the ground face down in
humble intercession. Afterward, Moses said to Korah and his
whole group: "Tomorrow morning the Lord will reveal who will
be the leader. The Lord will also show the one who is holy and
set apart as the high priest. The Lord will present Himself to
show whom He chooses to be the leader. So, Korah, you and
your whole group should do this: Each of you should get some
pans for burning incense. Tomorrow put fire and incense in
them. Then take these into the presence of the Lord. God will
choose the man who is to be the holy high priest."

Moses then said to Korah, "Listen now, you make-believe priest, will you
ever be satisfied? The God of Israel has separated Levites from
the rest of the Israelites to be priests. He permitted them to be

close to Him; they are privileged to perform service in the Lord's Holy Tent. Levites stand in front of the Jewish community to serve them. It is true that the Lord has brought you and all your fellow Levites near Him. But now, you want to be priests too!? No! Your complaint is *not* against Aaron; no, you and your entire group have gathered yourselves together against YAH-WEH!" Then Moses invited Dathan and Abiram, the sons of Eliab, to come to him. (Moses wanted to talk with these Reubenites separately, away from Korah, a Levite.) But they said, "We will not come! You took us away from a land where abundant food grows. You just want to boss us around. You have surely brought us here to this desert to kill us! You did *not* bring us into a land where plenty of food grows. You did *not* give us any land with fields and vineyards as you said you would. Will you cut out the eyes of these men? Would you blind them to the fact that you have *not* kept any of your promises?

"No! We will *not* come!"

Then Moses got very angry. He said to the Lord, "Do not accept their offering. I have not taken anything from them, not even one donkey. I have done no wrong to any of them!"

Then Moses said to Korah, "You and all your group must stand with your pans in the presence of the Lord tomorrow. Yes, you and they will stand there, also Aaron will stand there with his pan. Each of you are to take your pan and put incense in it. All of you will present these 250 pans before the Lord. You people must present your pans. Aaron will present his also."

The Next Day

So, each man got his pan, then put fire and incense into it. Then they stood at the doorway to the Meeting Tent. Moses and Aaron stood there too. (This was a test by fire, showing which men were accepted by God to be His priests.) Korah gathered all his group to oppose Moses and Aaron. And they all stood near the doorway to the Meeting Tent.

Then the glory of the Lord appeared to the whole community. The Lord spoke to Moses and Aaron: "Move away from this group of Korah! In a moment, I will consume them!"

Moses and Aaron fell face down on the ground. They cried out, "O God, You are the God over the spirits of every person. Please don't be angry with this whole group. Only *one* man (Korah, the ringleader) has sinned!"

Then the Lord spoke to Moses: "Tell the Jewish community to withdraw from around the tents of Korah, Dathan, and Abiram!" Moses stood up and went to Dathan and Abiram. The elders of Israel followed him. Then Moses warned the community: "Please move away from the tents of these evil men! Do not touch anything that belongs to them. If you do, then you might be destroyed along with all their sins!"

So, everyone cleared away from the tents of Korah, Dathan, and Abiram. (On was originally in the conspiracy against Moses, but probably withdrew when he realized the consequences of rebelling against Moses.) Dathan and Abiram were standing outside, at the entrance of their tents. Their wives, children, and little babies were with them.

Then Moses said, "Now you will know that the Lord has authorized me to do all these things. It was not *my* idea. If these men die a normal death—the way men usually die—then the Lord did *not* really send me! But if the Lord does something totally new, you will *know* these men have insulted the Lord; the ground will open up

its mouth and swallow them and everything that belongs to
them will go after them too! They will go down alive to Sheol."

When Moses finished saying all these words, the ground underneath the
men split open. The earth opened its mouth and swallowed
them and all their families—all the men who were on Korah's
side, and everything they owned—went down. They and everything they owned were buried alive in Sheol. The earth closed
over them. They died. They were gone from the Jewish congregation! When all the people of Israel around them heard their
screams, they ran away, saying, "The earth might swallow us up
too!" Then a fire came out from the Lord and destroyed the 250
men who had offered the incense.

Lord, You have put Your spirit on those men You call
To serve You full time as Your leaders.

I realize there are those who like the "honor" and
"power" of "church leadership," but they were not called
By You, nor are they spiritually qualified.

Moses was correct to test them by fire,
And the church must test false leaders
Who wrongly want to lead Your church today.

Lord, You said, "Do not despise inspired messages,
Put all things to the test: Keep what is good,
And avoid every kind of evil" (1 Thess. 5:20, 22 TEV).

Lord, I will carefully obey what You have said,
In the inspired Word of God.

Amen.

Then the Lord spoke to Moses: "Tell Eleazar the priest, the son of Aaron, to take all the incense pans along with the burning embers and scatter the ashes elsewhere. But, he must keep the incense pans because they are still holy.

"These men sinned, and thus, they lost their lives. Take their pans and hammer them into flat metal sheets and cover the altar with them. These objects are holy because they once presented them to the Lord. This will be a continual sign to the Israelites." So, Eleazar had some men hammer the pans into flat sheets to overlay the altar.

This is what the Lord had commanded Eleazar through Moses. These metal sheets were to remind the Israelites that only descendants of Aaron and his sons were allowed to burn incense in the presence of the Lord (only blood relatives of Aaron were permitted to be in the priesthood). Anyone else would die, like Korah and his followers.

The next day, the whole community of the Israelites gathered to complain against Moses and Aaron. They said, "You have put to death the people of the Lord!" The Jewish community gathered to oppose Moses and Aaron. But when they turned toward the Meeting Tent, they saw the cloud suddenly cover it. And, the glory of the Lord appeared. Then Moses and Aaron went to the front of the Meeting Tent and the Lord spoke to Moses, "Move away from this group! In one minute, I am going to destroy them!"

Then Moses and Aaron fell to the ground face down in intercession. Moses said to Aaron, "Quick! Get your censer pan. Get fire from off the altar and put incense into the pan. Hurry to the people to make atonement for their sin. The Lord is very angry with them. A plague has already started to spread!" So, Aaron got the burning censer and ran into the center of the congregation. The epidemic was already spreading among them. Aaron quickly offered the incense to atone for the sins of the people. Because Aaron stood between the living and the dead, the sickness stopped. However, 14,700 people died from that plague. This was in addition to those who died because of Korah's rebellion. When the epidemic was halted, Aaron went back to Moses at the entrance of the Meeting Tent.

Numbers 16

THE STORY OF KORAH, DATHAN, AND ABIRAM

Date 1471 B.C. ~ Place: Marching Through the Wilderness

F ew ministers of God have had as many attacks on their ministry as Moses. After all Moses had done for the people of Israel, a formidable rebellion was led by Korah against Moses' position and authority.

Korah accused Moses and Aaron, "You take too much upon yourselves, for all the congregation is holy, every one of them, and the Lord is among them. Why then do you exalt yourselves above the assembly of the Lord?" (Num. 16:3).

When a minister has his authority challenged, what should he do? "So when Moses heard it, he fell on his face" (Num. 16:4).

There seems to always be crisis in the ministry of God's Word. Sometimes it is jealousy passed from mouth to mouth to mouth in the congregation. Some didn't like the sermon, or the way a preacher dresses, or they criticize what a pastor doesn't do. Criticism spreads like a prairie fire, consuming everything in its path.

Korah, Dathan, and Abiram rallied 250 Levites to challenge Moses' authority.

Moses challenged the rebels to live up to the privilege God gave them, "Is it a small thing to you that the God of Israel has separated you from the congregation of Israel, to bring you near to Himself, to do the work of the tabernacle of the Lord, and to stand before the congregation to serve them?" (Num. 16:9).

Moses reminded them of their privileges: they knew God, they served Him in the Tabernacle, and they ministered to the people. All great privileges, but that wasn't enough. No! They wanted Moses' place, or maybe they didn't like Moses, and wanted old Moses deposed. Jealousy has devious reasons for attacking God's ministers.

The band of 250 reminded Moses of his failure. "You have not brought us into a land flowing with milk and honey, nor given us inheritance of fields and vineyards" (Num. 16:14). Too often we look on the human side of our leaders and we don't see all they've done for God and for us. God places each star in its place to light the dark sky, can't He place each minister in this dark world of sin to shine the light of Jesus?

Moses reminded the rebels, "Therefore you and all your company are gathered together against the Lord" (Num. 16:11).

Moses left the final decision with God. The rebels were to take census— as a priest must do—and appear before God at the gate of the Tabernacle. Then it would be God's choice, not man's choice. To this Moses added, "By this you shall know that the Lord has sent me to do all these works, for I have not done them of my own will" (Num. 16:28).

Moses sent for Dathan and Abiram to come join the other rebels at the Tabernacle door. When they wouldn't come, Moses and the elders went to them. This was not Moses' battle; he would let God decide the leader of Israel. Moses announced, "If the Lord creates a new thing, and the earth opens its mouth and swallows them up with all that belongs to them, and they go down alive into the pit, then you will understand that these men have rejected the Lord" (Num. 16:30).

God stamped out rebellion without mercy. If you have cancer, it must be cut out if you would live. "The earth opened its mouth and swallowed them up, with their households and all the men with Korah, with all their goods" (Num. 16:32). What about the 250 men with cancer? "A fire came out from the Lord and consumed the two hundred and fifty men who were offering incense" (Num. 16:35).

My Time to Pray

Lord, teach me to humbly walk with You and serve You,
May I never think of myself greater
Than the spiritual gifts You give me for service.

Lord, may I never be jealous of other people's position and gifts.
May I pray for them and support their ministry.
Keep me from having a jealous heart.

Amen.

Numbers 17

AARON'S WALKING STICK

And the Lord told Moses to tell the people, "Get twelve walking sticks from the ruler of each ancestral tribe. Then write the name of each man on his stick. Also write Aaron's name on the walking stick of Levi. Gather one stick for the head of each ancestral tribe.

"Put the twelve walking sticks in the Meeting Tent in front of the Ark of the Covenant where I will meet with you. I will choose the man I want to be My high priest by causing his stick to begin sprouting. This is how I will stop the grumblings of the Israelites; because they are always complaining against you and Aaron." So, Moses spoke to the Israelites, and each of the 12 rulers gave him a walking stick—one stick for each ancestral tribe. And, Aaron's walking stick was among theirs.

Lord, in chapter 16 You deal with the political rebellion against Moses,

Now in chapter 17 You are dealing with spiritual rebellion against Aaron.

Lord, I will recognize those You have called and anointed

For full-time Christian service. I will follow their leadership And learn from their teaching and example.

Lord, I pray for my spiritual leaders that they will Point me to You. Speak to me through them.

Amen.

Moses placed the sticks in the presence of the Lord in the Tabernacle. The next day, Moses went into the Tent of the Covenant, and behold Aaron's stick had grown leaves! (It represented the tribe of Levi.) It even put forth buds, blossomed with a flower, and had produced ripe almonds! Moses brought out all the walking sticks from the Lord's presence to the Israelites. They looked and each man took back his stick.

Then the Lord said to Moses, "Put back Aaron's walking stick in front of the Ark of the Covenant, because it must be kept as a proof to those people who are always turning against Me. This will stop their constant complaining against Me, or else they will die!" So Moses obeyed what the Lord commanded him to do.

Lord, the dry walking stick that bloomed and bore fruit
Shows that You are able to make dead bodies live,
That they will prosper and be fruitful in eternity.
I thank You for this picture that shows
Your resurrection promise and power.

Lord, I believe Your promise of resurrection throughout Scripture
I know one day I will be raised from death,
And that I'll live forever with You.

I thank You for the hope of life beyond the grave
Now I will live for You on this earth,

Because I have the hope of Heaven after death.

Amen.

The people of Israel then said to Moses: "Listen, we are about to die! We are lost. We are all lost! When anyone even comes close to the Tabernacle of the Lord, he dies. Will we all die?"

Numbers 18

THE DUTIES OF THE PRIESTS
AND THE LEVITES

And the Lord said to Aaron, "You, your sons, and your family are now
responsible for anything that goes wrong in the sanctuary. And
you and your sons are responsible for handling any infractions
against the priests.

"Bring with you your fellow Levites from the tribe of your father. They will
help you and your sons in serving in the Tabernacle. The Levites are
under your control. They are in charge of doing all the work that
needs to be done in the Tabernacle. However, they must *not* go near
the furniture in the sanctuary or near the altar. If they do, then both
you and they will die! They will work with you to take care of the
Meeting Tent and do all the work that needs to be done. No one
else may come near you. You must take charge of the sanctuary and
the altar so I won't become angry with the Israelites again. I Myself
have chosen your fellow Levites from among the Israelites as a gift
that is given to you from Me so they can serve in the Tabernacle.
Only you and your sons may serve as priests. Only you (and suc-
ceeding high priests) may serve at the altar or go behind the curtain.
I am giving you this gift of serving as a priest. If any unauthorized
person tries to take the place of the priest, he will be put to death!"

Offerings for the Priests

Then the Lord said to Aaron, "I am making you responsible for all the
holy, raised offerings that the Israelites give to Me. I give them to

you. They are for you and your sons as your share. They will be your continual portion and your share of the offerings will be that part which is not burned. The people will bring Me all kinds of gifts—all their food offerings, all their sin offerings, and all their penalty offerings which will be set apart for you and your sons. You must eat it in a holy place.

"I also give you other offerings—raised offerings and wave offerings—which the Israelites present to Me. I give these to you and your sons, and your daughters. This is your share; anyone in your family who is clean may eat it. And I give you all the best olive oil and all the best new wine and grain. What the Israelites give to Me, I give to you. These are the first fruits that they harvest. They bring to Me all the first fruits that they will harvest. These things will be yours. Anyone in your family who is 'clean' may eat these things. Everything in Israel that is dedicated to Me is yours.

"The first one born to any Jewish family will be given to Me. This is true for both human beings and animals, and that will be yours. But you must make a payment (redeem) every firstborn son and every firstborn animal. When they are 1 month old, you must make a payment of 2 ounces of silver as set by the standard of the sanctuary. But you must not make a payment for the first-born ox or the firstborn of a sheep or the firstborn of a goat. Those animals are holy. Sprinkle their blood on the altar and burn their fat as incense. This is an offering made by fire. The smell is pleasing to Me. But the meat will be yours. Also the chest that is presented and the right leg will be yours. Anything the Israelites present as holy gifts to Me, which the Israelites lift up to Me, I give them to you, your sons, and your daughters. It will always be your share. This law is a lasting promise from Me to you and your children."

The Lord also said to Aaron, "Your priests will not inherit any of the land." (The priests and the Levites were depending upon God and the contributions [tithes] of the other tribes for their entire livelihood. The priests and the Levites were completely devoted to the service of God.)

Offerings for the Levites

God continued speaking, "Israel will give 10 percent of what they make to Me. I give that one-tenth to the Levites. This is their payment for the work which they do serving at the Tabernacle. But the other Israelites must never go near the Meeting Tent. If they do, then they will die for their sin! Only the Levites should work in the Tabernacle. They are responsible for any sins committed against it. This is a constant rule from now on. The Levites will not get any land among the other Israelites. Instead, the Israelites will give 10 percent of everything they make to Me. And I will give that raised offering as one-tenth to the Levites as their inheritance. Therefore, I have said that they would have no land (inheritance) among the people of Israel."

Then the Lord spoke to Moses: "Tell the Levites, 'You will receive 10 percent of everything that the Israelites make. I give that to you as your inheritance. However, you must give back 10 percent of that to Me as a raised offering, that is, 10 percent of the 10 percent. I will accept your raised offering just as much as I accept the offerings of grain from the threshing floor from other Jews, or the offerings of new wine. (Like all the other Israelites, the Levites were commanded to pay their tithes to the priest.) In this way, you will also present a raised offering to Me (just as all the other Israelites do). You will receive 10 percent from the Israelites, then, give 10 percent of that to Aaron the priest as My share. Choose the best and the holiest part from what you

receive as the portion which you must give to Me.' Tell the
Levites: 'When you present your best, it will be accepted as
much as the grain of the threshing floor and as the wine of the
wine press. You and your families may eat the 90 percent portion anywhere. That is your pay for your work in the Tabernacle.
And when you give the best part to Me, then you will never be
guilty. If you do not profane the holy offerings of the Israelites,
then you will not die!'"

Numbers 19

RULES ABOUT CLEANLINESS

And the Lord spoke to Moses and Aaron: "This is the law (Torah) that I
command: Tell the Israelites to get a young, reddish-brown cow
with no physical defects. It must not have been used for work
("upon which a yoke has never come"). Give the cow to Eleazar
the priest. He will take it outside the camp and kill it. Then
Eleazar the priest must put some of her blood on his finger and
sprinkle the blood seven times in the direction of the front of the
Tabernacle. Then the entire cow must be burned while he watches. Her skin, her meat, her blood, and her waste must all be
burned up. Then the priest must take a cedar stick, attach a hyssop branch (Note: Hyssop is a small fragrant plant from the
mint family. It is bushy and makes a good paint brush or sprin-
kling device [see Lev. 14:4,6,49,51-52; Num. 19:18; Heb.
9:19]) with a red string to sprinkle her blood toward the burning cow.

"Then the priest must bathe himself and wash his clothes with water.
After that, he may come back into the camp. Then someone who
is 'clean' will collect the ashes from the cow, and store them in a
'clean' place outside the camp. The sons of Israel will use these
ashes in a special ceremony to atone for sin. The man who collected the cow's ashes must wash his clothes; he will be
'unclean' until the evening. This is a permanent rule for the
Israelites and the foreigners among them.

"Whoever touches a human corpse will be 'unclean' for seven days.
(Some have estimated that about 100 people died every day during this 38-year-long stay in the Sinai Desert.) He must purify

himself with water. He must do this on the third day, and again on the seventh day. Then he will be 'clean.' However, if he does not purify himself on the third day and the seventh day, then he cannot be 'clean.'

"Whoever touches a human corpse is 'unclean.' If he stays 'unclean' ("does not purify himself") and he goes to the Tabernacle, it becomes 'unclean' ("he has defiled the Tabernacle of Yahweh"). So, he must be separated from Israel. If the cleansing water is not sprinkled on him, then he will stay 'unclean.'

"This is the teaching (Torah) about someone who dies in his house. Anyone in the tent or anyone who comes into the tent will be 'unclean' for seven days. And every open container which has no cover on it becomes 'unclean.'

"If anyone in an open field touches someone who was killed by a sword or who has died a natural death, then he is 'unclean.' He will be 'unclean' for seven days. So, you must use the ashes from the burnt sin offering to make that person 'clean' again. Pour fresh water over the ashes into a jar. A 'clean' person must take a hyssop branch and dip it into the water. Then he must sprinkle it over the tent and on all its objects. And, he must sprinkle the people who were there. He must sprinkle anyone who touched a bone or the body of someone who was killed. He must sprinkle anyone who touched a corpse or a grave. Then someone who is 'clean' must sprinkle this water on the 'unclean' person. He must do this on the third day, and again on the seventh day. On the seventh day, that person becomes 'purified.' He must wash his clothes and take a bath in water. He will be 'clean' that evening. If anyone who is 'unclean' does not become 'purified,' then that person must be separated from the congregation. He was not sprinkled with the cleansing water. He stays 'unclean.' He would make My Tabernacle 'unclean.' This is a permanent rule. Whoever sprinkles the cleansing water must also wash his clothes. Anyone who touches that water will be 'unclean' until the evening. Anyone whom the unclean person touches becomes 'unclean.' And, whoever touches him will be 'unclean' until the evening."

Numbers 20

MOSES DEFIES GOD

In the first month of the 40th year after leaving Egypt, the whole community of Israelites arrived at the desert of Zin. They camped at
Kadesh. Miriam died, and she was buried there (four months
before Aaron's death [see Num. 33:38]). Now, there was no
water for the community. So, they gathered together against
Moses and against Aaron. The people argued with Moses. They
said, "We wish we would have died when our Hebrew brothers
died in the Lord's presence. Why did the two of you bring the
Lord's congregation into this desert? Are we and our livestock
supposed to die here? And why did you bring us up from Egypt
to this awful place? It has no grain, no figs, no vines, and no
pomegranates! And there is no water for us to drink!"

Then Moses and Aaron left that gathering and went to the Tabernacle
and lay on the ground face down. And the glory of the Lord
appeared to them, and spoke to Moses: "You and your brother
Aaron must get Aaron's walking stick and you must gather the
community. Speak to that rock in plain view of the people. It
will yield its water! You are to bring water out of that rock for
them. Give that water to the people and their animals."

So, Moses took Aaron's walking stick from the Ark of the Covenant. He
did just as the Lord told him.

Moses and Aaron assembled the congregation in front of the rock. Then
Moses said, "Now listen to me, you rebels! (God had told Moses
to speak to the rock, *not* to the people.) Do you want us to
bring water out of this rock for you?" Then Moses raised his

hand and hit the rock with the walking stick. Water started to gush out immediately. And the people and their animals drank from it. However, the Lord said to Moses and Aaron, "Because you did *not* obey Me, you did *not* honor Me in the sight of the people, therefore you two will not lead this congregation into the land that I will give them!" These were the waters of Meribah. (Hebrew means "arguing" or "quarreling.") Here the Israelites argued with the Lord, but the Lord showed them that He is holy.

The Edomites Would Not Let the Israelites Pass

From Kadesh, Moses sent messengers to the king of Edom, saying, "You know about all the troubles your brothers have had. Our ancestors went down into Egypt and lived there for many years. The people of Egypt were cruel to our ancestors. So they cried out to the Lord. He heard us and sent an angel to bring us out of Egypt. Now, look, we are here at Kadesh, a town on the border of your land. Please let us pass through your country. We will not touch any fields of grain or vineyards. We will not drink water from the wells. We will travel only along the King's Road. (This famous road had been used since the Early Bronze Age. It led from the Gulf of Aqaba in the south up through Edom to Damascus.) We will not turn right or left until we have passed through your country."

But the king of Edom answered: "You may *not* pass through here! If you try, then I will come and meet you with swords."

The Israelites answered: "We will go along the main road. If we or our animals drink any of your water, then we will pay for it. We only want to walk through. That is all."

But the king answered: "You may *not* pass through here!" Then the Edomites went out to oppose the Israelites with a large and powerful army. The Edomites refused to let them pass through their country. So, the Israelites turned back.

Aaron Dies on Mount Hor

The entire community of the Israelites moved from Kadesh to Mount Hor, near the boundary of Edom. The Lord spoke to Moses and Aaron at Mount Hor: "Aaron is going to die. He must *not* go into the land that I am giving the Israelites. Because both of you rebelled against My instruction at the waters of Meribah.

"Moses, get Aaron and his son Eleazar and take them up on Mount Hor. Take off Aaron's special priestly clothes (Moses had personally vested Aaron with these garments [see Lev. 8:7-9]) and put them on his son Eleazar, because Aaron will die there—he will join his ancestors." Moses obeyed the Lord's command. Together they climbed Mount Hor. And the whole congregation saw them go up there. Moses removed Aaron's priestly clothes. With them, Moses dressed Eleazar, Aaron's son. And Aaron died there on top of the mountain. (See Deuteronomy 10:6. Moserah must be another name for Mount Hor or Aaron's body was moved and re-buried at Moserah.) Then Moses and Eleazar came back down from the mountain.

Then all the people learned that Aaron was dead. (Aaron was 123 years old [see Num. 33:38-39].) So, everyone of Israel cried over him for 30 days.

Numbers 20:1-13

THE STORY OF MOSES' SIN AT MERIBAH

Date: 1452 B.C. ~ Place: Desert of Zin

The 40 years of wanderings are almost over. Soon Israel will enter the land flowing with milk and honey. Most of those who rebelled at Kadesh-Barnea are dead, their corpses buried in the sand. The glory cloud had led them to criss-cross the desert many times. Now the cloud led them back to Kadesh. When Israel came to Kadesh the first time there was water to drink, but this time there was none.

A footnote occurs here—Miriam died. Moses' older sister, who watched when baby Moses was set afloat in the Nile River, was gone. It was Miriam who said to Pharaoh's daughter, "I'll find a nurse maid for baby Moses." But her soul was now with the Lord.

After being encamped for some months, there was no water. The sons of those who rebelled at Kadesh-Barnea now came to Moses with their own rebellion and complaints. "Why have you brought up the assembly of the Lord into this wilderness, that we and our animals should die here?" (Num. 20:4). They claimed God's unfulfilled promises, "It is not a place of grain or figs or vines or pomegranates; nor is there any water to drink" (Num. 20:5).

Although the glory cloud sat over the Tabernacle for all to see God's presence with them, and although they gathered manna daily, yet the unbelief of their hearts seeped out through their criticism. God was with them, but they couldn't trust Him.

Moses did what he previously did when challenged. "So Moses and Aaron...fell on their faces. And the glory of the Lord appeared to them"

(Num. 20:6). We should be careful when we trust our old methods of prayer, but we stop trusting the God who makes prayer fresh every day.

God told Moses, "Take the rod; you and your brother Aaron gather the congregation together. Speak to the rock before their eyes, and it will yield its water; thus you shall bring water for them out of the rock..." (Num. 20:8).

Moses heard only the first thing God said, "Take the rod." Perhaps he forgot the other things God told him to do. God said "speak" and Moses heard "smite."

Then Moses became guilty...he fell at the point of his strength, not the point of his weakness. Hadn't God said, "Moses was very humble, more than all men who were on the face of the earth" (Num. 12:3)? Wow! God said Moses was the humblest man on earth.

In his pride Moses said, "Must we bring water for you out of this rock?" (Num. 20:10). What arrogance! Moses thought he was doing it. He didn't give credit to God. Doesn't Paul tell us, "Let him who thinks he stands take heed lest he fall" (1 Cor. 10:12).

When we arrogantly think we are strong, then we are weak. The flesh blinds us to our sin of self, and we fall at our strength. Didn't Abraham, the man of faith, lie about his wife because he couldn't trust God? Didn't David, a man after God's own heart, chase a skirt? Didn't strong Elijah sit under a juniper tree and pray to die? Didn't bold Peter deny the Lord Jesus when confronted by a maid?

Lord, You know my strengths, keep me from selfishly bragging about them.

Moses was not to strike the rock, but speak to it. Don't we do the same thing when we trust our strength to strike, rather than trusting God's Word to speak? Moses' greatest sin was that it was done before the eyes of the multitude. That doesn't mean private sins are not as bad as public sins, but our public sins have much greater consequences.

God didn't punish the people because of their leader's sin. No! The water gushed out "abundantly." They had complained, and they got water. But

Moses was punished, "Because you did not believe Me, to hallow Me in the eyes of the children of Israel" (Num. 20:12).

Because of Moses' sin, God said, "You shall not bring this assembly into the land which I have given them" (Num. 20:12). One of the key verses of Hebrews is, "They could not enter in because of unbelief" (Heb. 3:19). The way we express unbelief is by our disobedience of God. Unbelief and disobedience are the same doorway; you enter by disobedience, but you exit in unbelief.

All God wanted was for Moses to speak to the rock. Have you ever thought that speaking to the rock is a lot easier than smiting the rock? When we speak, God does the work. When we smite, we must do the outward work.

Then maybe, we try to meet new challenges by the old methods we used before. Forty years earlier Moses struck the rock and water came forth; now Moses tries the same thing again, but it doesn't work. Why? Because God gave different instructions. Remember, you can't use yesterday's tools in today's world—and be in ministry next year.

God doesn't repeat Himself, and He puts new wine in new wineskins; He doesn't put new wine in old wineskins.

Perhaps the greatest sin here was ignoring the type. The rock is a symbol of Christ who is our foundation. "That rock was Christ" (1 Cor. 10:4). The first smiting of the rock is symbolic of the death blow Christ received when He died for our sins. Christ was once offered to bear the sins of many (see Heb. 9:28), and "For the death that He died, He died to sin once for all; but the life that He lives, He lives to God" (Rom. 6:10). The death of Christ is a finished act; now we speak to Christ in prayer and supplication. "Whatever you ask in My name, that I will do..." (John 14:13).

Don't forget Moses stood for the Lord, Moses gave us the Law, and he communicated the Law. But the Law could never bring us into the land of mercy and forgiveness. Moses was punished for disobedience just as every person who broke the Law was punished.

But grace brought us into the land of promise. The Israelites leader was Joshua (Hebrew name), but the one whose name was Jesus (Greek name for Joshua) brought us into the very heart of God.

Just as we must reap what we sow, so Moses was not permitted to lead Israel into the Promised Land. Yet, Christ brought us beyond the Law.

When Christ stood on the Mount of Transfiguration, Moses stood there with Christ. Isn't it better to enter the land with Jesus Christ and see Him glorified, than to go into Canaan with other humans? Let's learn with Paul, "His grace is sufficient for us."

My Time to Pray

Lord, it's inconceivable that Moses sinned against You,
And You didn't permit him to enter Canaan.

Yet Your word is clear, Moses sinned publically
And You kept him from the Promised Land.

Lord, teach me to instantly obey Your Word,
And seek Your will with all my heart.

Lord, I will be Your servant and obey You,

I will quickly obey Your word.

Amen.

Numbers 21

THE ISRAELITES DEFEAT THE CANAANITES

The Canaanite king of Arad lived in the southern Negev. He heard that the Israelites were coming on the road to Atharim. So, he attacked and captured some of them.

Then the Israelites solemnly vowed to the Lord: "If You will truly defeat these people, then we will completely destroy their towns." The Lord listened to the Israelites, and permitted them to defeat the Canaanites. The Israelites completely destroyed them and their cities. So, the place was named Hormah.

The Brazen Serpent

The Israelites traveled from Mount Hor on toward the End Sea (the eastern part, now called the Gulf of Aqaba). They did this so they could go around the country of Edom. However, the people became impatient along the way and complained against God and against Moses. They said, "Why did you bring us up out of Egypt? Do you want us to die in this desert? There is no normal food, nor is there much water here! We hate this worthless manna." So, the Lord sent poisonous snakes (with a fiery bite) among the people. They bit some of them, and many of them died.

Then the people came to Moses and said, "We have sinned, because we complained against the Lord and against you. Pray to the Lord, so that He will take away these snakes!" So, Moses prayed for the people.

The Lord said to Moses, "Make a snake-like object out of brass for your-selves. Then put it up on a pole. I want them to ponder their sins. I merely used this crude sculpture of a poisonous snake as a test to see if the individual would obediently look at it with faith. If anyone has been bitten by a poisonous snake, he must look at the bronze snake and trust Me. Then that person will live!" So Moses made the bronze snake, and put it up on a pole. Whenever a poisonous snake bit anyone, if he or she looked at that bronze snake and trusted God, that person lived.

The Israelites Travel From Mount Hor to Mount Pisgah

The Israelites went and camped at Oboth. Then they went from Oboth and camped at Iye-abarim. This was in the desert, east of Moab. From there they went and camped in the Zered Valley where the creek begins among the mountains to the east of Moab. Flowing westward it empties into the Dead Sea. From there, they went and camped across the Arnon River. This was in the desert just inside the border of the Amorites. The Arnon River was the boundary between the Moabites and the Amorites. That is why the Book of the Wars of the Lord says: "And…He conquered Waheb in Suphah, of the dry riverbeds of the Arnon River, and the slopes of the ravines that lead to the settlement of Ar. These places are at the border of Moab."

The Israelites went from there to Beer, the well where the Lord said to Moses: "Gather the people; I will give them water." (However, this time, they had to dig the well themselves.)

Then the Israelites sang this song:

> Pour out water, O well!
> Sing about it!

Princes dug this well.

Important men dug this well.

Their scepters were their authority to dig this well.

The people went from the desert to Mattanah. From Mattanah, they went to Nahaliel and on to Bamoth. From Bamoth, they went to the valley of the pastures of Moab. From there they could see the top of Mount Pisgah.

The Israelites Defeat the Amorites

The people of Israel sent messengers to Sihon, the king of the Amorites. They said to him: "Let us pass through your country. We will not go through any fields of grain or into vineyards. We will not drink water from the wells. We will travel only along the King's Road. (This famous road had been used since the Early Bronze Age, leading from the Gulf of Aqaba up through Edom to Damascus.) We will stay on it until we have passed through your country."

But King Sihon would *not* permit the Israelites to pass through his country. Instead, Sihon gathered his army together and marched out to engage Israel in battle in the desert. They fought against Israel at Jahaz. Israel killed Sihon with the edge of the sword. Then they captured his land from the Arnon River to the Jabbok River. They took his land as far as the Ammonite border, which was strongly defended. Israel captured all the Amorite towns and lived in them. They took Heshbon (the capital city) and all the villages around it. (Heshbon was the city where Sihon the Amorite king lived. In the past, he had fought against the king of Moab, and taken away all the land as far as the Arnon River. That is why the poets say:

"Come to Heshbon,
> And rebuild it.

Rebuild Sihon's city.

A fire began in Heshbon.

Flames came out of Sihon's city
> And destroyed it.

It scorched the lords of the Arnon highlands.

How terrible for you, Moab!
> The people of Chemosh are ruined!

His sons ran away.
> His daughters were captured

By Sihon, king of the Amorites.
> But we defeated those Amorites

And the boasts of the Amorites fade into oblivion.
> We ruined their downs

And, we destroyed them as far as Nophah, near Medeba."

So, Israel lived in the land of the Amorites. Moses sent spies to the town of Jazer. Then they captured the towns around it. They forced out the Amorites who lived there. Then the Israelites went up the road toward Bashan. Og, the king of Bashan, and his army marched out to engage the Israelites in battle. They fought at Edrei. The Lord said to Moses, "Don't be afraid of him. I will hand him, his whole army, and his land over to you. Do to him what you did to Sihon, the Amorite king who lived at Heshbon."

So, the Israelites killed Og, and his sons, and all of his army. No one was left alive. So they seized his land.

Numbers 22

BALAAM THE FALSE PROPHET

Then the people of Israel went to the plains of Moab and camped near the Jordan River across from Jericho. Balak, the son of Zippor, saw everything that the Israelites had done to the Amorites, and Moab was truly terrified of them. The Moabites said to their elders, "This horde will take everything around us, just like a bull eating grass in a field."

Balak, the son of Zippor, was the king of Moab at that time. He sent messengers to Balaam (a famous "soothsayer" who prophesied for a business, not a religion), the son of Beor, at Pethor. He sent to the Euphrates River, in the land of Amaw, to summon him. Balak said, "Listen, a whole nation has come out of Egypt! They cover the earth, and they are camping next to me. They are too powerful for me, so come and put a curse on them for me! Perhaps then I can defeat them and force them to leave this area. I know that if *you* bless someone, the blessings happen. And if *you* put a curse on someone, it also happens."

The elders of Moab and the elders of Midian traveled to Balaam with money in their hands. When they found Balaam, they told him what Balak had said.

Balaam said to them, "Stay here tonight; I will give you an answer according to whatever the Lord may speak to me." So, the Moabite chiefs stayed with him.

God came to Balaam and asked him, "Who are these men with you?" Balaam told God, "The king of Moab, Balak, the son of Zippor, sent them to me. They told me, 'Listen, a whole nation has come out of Egypt! They cover the earth. Come now and put a curse on them for me! Perhaps then I will be able to defeat them and force them out.'"

But God said to Balaam, "Do *not* go with them! Do not put a curse on Israel, because they are blessed."

The next morning Balaam got up and told Balak's chiefs, "Go back to your own country. The Lord has refused to allow me to go with you!"

So, the Moabite chiefs went back to Balak and told him, "Balaam refused to come with us!"

So, Balak sent different chiefs. This time, he sent more of them. And they were more important than the first ones. These men went to Balaam and said, "Balak, the son of Zippor, says this: 'Please don't let anything stop you from coming to me! I will pay you very well. I will do *anything* that you tell me! But, please come. Put a curse on these people for me!'"

But Balaam answered the servants of Balak: "If King Balak were to give to me all of his palace full of silver and gold, I still could not go beyond the command of the Lord my God, to do anything—great or small! Please, you men, stay here for tonight. I will find out anything more that the Lord might say to me."

That night God came to Balaam and told him, "These men have come to summon you. Get up and go with them. However, you must do *only* what I speak to you."

Balaam got up the next morning, put a saddle on his donkey, and went with the Moabite chiefs.

Balaam and His Donkey

God became angry because Balaam went. (See 2 Peter 2:15-16. Balaam had already decided in his own heart that he would curse the people of Israel for money.) Balaam was riding on his donkey, and he had two servants with him. The Angel of the Lord stood in the road to kill him. The donkey saw the Angel of the Lord standing in the road with a drawn sword in his hand. So, the donkey swerved off the road and went into the field. Therefore, Balaam started hitting the donkey to make it go back on the road.

Later, the Angel of the Lord stood in a narrow path between two vineyards. There were walls on both sides. Again, the donkey saw the Angel of the Lord so the donkey thrust herself up against one wall. This scraped Balaam's foot against the wall. That is why Balaam hit her again. The Angel of the Lord did it again later on—the Angel stood in a very narrow place; it was too narrow to turn either left or right.

The donkey saw the Angel of the Lord, so she lay down underneath Balaam. Balaam was very angry and he started hitting the donkey with his stick. Then the Lord caused the donkey to speak. She said to Balaam, "What have I done to make you beat me three times?"

But the donkey said to Balaam, "I am your donkey, aren't I? You have ridden me all your life until this very day. Have you ever known me to act like this before?"

"No," Balaam said. Then the Lord opened Balaam's eyes to see the Angel. The Angel of the Lord was standing in the road with his sword in his hand. Then Balaam bowed face down on the ground.

The Angel of the Lord asked Balaam, "Why have you beaten your donkey three times? Listen, I have come out to kill you, because your way is not My way! The donkey saw Me; she turned away from Me three times. If she had not turned away from Me, then I would have certainly killed you by now! However, I would have let the donkey live."

Then Balaam said to the Angel of the Lord, "I have sinned! I did not realize that You were standing in the road to stop me. Now, since You see that this trip is such a bad idea, I'm just going to turn myself around and go back!" The Angel of the Lord said to Balaam, "No, go on with these men. (God had a purpose for Balaam.) However, say *only* the message that I speak to you; that is all you can say." So, Balaam went with the chiefs of Balak.

Balak Greets Balaam

Balak heard that Balaam was arriving. So, Balak went out to meet him at a town in Moab. It was on the boundary line, the Arnon River, at the border of his country. Balak said to Balaam, "I had asked you to come quickly before. Why didn't you come to me? I can afford to pay you well, can I not?"

But Balaam gave this answer to Balak: "Look, I have come to you now. However, I am not at liberty to speak anything! Whatever the message is that God puts in my mouth, *that* is what I will speak!" Then Balaam went with Balak. They came to Kiriath-Huzoth. Balak offered cattle and sheep as a sacrifice. He gave some meat to Balaam and the chiefs who were with him. The next morning, Balak took Balaam up to Bamoth-Baal. (This name means "the high places of baal" for worshiping Baal-Peor.) From there he could see the far edge of the Israelite people.

Numbers 23

BALAAM BLESSES ISRAEL THE FIRST TIME

Balaam said to Balak, "Build seven altars here for me. And, prepare seven bulls and seven male sheep for me." Balak did what Balaam asked. Then Balak and Balaam offered one ram and one bull on each of the altars.

Then Balaam said to Balak, "Stay here beside your whole burnt offering. I will go. Perhaps the Lord will come to meet me? I will tell you whatever He shows to me." Then Balaam went to a higher place. And God did come to Balaam there. Balaam said to God, "I have prepared seven altars. And I have offered one bull and one ram on each altar."

The Lord told Balaam what he should say. Then the Lord said, "Go back to Balak. And you must give him My message." So, Balaam went back to Balak. Balak and all the chiefs of Moab were still standing beside his whole burnt offering. Then Balaam gave them this message: "Balak brought me here from Syria. The king of Moab brought me from the mountains of the East. Balak said, 'Come, put a curse on the people of Jacob for me! Come, wish evil upon Israel!'

"But God has not cursed them," Balaam said, "Therefore, I cannot curse them." The Lord has not wished evil upon them. So, I cannot do so, either. I see them from the top of the rocks. I observe them from the high spots. Look, they are living securely as an isolated people. They are not listed among the nations. No one can count them, just as no one can count the dust. None can count even one-fourth of Israel. (The camp of Israel was divided into four divisions, three tribes in each division.) Let me die like good people do. Let me end up like them!"

And Balak said to Balaam, "What have you done to me? I brought you to put a curse on my enemies! But, you have done nothing but bless them!"

And, Balaam answered, "I must say whatever the Lord tells me to say!"

Balaam Blesses Israel a Second Time

Then Balak said to Balaam, "Please come with me to another place. You can see the Israelite people from there. However, you can only see the outer fringes from here. But you will see all of them from there. Put a curse on them for me from there!" So Balak took Balaam to the field of Zophim on top of Mount Pisgah. There Balak built seven altars. And he offered one bull and one ram on each altar.

So Balaam said to Balak, "Stay here next to your whole burnt offering. I will meet with God over there."

So, the Lord met with Balaam, and told Balaam what to say. Then God said, "Go back to Balak and give him My message."

So Balaam went to Balak, who was still standing next to his whole burnt offering along with his Moabite chiefs. Balak said to Balaam, "What has the Lord spoken?"

Then Balaam gave him this message: "Get up, O Balak, and listen! Pay attention to me, O son of Zippor! God is not a man, that He should tell a lie. God is not a human being, that He can change His mind. Whatever He says that He will do, He does. He always keeps His promises. Look, I have given them a blessing. Yes, God has blessed them, and I cannot reverse it. God has found nothing wrong in Jacob. He saw no fault in Israel. The Lord, their God, is with them. They praise their King. God brought them out of Egypt. They are as strong as wild ox. No spells will work on the people of Jacob. No fortune telling works against Israel. People now say this about them, 'Look what God has done!' Look, the people will rise up like an old lion. They get up like a strong lion. Lions don't lie down until they have eaten prey. They drink the blood of their victims."

Then Balak said to Balaam, "You have not cursed these people at all! So, please stop blessing them!"

Balaam answered Balak, "I told you before: 'I can only speak what the Lord speaks!'"

Balaam Blesses Israel a Third Time

Then Balak said to Balaam, "Please come, I will take you to another place. Perhaps God will be pleased to permit you to put a curse on them for me." So, Balak took Balaam to the top of Mount Peor that overlooks the desert.

Balaam told Balak, "Build seven altars for me here. Then prepare for me seven bulls and seven rams." Balak did what Balaam asked. Balak offered up one bull and one ram on each altar.

Numbers 24

BALAAM AND BALAK (CONTINUED)

Balaam saw that the Lord wanted to bless Israel. So, Balaam did not go to look for omens. He looked toward the desert. Balaam looked up and saw the Israelites camped, tribe by tribe. Then the Spirit of God was on him. Then Balaam gave them this message:

"This is the message or, 'prophecy,' of Balaam, the son of Boer: This is the message of a man who sees clearly. This is the message of a man who can hear the words of God. I see a vision from the Almighty One (El Shaddai). My eyes are wide open as I fall in front of Him. Your tents are beautiful, O people of Jacob! So are your homes, O Israel! Your tents spread out like valleys. (Orderly because they had followed God's instructions.) They spread out like gardens beside a river. They are like aromatic spices planted by the Lord. They are like cedar trees growing by the water. Israel's water buckets will always be full. Their crops will have plenty of water. Their king will be greater than Agag. Their kingdom will be very great. God brought them out of Egypt.

"They are as strong as a wild ox. They will defeat their enemies. They will crush their bones. They will smash their arrows. Like a lion, they lie down very quietly, waiting to attack. No one would disturb him. Anyone who blesses you will be blessed. And, anyone who curses you will be cursed!"

Then Balak became very angry at Balaam, pounding his fist. He said to Balaam, "I summoned you here to curse my enemies, but, look, you have truly blessed them three times! Now, get out of here!

Go home! I said I would pay you well. But, look, the Lord has caused you to lose your reward!"

Balaam told Balak, "You sent messengers to me and I told them: 'Balak could give me his palace full of silver and gold, but I still cannot go beyond the Lord's commands. I cannot do anything—good or bad—on my own. Whatever the Lord says, *that* is what I must speak!' Now, look, I am going back to my own people. Come, I will tell you what these people will do to *your* people in the future."

Then Balaam gave him this message: "This is the message of Balaam, the son of Beor: This is the message of a man who sees clearly. This is the message of a man who can hear the words of God. I have certain knowledge of the Most High God. I see a vision from the Almighty One (El Shaddai). My eyes are wide open as I bow in front of Him. I see Someone who will come some day. I see Someone who will come, but not soon. A Star will come from Jacob. A Ruler will rise from Israel. He will crush the heads of the Moabites. He will smash the skulls of the sons of Sheth. Edom will be conquered. His enemies, Seir, will be conquered. However, Israel will grow wealthy. He of Jacob will dominate. He will destroy those who are left in the city."

Then Balaam saw Amalek and gave this message: "Amalek was once a leading nation. But Amalek will be destroyed at the end!"

Then Balaam saw the Kenites and gave this message: "Your home seems safe. It is like a nest on a cliff. However, you Kenites will be burned up! Assyria will carry you off!"

Then Balaam gave this message: "Alas, no one can live when God does this. Ships will sail from the shores of Cyprus. They will defeat Assyria and Eber. Destruction will come to them, too!"

Then Balaam got up and returned home. (According to Numbers 31, Balaam must have returned, seeking Balak's favor [see Num. 31:8,16].)

Numbers 25

THE ISRAELITES ARE SEDUCED BY THE MIDIANITES

The people of Israel were still camping at Shittim. The men began sinning sexually with Moabite women. The women invited them to the sacrifices of their false gods. The Israelites ate food there and worshiped these gods. So, the Israelites began to worship Baal-Peor. (The Hebrew word *baal* means "lord"—the false god. Baal-worship involved "sacred" prostitution and child sacrifice.) And, the Lord was very angry with them. The Lord said to Moses, "Get all the elders of the people. Post the bodies of the sinners up in broad daylight in My presence. Then I will not be angry with the people of Israel anymore."

So, Moses said to Israel's judges, "Each of you must put to death the men of your tribe who have become worshipers of Baal-Peor!" Moses and the Israelites were gathered at the entrance to the Tabernacle. They were crying there. So, they assembled there to plead for mercy from God. And that must have been the moment when Zimri, an Israelite man, committed a very public outrage. He brought a Midianite woman to his brothers in plain sight of Moses and all the people. Phinehas, the son of Eleazar and the grandson of Aaron the high priest, saw this. So, he left the meeting and grabbed a spear. He followed the Israelite man into the man's tent and drove his spear through both of them— the Israelite man and the belly of the Midianite woman. Then the terrible disease among the Israelites stopped. This outbreak had killed 24,000 people.

The Lord spoke to Moses: "Phinehas, the son of Eleazar, the grandson of Aaron the high priest, has spared the Israelites from My punishment. He refused to tolerate the worshiping of any god but Me among them. He tried to uphold My honor. Therefore, I will not destroy them. So, tell Phinehas that I am making My covenant of peace with him! He and all his descendants will have a covenant. They will always be priests, because he showed great zeal for My honor. He canceled the sins of the Israelites."

The Israelite man who was killed with the Midianite woman was named Zimri, the son of Salu. Salu was the chief of a family group among the Simeonites. And the name of the Midianite woman who was put to death was Cozbi, the daughter of Zur. Zur was the chief of a Midianite family group.

Then the Lord spoke to Moses: "Attack the Midianites. Kill them! They are your enemies. They tricked you at Peor, and Cozbi their sister, the daughter of the Midianite chief, caused Israel to sin. She was killed when the epidemic came. It came because the people were worshiping the false god at Peor."

Numbers 26

THE ISRAELITES ARE COUNTED
A SECOND TIME

After the epidemic, the Lord spoke to Moses and Eleazar, the son of
Aaron the high priest: "Count the heads of every family of all the
people of Israel. About 38 years has elapsed since the last census. Count all the men who are 20 years old or older. They will
serve in the army of Israel."

Moses and Eleazar the high priest spoke to the people on the plains of
Moab near the Jordan River, across from Jericho. They said,
"Count the men who are 20 years old or older. This is what the
Lord commanded Moses."

Here are the Israelites who came out of the land of Egypt: The tribe of
Reuben was counted. (Reuben was the first son born to Israel.)
The Hanochite clan came from Hanoch. The Palluite clan came
from Pallu. The Hezronite clan came from Hezron. The Carmite
clan came from Carmi. The total number of the clans of the
Reubenites was 43,730 men.

The son of Pallu was Eliab. Eliab's sons were: Nemuel, Dathan, and
Abiram. Dathan and Abiram were the ones who turned against
Moses and Aaron. They followed Korah when he turned against
the Lord. The earth opened up and swallowed them and Korah.
They died when the fire burned up the 250 men. This was a
warning sign to all Israel. But the children of Korah did not die.

These were the clans in the tribe of Simeon: The Nemuelite clan came
from Nemuel. The Jaminite clan came from Jamin. The Jachinite

PRAYING FOR YOUR SECOND CHANCE

clan came from Jachin. The Zerahite clan came from Zerah. The
Shaulite clan came from Shaul. The total number of men in the
clans of Simeon was 22,200.

These were the clans in the tribe of Gad: The Zephonite clan came from
Zephon. The Haggite clan came from Haggi. The Shunite clan
came from Shuni. The Oznite clane came from Ozni. The Erite
clan came from Eri. The Arodite clan came from Arod. The
Arelite clan came from Areli. The total number of men from the
clans of Gad was 40,500.

These were the clans in the tribe of Judah: The Shelanite clan came
from Shelah. The Perezite clan came from Perez. The Zerahite
clan came from Zerah. These were the sons of Perez: The
Hezronite clan came from Hezron. The Hamulite clan came
from Hamul. The total number of the men from the clans of
Judah was 76,500. Two of Judah's sons, Er and Onan, died in
the land of Canaan.

These were the clans in the tribe of Issachar: The Tolaite clan came from
Tola. The Punite clan came from Puwah. The Jashubite clan
came from Jashub. The Shimronite clan came from Shimron. The
total number of men from the clans of Issachar was 64,300.

These were the clans in the tribe of Zebulun: The Seredite clan came
from Sered. The Elonite clan came from Elon. The Jahleelite clan
came from Jahleel. The total number of men from the clans of
Zebulun was 60,500.

These were the descendants of Joseph, through Manasseh and Ephraim,
by their clans: these were the descendants of Manasseh. The
Machirite clan came from Machir. (Machir was the father of
Gilead.) The Gileadite clan came from Gilead. The Iezerite clan
came from Iezer. The Helekite clan came from Helek. The
Asrielite clan came from Asriel. The Shechemite clan came from

Shechem. The Shemidaite clan came from Shemida. The Hepherite clan came from Hepher. Zelophehad, the son of Hepher, had no sons. He had only daughters. Their names were: Mahlah, Noah, Hoglah, Milcah, and Tirzah. The total number of men from the clans of Manasseh was 52,700.

These were the descendants of Ephraim by their clans: the Shuthelahite clan came from Shuthelah. The Becherite clan came from Becher. The Tahanite clan came from Tahan. And these were the descendants of Shuthelah: the Eranite clan came from Eran. These were the clans of the Ephraimites. The total number of men was 32,500. These were the descendants of Joseph by their clans.

These were the descendants of Benjamin by their clans: the Belaite clan came from Bela. The Ashbelite clan came from Ashbel. The Ahiramite clan came from Ahiram. The Shuphamite clan came from Shupham. The Huphamite clan came from Hupham. These were the descendants of Bela through Ard and Naaman. The Ardite clan came from Ard. The Naamite clan came from Naaman. These were the descendants of Benjamin by their clans. The total number of men was 45,600.

These were the descendants of Dan by their clans: the Shuhamite clans came from Shuham. These were the clans of Dan. The total number of men in the Shuhamite clans of Dan was 64,400.

These were the descendants of Asher by their clans: the Imnite clan came from Imnah. The Ishvite clan came from Ishvi. The Beriite clan came from Beriah. These were the descendants of Beriah by their clans. The Heberite clan came from Heber. The Malchielite clan came from Malchiel. Asher also had a daughter named Serah. These were the clans of the Asherites. The total number of men was 53,400.

These were the descendants of Naphtali by their clans: the Jahzeelite clan came from Jahzeel. The Gunite clan came from Guni. The Jezerite clan came from Jezer. The Shillemite clan came from Shillem. These were the clans of Naphtali. The total number of men was 45,400.

So, the total number of the men of Israel was 601,730. Then the Lord spoke to Moses: "Divide the land for inheritance among these people by the number of names. A large tribe will get more land. A small tribe will get less land. The amount of land that each tribe gets will depend on the proportionate number of its people. Only, divide the land by picking lots. And the land which each tribe gets will be named for that tribe. Divide the land by the authority of the lots. Divide it between large and small groups."

The tribe of Levi was also counted. These were the clans of Levi: the Gershonite clan came from Gershon; the Kohathite clan came from Kohath; the Merarite clan came from Merari; the Libnite clan; the Hebronite clan; the Mahlite clan; the Mushite clan; and the Korahite clan. (Kohath was the forefather of Amram.) Amram's wife was named Jochebed. She was from the tribe of Levi and was born in Egypt. She and Amram had two sons— Aaron and Moses—and their sister Miriam.

Aaron was the father of: Nadab, Abihu, Eleazar, and Ithamar. But Nadab and Abihu died. They died because they made an offering in the presence of the Lord with unauthorized fire. The total number of male Levites that were 1 month old or older was 23,000. But these males were not counted with the other Israelites. They did not receive any of the land that the Lord gave the other Israelites. Moses and Eleazar the high priest counted all these people. They counted the Israelites on the plains of Moab next to the Jordan River across from Jericho. Moses and Aaron the high priest had counted the Israelites in the desert of

Sinai. But no one whom Moses counted on the plains of Moab was in the first counting. The Lord had told the Israelites that they would all surely die in the desert. Caleb, the son of Jephunneh, and Joshua, the son of Nun, were the only exceptions.

Numbers 26

THE STORY OF COUNTING THE MULTITUDE

Date: 1452 B.C. ~ Place: Marching Through the Wilderness

Moses sat on a rock, just high enough over the heads of the men in front of him that he could look into all their eyes. These were young eyes...eyes tested in the desert for almost 40 years.

I'll have to start all over again, Moses said to himself. He was thinking of the task of counting the Israelites with his brother Aaron almost 40 years ago. It was a long, tedious task—the men of Israel counted, men who could be counted on for warfare.

Aaron is dead, Moses thought, *so I won't have his skills to help me. Aaron was invaluable 38 years ago because he grew up with these people. I didn't; I grew up in Pharaoh's palace. Aaron knew many of the aunts, uncles, and cousins.*

The Jews had intermarried from family to family, and clan to clan, and tribe to tribe. The intermarriage caused census problems. When there was a question where a man should be counted, Aaron had the answer.

"ELEAZAR," Moses yelled out to the older son of Aaron who was now high priest. "Eleazar, you'll have to be as wise as your father when we number the men this time."

Two years after Israel left Egypt, they were numbered in preparation for war. Now, 38 years later, they were preparing to cross the Jordan to conquer the land flowing with milk and honey. Each man needed to know who would stand by him in battle, and because these fighting men were brothers, they would fight as courageously for a relative as they would for themselves.

Moses rose to speak, "God told me to number you, just as we numbered your fathers 38 years ago. We number each one because each is important to the Lord. You are not lost in an army of fighting men; you will be enrolled in a family book of the living God."

Then men needed to be numbered so they could be arranged in ranks and squads, so they could be disciplined, and they could be taught to fight together.

Most would think the number would grow over 38 years. But no! The number of fighting men decreased. It's not because the desert wanderings were rigorous or demanding. The Jews were hardy. In slavery the conditions would have been more rigorous and demanding than wilderness wanderings. But look what happened in Egypt. "But the more they (Egyptians) afflicted them, the more they multiplied and grew" (Exod. 1:12). It was not hardiness but sin that depleted their ranks.

Isn't that the way with churches today? Sin and unbelief destroy a church, but persecution makes it stronger. Look at the unparalleled growth of the church in China under Communist oppression.

"Men," Moses' strong voice pierced the air, "You are the future of Israel, you will carry out God's promise to conquer the land of our future."

With that announcement, each man knew he couldn't rely on the wisdom and guidance of his father. As good as their fathers were, they died in the desert because of unbelief and rebellion. They were now called on to do what their fathers didn't do. They were called to conquer Israel's enemies.

No man can climb the hill of aging to sit on its top of immortality. All must die; sons must carry on. Only God is eternal.

Each man would be numbered. What if he was lost in battle? His place would be empty; no one would answer "HERE" when his number was called (Israel probably didn't take roll as a modern army does each day). But the numbering ensured each soldier of his place in the army and his importance to God.

If a man were lost in battle, it would not go unnoticed. The leaders would know when any soldier was lost. In the armies of the world, the individual is not important—they measure might by their mass. But not one of God's warriors falls without His notice. As a matter of fact, a soldier is safe though thousands fall beside him, until God's appointed time to call him home. A wise God fixes the date for the death of each of His followers. None are killed prematurely. Not one sparrow falls to the ground without His knowledge; so know for sure, not one believer is lost until the Lord of the living says, "Return ye child of man" (see Ps. 90:3).

It's good we don't live as long a time as Methuselah (see Gen. 5:27). Old embryonic habits have a way of creeping out of hiding. Discontent, selfishness, and doubts throw off their shackles after festering for a time. Just as Samson, David, and others had to constantly fight the Philistines, so we must constantly fight the world, the flesh, and the devil. When fighting gets tiring, we let up and let them back in. Oh, that God would take us home earlier when we were victorious.

The fathers of men standing before Moses had died in rebellion and been buried in the desert. The lessons they learned as slaves in Egypt were hard to forget. Slavery made them fearful, selfish, and they panicked often. They were their own victims of discontent. As slaves, they hadn't learned discipline and courage. Instead, they learned to accept defeat and embrace pessimism. All of Israel that came out of Egypt had to die. Living as long as Methuselah would not have changed their outlook on life.

The new blood of a new generation had to take over. As children they saw the Red Sea pushed back and they saw the Shekinah cloud lead them. Their fathers had said, "Where is God?" The sons knew God was with them for they ate manna 40 years, drank water from the rock, and followed the glory cloud.

There on the high hill with old Moses was young Eleazar, their new high priest. The new generation saw their new leader. They were learning that when one dies, another fills his rank and takes his place. The march goes on, the battle continues. Yesterday Aaron died, but life and ministry go on. Today, Eleazar stands with Moses.

"Don't look back," Moses told the men.

The glory cloud was over them, the Tabernacle was in the center of them, the brazen altar was there to forgive their sins, and a brighter day was coming. God had prepared them 40 years for today. They would be counted and cross over into the Promised Land to finally conquer it for their own.

Numbers 27

THE DAUGHTERS OF ZELOPHEHAD

Zelophehad was the son of Hepher, the son of Gilead. Gilead was the son of Machir. Machir was the son of Manasseh. (This was the abbreviated genealogy.) Zelophehad belonged to the tribe of Manasseh, who was the son of Joseph. The names of Zelophehad's daughters were: Mahlah, Noah, Hoglah, Milcah, and Tirzah. These daughters went to the entrance of the Tabernacle and stood in front of Moses, Eleazar the high priest, the rulers, and all the people. The daughters said, "Our father died in the desert. He was *not* one of Korah's group who was against the Lord. Our father died because of his own sin. But he had no sons. Why should our father's name die out just because he had no son? Give property to us among our father's relatives!"

Then Moses brought their case into the presence of the Lord, who said, "The daughters of Zelophehad are right. They *should* receive what their father was entitled to. Give them property among their father's relatives. Tell the Israelites: 'If a man dies and he had no son, then everything he owned should go to his daughter. If he had no daughter, then everything he owned should go to his brothers. If he had no brothers, then everything he owned should go to his father's brothers. If his father had no brothers, then everything he owned should go to the nearest relative within his clan and that person will own it.'" This is a law among the people of Israel, just as the Lord has given this command to Moses.

Joshua Is Chosen to Succeed Moses

Then the Lord said to Moses, "Climb this mountain in the Abarim
Mountains. Observe the land which I have given to the
Israelites. After you have seen it, you will die, just as your brother Aaron died. During the time of trouble with the people, both
of you acted against My command in the desert of Zin. You did
not honor Me as holy in front of the people at the waters of
Meribah."

Then Moses said to the Lord, "The Lord is the God of the spirits of all
people. May He choose a good leader over these people. He
must go in and out ahead of them. He must lead them out like
sheep and bring them in. The Lord's people must *not* be like
sheep without a shepherd to lead them."

Then the Lord said to Moses, "Take Joshua, the son of Nun. My Spirit is
in him. Put your hand on him. Have Joshua stand in front of
Eleazar the high priest and all the people. Then as they watch,
give Joshua his orders. Let him share your honor. Then all the
Israelites will obey him. Joshua must stand in the presence of
Eleazar the high priest. And Eleazar will receive revelation from
Me by using the Urim and Thummim. At Joshua's command, all
the Israelites will go out. At Joshua's command, they will all
come in."

Moses did exactly what the Lord commanded him. Moses had Joshua
stand in the presence of Eleazar the high priest and in the presence of all the people. Then Moses put his hands upon Joshua
and gave orders to him. This was just as the Lord had commanded through Moses.

Numbers 28

THE DAILY OFFERINGS TO YAHWEH

And the Lord spoke to Moses: "Give this command to the Israelites. Tell them, 'Bring food offerings to Me made by fire. The smell is pleasing to Me. Be sure to bring them at the proper times.' Say to them, 'These are the fire offerings which you must bring to Me. Bring two male, year-old lambs as a whole burnt offering every single day. They must have no physical defects. Offer one lamb in the morning and the other lamb at twilight. Also bring a food offering of 2 pounds of flour. It must be mixed with 1 quart of oil from pressed olives. This is the daily, whole burnt offering which began at Mount Sinai. This is an offering made by fire which is pleasing to the Lord. Offer 1 quart of wine with each lamb as a drink offering. Pour it out to Me at the sanctuary. Offer the second lamb at twilight. As you do in the morning, you must also offer a food offering and its drink offering. This offering is made by fire. The smell of it is pleasing to Me.'"

The Sabbath Offerings

"On the Sabbath day, you must offer two male, year-old lambs. They must have no physical defects. Also give its drink offering and a food offering. The food offering must be 4 pounds of flour mixed with olive oil. (The offering was to be doubled on the Sabbath.) This is the whole burnt offering for the Sabbath. It is in addition to the daily, whole burnt offering and its drink offering."

PRAYING FOR YOUR SECOND CHANCE

The Monthly Offerings

"On the first day of each month, bring a whole burnt offering to Me.
This will be: two young bulls, one male sheep, and seven male
lambs, each 1 year old. They all must have no physical defects.
Give a food offering with each bull. It must be 6 pounds of flour
mixed with olive oil. Also give a food offering with the ram. It
must be 6 pounds of flour mixed with olive oil. Also give a food
offering with the ram. It must be 4 pounds of flour mixed with
olive oil. In addition, give a food offering with each lamb. It
must be 2 pounds of flour mixed with olive oil. This is a whole
burnt offering made by fire. The smell is pleasing to Me. The
drink offering with each bull will be 2 quarts of wine. With the
ram it will be 1½ quarts. And with each lamb it will be 1 quart
of wine. This is the whole burnt offering that must be offered
each month of the year, in addition to the daily, whole burnt
offerings and its drink offerings. This is also in addition to a sin
offering to the Lord, which is one male goat."

The Offerings During the Passover Festival

"The Passover of the Lord will be on the fourteenth day of the first
month of the year.

"The Feast of Unleavened Bread begins the day after the Passover, on
the fifteenth day of that month. It lasts for seven days. You may
eat only bread which has been made without yeast. Have a holy
convocation on the first day of the festival. Do not work on that
day! Bring this offering made by fire, the whole burnt offering to
Me: two young bulls, one ram, and seven male lambs, each 1
year old. They all must have no physical defects. Also, bring a
food offering with each bull. It must be 6 pounds of flour mixed
with olive oil. Bring a food offering with the ram. It must be 4

pounds of flour mixed with olive oil. Bring one goat as a sin offering. It will atone for your sins. Bring these offerings in addition to the whole burnt offerings that you offer every morning. So, bring food offerings each day for seven days. The offering is made by fire. And its smell is pleasing to Me. Do it in addition to the daily, whole burnt offering and its drink offering. On the seventh day (the last day of the Feast of Unleavened Bread), have a holy convocation. Do not work on that day!"

The Offerings During the Harvest Festival

"On the first day of the first fruits offer a new food offering to Me. This is attached to Pentecost. Have a holy convocation. Do not work on that day! Give this whole burnt offering to Me: two young bulls, one ram, and seven male lambs each 1 year old. This smell is pleasing to Me. Also, give a food offering with each bull. It must be 6 pounds of flour mixed with olive oil. With the ram, it must be 4 pounds of flour. With each of the seven lambs offer 2 pounds of flour. Offer one male goat to atone for your sins. Bring these offerings and their drink offerings in addition to the daily, whole burnt offering and its food offering. The animals must have no physical defects."

Numbers 29

THE OFFERINGS DURING
THE FESTIVAL OF THE TRUMPETS

"Have a holy convocation on the first day of the seventh month. Do not work on that day, because it is the day when you blow the trumpets. Bring these whole burnt offerings to Me: one young bull, one ram, and seven male lambs, each 1 year old. None of them must have any physical defects. The smell will be pleasing to Me. Bring a food offering with the bull: 6 pounds of flour mixed with olive oil. Offer 4 pounds with the ram, and offer 2 pounds with each of the seven lambs. Then offer one male goat for a sin offering, it will atone for your sins. These offerings are in addition to the monthly and daily, whole burnt offerings. These food offerings and their drink offerings must be offered by fire to Me. And the smell is pleasing to Me."

The Offerings During the Day of Atonement

"Have a holy convocation the tenth day of this seventh month. On that day, do not eat (fast) and do not do any work! Bring these whole burnt offerings to Me: one young bull, one ram, and seven male lambs. None of them must have any physical defects. The smell will be pleasing to Me. Give a food offering with the bull. It must be 6 pounds of flour mixed with olive oil. With the ram, bring 4 pounds of food offering. And, with each of the seven male lambs, bring a 2-pound food offering. Offer one male goat as a sin offering, that is in addition to the sin offering which atones for your sins. It will also be in addition to the daily, whole burnt offering and its accompanying food offering and drink offerings."

The Offerings During the Festival of Tents

"Have a holy convocation on the fifteenth day of the seventh month. Do not do any work on that day. Celebrate the festival to Me for seven days.

"Bring these whole burnt offerings to Me: thirteen young bulls, two rams, and fourteen male lambs, each 1 year old. None of them must have any physical defects. Offer them by fire and the smell will be pleasing to Me. Also offer 6 pounds of flour mixed with olive oil as a food offering with each of the thirteen bulls. With each of the two rams, offer a 4-pound food offering. And, with each of the fourteen lambs, offer a 2-pound food offering. Then offer one male goat as a sin offering in addition to the daily, whole burnt offering with its food offering and drink offering.

"One the second day of this festival, bring an offering of twelve young bulls, two rams, and fourteen male lambs, each 1 year old. None of them must have any physical defects. Bring the food offering and drink offerings for the bulls, the rams, and the lambs, according to predetermined numbers. Bring one male goat as a sin offering, in addition to the daily, whole burnt offering with its food offering and drink offerings.

"On the third day, offer eleven bulls, two rams, and fourteen male lambs each 1 year old. None of them must have any physical defects. Also bring their accompanying food offering and drink offerings for the bulls, the rams, and the lambs, according to the predetermined number. Bring one male goat as a sin offering, in addition to the daily, whole burnt offering with its accompanying food offering and drink offering.

"On the fourth day, offer ten bulls, two rams, and fourteen male lambs, each 1 year old. None of them must have any physical defects. Also, bring their accompanying food offering and drink offerings for the bulls, the rams, and the lambs, according to their predetermined number. Bring one male goat as a sin offering, in addition to the daily, whole burnt offering with its accompanying food offering and drink offering.

"On the fifth day, offer nine bulls, two rams, and fourteen male lambs, each 1 year old. None of them must have any physical defects. Also bring their accompanying food offering and drink offerings for the bulls, the rams, and the lambs, according to their predetermined number. Bring one male goat as a sin offering in addition to the daily, whole burnt offering with its food offering and drink offerings.

"On the sixth day, offer eight bulls, two rams, and fourteen male lambs, each 1 year old. None of them must have any physical defects. Also bring their accompanying food offering and drink offerings for the bulls, the rams, and the lambs, according to their predetermined number. Bring one male goat as a sin offering, in addition to the daily, whole burnt offering with its accompanying food offering and drink offerings.

"On the seventh day, offer seven bulls, two rams, and fourteen male lambs, each 1 year old. None of them must have any physical defects. Also, bring their accompanying food offering and drink offerings for the bulls, the rams, and the lambs, according to their predetermined number. Bring one male goat as a sin offering, in addition to the daily, whole burnt offering with its accompanying food offering and drink offering.

"On the eighth day, have a closing meeting of the solemn assembly. Do not do any work on that day! You must bring a whole burnt offering, and a fire offering. The smell of it will be pleasing to

Me. Offer one bull, one ram, and seven male lambs, each 1 year old. None of them must have any physical defects. Bring their accompanying food offering and drink offerings for the bull, the ram, and the lambs, according to their predetermined number. Also offer one male goat as a sin offering in addition to the daily, whole burnt offering with its accompanying food offering and drink offering.

"At your set festivals, you must bring these to Me: your whole burnt offerings, your food offerings, your drink offerings, and your peace offerings. These are in addition to other vow offerings and special gifts that you want to give to Me." Moses told the Israelites everything that the Lord had commanded him.

Numbers 30

RULES ABOUT VOWS

Then Moses spoke with the leaders of the Israelite tribes to tell them the thing that the Lord had commanded: "A person may make a vow to the Lord, by promising to do something special. If he does, then he must keep his promise and do what he said he would do. A young woman who is still living at home might make a vow to the Lord, by pledging to do something special. Her father might hear about the vow or pledge and say nothing. Then she must stand behind her vows and keep her pledge. But when her father hears about the vow or the pledge, he may not allow it. Then the vow or the pledge does not have to be kept because her father would not allow her to do it. So, I will set her free from her vow.

"A woman might make a pledge or a careless promise (a rash utterance) but gets married later. Her husband might hear about it and say nothing. Then she must keep her promise or the pledge that she made. However, when her husband hears about it, he might not allow it, and cancel her pledge or the careless promise that she made. I will free her from keeping it.

"When a widow or a divorced woman makes a vow, she must do whatever she promised. If a woman makes a promise or pledge while she is married, when her husband hears about it, he might say nothing, and, not stop her—then she must keep her vow or pledge. But if her husband hears about it, he may cancel it. Then she does not have to do what she said, because her husband has canceled it. I will set her free from it. A woman's husband may make her keep, or cancel, any vow or any pledge that she has made. However, if her husband says nothing to her about it for several days, then she *must* keep her vows. But, if he cancels them long after he heard about them, then *he* is responsible for her breaking her vow."

These are the rules for husbands and wives that the Lord commanded Moses. They are also for fathers with minor daughters who are living at home.

Numbers 31

WAR AGAINST THE MIDIANITES

And the Lord spoke to Moses: "Pay back (execute vengeance upon) these Midianites for what they did to the Israelites. After that, you will die!" So Moses said to the people: "Get some men ready for war. The Lord will use them to pay back the Midianites. Send 1,000 men from each of the tribes of Israel to war." So 12,000 men got ready for war. There were 1,000 men from each tribe.

Moses sent those 1,000 men from each tribe to war. Phinehas, the son of Eleazar the high priest, was with them. He took with him the holy items—the trumpets to blow under his command. They fought the Midianites, just as the Lord had commanded Moses, and they killed every Midianite man. Among those whom they killed were: Evi, Rekem, Zur, Hur, and Reba. (They were the five kings of Midian.) They also killed Balaam, the son of Beor, with a sword. The Israelites captured the Midianite women and their young children. They also took all their flocks, herds, and goods. Then they burned all of the Midianite towns and their villages. Then they brought all the people and the animals and the goods back to Moses and Eleazar the high priest and all the Israelites. The camp was on the plains of Moab near the Jordan River across from Jericho. Moses, Eleazar the high priest, and all the rulers of the people went outside the camp to meet them.

Moses was angry with the army officers who returned from the battle— the commanders over 1,000 men and the captains over 100 men. Moses asked them, "You have let the women live!? Listen, the women were the ones who followed Balaam's advice. They turned the Israelites away from the Lord in the incident at Mount Peor. The women were responsible for the terrible disease that struck the people. Now kill all the little Midianite boys! And kill every Midianite female who has had sex! But save the little girls for yourselves who have not had sex with a man. And all of you men who killed anyone or touched a corpse must stay outside the camp for seven days. On the third and seventh days, you and your captives must make yourselves clean. You must purify all of your clothes. And you must clean anything made of leather, goat's hair, or wood."

Then Eleazar the high priest spoke to the soldiers who had gone to war, telling them, "These are the teachings that the Lord gave to Moses. Put any gold, silver, copper, iron, tin, or lead into the fire. Put into the fire anything that will not burn. It will be clean. Then purify those things with the cleansing water, and whatever cannot withstand the fire. On the seventh day, you must wash your clothes. Then you will be clean. After that, you may come into the camp."

The Treasures Taken in Battle

Then the Lord spoke to Moses: "You, Eleazar the high priest, and the leading fathers of the community should take a count of the goods, people, and animals that were captured. Then divide those things among the soldiers who went to war and the rest of the people. Tax the soldiers who went to war. The Lord's share is: 1 item out of every 500 things. This includes people, cattle, donkeys, sheep, or goats. Take it from the soldiers' half, and give it to Eleazar the high priest. It is a raised offering to Me. (This was a thanksgiving offering to God for preserving them in battle and giving them victory.) And from the people's half, take 1 item out of every 50. This includes people, cattle, donkeys, sheep, goats, or other animals. Give that to the Levites. They guard My Holy Tent." So, Moses and Eleazar the high priest did as the Lord commanded Moses. The soldiers had taken: 675,000 flock animals, 72,000 cattle, 61,000 donkeys, and 32,000 girls. (These were the females who had not had sex with a man.)

The soldiers who went to war got 337,500 flock animals. They gave 675 of them to the Lord. They got 36,000 cattle, and gave 72 of them to the Lord. They got 30,500 donkeys, and gave 61 of them to the Lord. They got 16,000 people, and gave 32 of them to the Lord. Moses gave them as a raised offering to the Lord, to Eleazar the high priest, as God's share, just as the Lord had commanded Moses.

Moses separated out the people's half from the soldiers' half. The people received: 337,500 flock animals, 36,000 cattle, 30,500 donkeys, and 16,000 persons.

From the people's half, Moses took 1 thing out of every 50 for the Lord. This included the animals and the people. Then he gave them to the Levites who guarded the Lord's Holy Tent. This was exactly what the Lord had commanded Moses.

Then the officers of the army came close to Moses. They were the commanders of 1,000 men and the captains of 100 men, and they told Moses, "We, your servants, have counted our soldiers under our command. Not one of them is missing! (No casualties among the Israelite soldiers!) So, we brought a gift to the Lord. We have brought the gold things that each of us found—arm bands, bracelets, signet rings, earrings, and pendants. These are to atone for our sins in the presence of the Lord. So, Moses and Eleazar the high priest received all the crafted gold items from them. The commander of 1,000 men and the captains of 100 men gave gold that weighed about 420 pounds! Each soldier had taken some plunder for himself. Moses and Eleazar the high priest received the gold from the commanders and captains and put it in the Meeting Tent as a memorial in the presence of the Lord for the people of Israel.

Numbers 32

TWO TRIBES REMAIN EAST OF THE JORDAN RIVER

The people of Reuben and Gad had a lot of cattle. They saw the lands of Jazer and Gilead were good for cattle. So, both tribes came to Moses, Eleazar the high priest, and the rulers of the people saying: "We, your servants, have many cattle. The Lord has captured for the Israelites a land that is good for cattle. This is the land around Ataroth, Dibon, Jazer, Nimrah, Heshbon, Elealeh, Sebam, Nebo, and Beon." They continued, "If it pleases you, we would like for this land to be given to us. Don't make us cross the Jordan River."

Moses said to the people of Gad and Reuben, "Should your brothers go to war while you stay here? No! You would discourage the Israelites. They would not want to cross over into the land that the Lord has given them! Your fathers did the same thing when I sent them from Kadesh-Barnea to look at the land. They went up to the Valley of Eshcol and saw the land. Then they discouraged the Israelites from going into the land which the Lord had given to them! The Lord became very angry on that day. He made this vow: 'None of the people who came up from Egypt and who are 20 years old or older will see ever this land! I promised it to Abraham, Isaac, and to Jacob. But these descendents have not followed Me completely.' Only Caleb, the son of Jephunneh the Kenizzite, and Joshua, the son of Nun, followed the Lord completely. "The Lord was very angry with Israel. So, He made them wander in the desert for 40 years. Finally, all that generation who had done wrong in the sight of the Lord died. And now look, you are acting just like your fathers! You sinful people are making the Lord even more angry at Israel! If you quit following the Lord, He will once again leave Israel in the desert. So, you would hurt all these people!"

But the Reubenites and the Gadites got closer to Moses to say, "No! We will build pens for our animals, and we will rebuild towns for our families here. Then our families will live in strong, walled cities where they will be safe from the people who live in this land. Then we will prepare for war. (We ourselves will go armed. About 40,000 soldiers crossed over the Jordan River.) We will hurry to help the other Israelites to get their land. We will *not* return home until every Israelite has received his land. We will not get any of the land west of the Jordan River. Our part of the land is on the eastern side of the Jordan River."

So Moses told them, "You must do these things. You must go in the presence of the Lord in battle. You must cross the Jordan River completely armed in the presence of the Lord, until He forces out His enemies from the land. After the Lord helps us capture the land, you may return home. Then you will have done your duty to the Lord and to Israel. Then you may have this land as your own in the presence of the Lord.

"But, if you don't do these things, listen, you will be sinning against the Lord! And know for certain that you *will* be punished for your sin! Build for yourselves towns for your families and pens for your flock animals. But then, you *must* do what you promised!"

The Gadites and the Reubenites said to Moses, "We, your servants, will do what you, our master, commands! Our wives, our children, our cattle, and all of our animals will stay in the towns of Gilead. But we, each of your servants, will prepare for battle and go over and fight in the presence of the Lord, just as you, our master, have said."

So, Moses gave orders about them to Eleazar the high priest, to Joshua the son of Nun, and the leaders of the tribes of Israel, saying, "The Gadites and the Reubenites will prepare for battle! They *will* cross over the Jordan River with you. They will go in the presence of the Lord, and they will help you conquer the land which is in front of you. If they do that, then give them the land of Gilead as their own. But, if they do not go over armed with you, then they will not receive Gilead. Their land will be in Canaan among you." The Gadites and Reubenites answered, "As the Lord has spoken to us, thus we will do! We ourselves will cross over into the land of Canaan armed in the presence of the Lord. However, *our* land will be on the eastern side of the Jordan River."

So, Moses gave that land to the Gadites, to the Reubenites, and to the eastern half-tribe of Manasseh. That land had been the kingdom of Sihon, the king of the Amorites, and it included the kingdom of Og, the king of Bashan. It also included all of the towns and the land that surrounded them.

The Gadites rebuilt the cities of Dibon, Ataroth, Aroer, Atroth-Shophan, Jazer, Jogbehah, Beth-Nimrah, and Beth-Haran. These were strong, walled cities. And they built sheep pens.

The Reubenites rebuilt Heshbon, Elealeh, Kiriathaim, Nebo, Baal-Meon, and Sibmah. They renamed Nebo and Baal-Meon after they rebuilt them.

The descendents of Machir, the son of Manasseh, went to Gilead and captured it. They forced out the Amorites who lived there. So, Moses gave Gilead to the clan of Machir, the son of Manasseh, and they settled there.

Jair, the descendent of Manasseh, went out and captured the villages there, calling them the "Towns of Jair."

Nobah went and captured Kenath and the villages around it. Then he named it "Nobah" after his own name.

Numbers 33

THE JOURNEY FROM EGYPT TO MOAB

These are the places where the Israelites traveled, as Moses and Aaron led them out of the land of Egypt by their divisions. At the command of the Lord, Moses recorded the places where they started and the places they went, stage by stage. These are the stages according to their starting places.

On the fifteenth day of the first month, they traveled from Ramses. The Israelites marched out boldly in full view of all the Egyptians. The Egyptians were burying all of their firstborn sons that the Lord had killed by passing judgment on their gods. The Israelites traveled from Ramses, and they camped at Succoth. They traveled from Succoth, and camped at Etham at the edge of the desert. The traveled from Etham and went back to Pi-Hahiroth, east of Baal-Zephon. There they camped near Migdol. They traveled from Pi-Hahiroth and crossed through the Red Sea into the desert. After going two days through the desert of Etham, they camped at Marah. They traveled from Marah to Elim, where there were 12 springs of water and 70 palm trees. They traveled from Elim and camped near the Red Sea and from the Red Sea, they camped in the desert of Zin. They crossed the desert of Zin and camped at Dophkah. Then they camped at Alush, and next they camped at Rephidim where people had no water to drink.

They traveled from Rephidim and camped in the desert of Sinai. They traveled from the desert of Sinai and camped at Kibroth-Hattaavah. They traveled from Kibroth-Hattaavah and camped at Hazeroth. They traveled from Hazeroth and camped at Rithmah, (Kadesh).

They traveled from Rithmah and camped at Rimmon-Perez. They traveled from Rimmon-Perez and camped at Libnah. They traveled from Libnah and camped at Rissah. They traveled from Rissah and camped at Kehelathah. They traveled from Kehelathah and camped at Mount Shepher. They traveled from Mount Shepher and camped at Haradah. They traveled from Haradah and camped at Makheloth. They traveled from Makheloth and camped at Tahath. They traveled from Tahath and camped at Terah. They traveled from Terah and camped at Mithkah. They traveled from Mithkah and camped at Hashmonah. They traveled from Hashmonah and camped at Moseroth. They traveled from Moseroth and camped at Bene-Jaakan. They traveled from Bene-Jaakan and camped at Hor-Haggidgad. They traveled from Hor-Haggidgad and camped at Jotbathah. They traveled from Jotbathah and camped at Abronah. They traveled from Abronah and camped at Ezion-Geber. They traveled from Ezion-Geber and camped at Kadesh in the desert of Zin. They traveled from Kadesh and camped at Mount Hor. This was on the border of Edom.

And Aaron, the high priest, obeyed the Lord and went up onto Mount Hor to die there. He died on the first day of the fifth month in the 40th year after the Israelites left the land of Egypt. Aaron was 123 years old when he died on Mount Hor.

The Canaanite king of Arad lived in the Negev where he heard that the Israelites were coming.

Israel traveled from Mount Hor and camped at Zalmonah. They traveled from Zalmonah and camped at Punon. They traveled from Punon and camped at Oboth. They traveled from Oboth and camped at Iye-abarim, on the border of Moab. They traveled from Iye-abarim and camped at Dibon-Gad. They traveled from Dibon-Gad and camped at Almon-Diblathaim. They traveled from Almon-Diblathaim and camped in the mountains of

Abarim, near Mount Nebo. They traveled from the mountains of Abarim and camped on the plains of Moab near the Jordan River across from Jericho. They camped next to the Jordan River on the plains of Moab. Their camp went from Beth-Jeshimoth to Abel-Shittim.

At the plains of Moab, next to the Jordan River across from Jericho, the Lord spoke to Moses to tell the Israelites, "Cross the Jordan River and go into Canaan. Drive out from ahead of you all the people who live there. Destroy all of their carved statues. Destroy their metal idols. Demolish all of their places of worship. Take possession of the land and settle there, because I have given this land to you to own. Use lots to divide up the land. You will inherit the land by clans. Give larger portions to larger clans. Give smaller portions to smaller clans. The land will be given as the lots decide. Each tribe of your forefathers will get its own land.

"But, if you do *not* drive out those people who live in the land from ahead of you, then the ones whom you allow to stay will become like pricks in your eyes and like thorns in your sides. They will always cause you trouble on the land where you live. Then I would destroy *you* as I had planned to destroy them!"

Numbers 34

BOUNDARIES OF THE PROMISED LAND

And the Lord told Moses to say to the people of Israel: "Soon, when you enter the land of Canaan, it will be yours. These will be its borders: On the south side, you will receive part of the desert of Zin, along the border of Edom. On the east side, your southern border will start at the south end of the Dead Sea. The border will cross from the south to Scorpion Pass, 'the Ascent of Akrabbim.' It will go through to the desert of Zin and end south of Kadesh-Barnea. Then it will go out to Hazar-Addar and go on over to Azmon. From Azmon, the border will go to the brook of Egypt. It ends at the Mediterranean Sea.

"Your western border will be the Mediterranean Sea.

"Your northern border will begin at the Mediterranean Sea and you will mark out a line to Mount Hor. From Mount Hor, you will mark out a line to Lebo-Hamath. Then it will end at Zeded. Then the border will go out to Ziphron, and it will end at Hazar-Enan. This will be your northern border.

"You must mark out a line for your eastern border. It will begin at Hazar-Enan and go to Shepham. From Shepham, the border will go down from east of Ain to Riblah. It will go along the hills east of Lake Galilee. Then the border will go down along the Jordan River, and it will end at the Dead Sea. These are the borders around your country."

So, Moses gave this command to the Israelites: "This is the land you will receive. Lots will divide it among 9½ tribes. The Lord commanded that it should be theirs. The tribes of Reuben and Gad and the eastern half-tribe of Manasseh have already received their land. They got it according to the households of their fathers. The 2½ tribes received land east of the Jordan River, across from Jericho."

Then the Lord spoke to Moses: "These are the names of the men who will divide up the land for inheritance: Eleazar the high priest and Joshua, the son of Nun. Also, take one ruler from each tribe. They will divide up the land. These are the names of the men: from the tribe of Judah—Caleb, the son of Jephunneh; from the tribe of Simeon—Shemuel, the son of Ammihud; from the tribe of Benjamin—Elidad, the son of Chilson; from the tribe of Dan—Bukki the ruler, the son of Jogli; from the tribe of Manasseh the son of Joseph—Hanniel the ruler, the son of Ephod; from the tribe of Ephraim—Kemuel the ruler, the son of Shiphtan; from the tribe of Zebulun—Elizaphan the ruler, the son of Parnach; from the tribe of Issachar—Paltiel the ruler, the son of Azzan; from the tribe of Asher—Ahihud the ruler, the son of Shelomi; from the tribe of Naphtali—Pehahel the ruler, the son of Ammihud." The Lord commanded these men to divide up the land of Canaan to the Israelites.

Numbers 35

The Levites Are Given Land

The Lord spoke to Moses on the plains of Moab, across from Jericho by the Jordan River, saying, "Command the Israelites to give towns to the Levites to live in. These will be towns in the land which they will receive. Also, give the Levites the pasture land around these towns. Then the Levites will have towns where they can dwell, and pasture land for their cattle, sheep, and other animals. The pasture lands that you give to the Levites will extend 1,500 feet from the wall of the town. Also measure out 3,000 feet in each direction from the town wall. Measure out 3,000 feet east of the town, 3,000 feet south of the town, 3,000 feet west of the town, 3,000 feet north of the town. The town will be in the center. This will be their pasture land surrounding the towns of the Levites.

"Six of the towns that you give to the Levites will be special towns for safe havens. (These cities of refuge were asylums where an accused person could flee to until passion subsided. Then a fair trial would be conducted by the impartial priests and Levites to determine whether the homicide was premeditated or unintentional.) A person might accidently kill someone. If he does, then he may run to one of those towns for refuge. You Israelites must also give 42 other towns to the Levites. Give to the Levites a total of 48 towns, along with their surrounding pasture lands. Each tribe must give some of its towns to the Levites. The number of towns that they give will depend on the size of their land. The larger tribes of Israel must give more towns. The smaller tribes must give fewer towns."

The Cities of Refuge

Then the Lord told Moses to speak to the Israelites: "You will cross the
Jordan River and go into the land of Canaan. You must choose
certain cities to be cities of refuge. If a person accidentally kills
someone, then he may run to one of these cities for safety. There
he will be safe from the corpse's relative who has the duty of
punishing the killer. The six cities that you give will be cities of
refuge. Give three cities east of the Jordan River. And give three
cities in the land of Canaan which will be cities of refuge. These
six towns will be places of safety for the Israelites. And, they will
be for foreigners and other people living among you. Any of
these people may also run to one of these cities, if he accidentally kills someone. However, if a person uses an iron tool to kill
someone, then he is a murderer. He must certainly be put to
death for murder. A person might take a rock that could kill
someone. If he kills a person with it, then he is a murderer. He
must certainly be put to death for murder. A person might pick
up a piece of wood that could kill someone. If he kills someone
with it, then he is a murderer. He must certainly be put to death
for murder. A relative of the corpse ('the avenger,' Hebrew: *go'el*)
must put the murderer to death. When he finds the murderer,
outside any city of refuge, he must kill him. A person might
shove someone with malice and kill him. Or, lurking, one throws
something at someone and kills him. Or, he hits someone with
his hand and kills him. If he did that out of hatred, he is a murderer. He must certainly be put to death for murder! A relative
of the corpse must kill that murderer when he finds him.

"However, a person might suddenly shove someone, and he did *not* hate
that person. Or, he throws something and hits someone, and he
was *not* ambushing him. Or, he drops a rock that could kill

someone, falling upon someone he did not see, and kills that person. He didn't plan to hurt anyone, and he did not hate that person whom he killed. If that happens, then the community must decide what to do. They must decide between the relative of the corpse and the one who struck the fatal blow.

"Here are the rules:

The community must protect the man-slayer from the corpse's relative. If the man-slayer is found to be innocent, they must send the man-slayer back to the city of refuge to which he fled. He must stay there until the high priest dies. That man must never go outside the city limits of his city of refuge. If a relative of the corpse finds him outside that city, then the relative may kill him. And the avenger will *not* be charged with murder. The man-slayer *must* stay inside his city of refuge until the high priest dies. After the high priest dies, the man may go back to his own land. These laws are for you from now on, wherever you live.

"A killer may be put to death only if he *is* a murderer. And there must be witnesses. No one may be put to death with only one witness. A murderer should die. Do *not* receive a money payment to spare his life. He must certainly be put to death! A person might run to a city of refuge. Do *not* receive a money payment to let him go back home *before* the high priest dies. Do not let murder pollute the land where you live. There is only one way to atone for the sin of killing an innocent person—the murderer must surely be put to death! I am the Lord. I live among the Israelites. I live in that land with you, too. So, do not pollute it with murder."

Numbers 36

LAND IS GIVEN TO
THE DAUGHTERS OF ZELOPHEHAD

The elders of Gilead's clan came closer and spoke to Moses and the
rulers, the heads of the fathers of the Israelites. Gilead was the
son of Machir, among the clans of the sons of Joseph. Machir
was Manasseh's son. The elders of Gilead's clan said, "The Lord
commanded you to give the land to the Israelites by picking lots.
And the Lord commanded you to give the land of Zelophehad,
our brother, to his daughters. Zelophehad's daughters may
marry men from other tribes of the sons of Israel. Then that land
of our fathers would leave our family. And the people of the
other tribes would obtain that land. The time of Jubilee for the
year will come for the Israelites. Then their land will go to other
tribes. It will go to the tribes of the persons whom they marry.
So, their land would be taken away from us. That was land that
we received from our forefathers!"

Then Moses gave the Israelites this command from the Lord: "These
men from the tribe of the sons of Joseph are saying what is correct! This was the Lord's command to Zelophehad's daughters:
'You may marry anyone you wish, but only from a clan of your
own tribe. In this way, the land of the Israelites will not pass
from tribe to tribe. Each Israelite will keep the land within the
tribe that belonged to his ancestors. A woman who inherits her
father's land may marry, but she must marry someone from a
clan of her own tribe. In this way, every Israelite will keep the
land that belonged to his ancestors. The land must not pass
from one tribe to a different tribe. Each Israelite tribe will keep

the land that is received from its own ancestors.' The daughters of Zelophehad did exactly as the Lord commanded Moses."

So, Zelophehad's daughters—Mahlah, Tirzah, Hoglah, Milcah, and Noah—married their cousins. These were their father's relatives. Their husbands were from the clan of Manasseh, the son of Joseph. So, their land stayed within their father's clan and tribe. These were the laws and commands that the Lord gave to the Israelites. God gave them through Moses when they were on the plains of Moab next to the Jordan River, across from Jericho.

PRAYERS FROM DEUTERONOMY

Preface

FROM MOSES' HEART TO US TODAY— THE GOD OF THE SECOND CHANCE

Three million people were camped on the east side of the Jordan River. Every day, people would walk to the high places in their camp to look over that water barrier to see the land God had promised to them.

It had been 40 years, 11 months, and 1 day since they left Egypt. Every Jewish heart was homesick for the land that flowed with milk and honey.

"Why don't we go now?" people asked up and down the streets of the camp. "Why is Moses waiting?"

Moses felt pressure from several sources, but he knew the people were not spiritually ready. They didn't know the laws by which they had to live in the land. They didn't know all the mistakes their parents had made. They would probably repeat them if he didn't warn them. Moses had to tell them, but Moses wanted to do more than give them a message. Moses wanted to get into their heads and hearts; he wanted this new generation to feel deeply what God said about holiness and how God judged the sins of their parents.

How can I make the people fully understand what God has said? Moses asked himself.

Then Moses decided to do what men of God have always done—he'd preach to the people. Writing the message was not enough; most Israelites couldn't read, and if they could, they'd only get a head knowledge. God's message would not capture their will and desire.

Moses decided to preach with passion, telling the disasters of their parents so the listeners would cry, or shake with terror, but above all they would repent before doing evil. They would commit themselves to right-eousness.

Moses decided to remind the people of their victories and the interven-tion of God so everyone would love God and commit themselves to fol-low God.

I won't tell about building the Tabernacle—the people already know about it, Moses thought to himself. *I won't tell about the rules for the priests; that doesn't concern them. I will not tell them about the feast days because we celebrate them.*

Moses decided to add a section about the king they would have someday, and how they should respond to prophets when God sends them.

I'll tell all that, the old Moses thought. *Then I'll write everything I say to the people in a book—it'll be the fifth book I've written.*

When I finish this fifth book, I will put all of them in the Ark of the Covenant. Moses wanted everything he wrote to be available to future generations, those who wouldn't hear his sermons.

Then it was time for Moses to address the people. He was 120 years old, and he thought, *I must manage my energy,* for energetic speaking wore him out. It took all his strength to speak so loudly for all the gathered leaders to hear. He poured all his heart, soul, and passion into his mes-sages. When he finished each message, Moses was helped back to his tent where he fell asleep as he rested his head on a pillow.

These sermons are important, Moses thought. *This generation must know everything that happened since the Exodus from Egypt.* He would tell this modern generation how their fathers rebelled against God in the wilder-ness and were judged. So Moses spoke with passionate fury so they wouldn't make the same mistake.

Moses gave them threats, he gave them promises, he gave them his heart. Moses stirred their hearts to a loving compliance with God's laws.

God had promised the land *unconditionally* to Abraham and his seed. But Moses gave this new generation a *conditional covenant,* that if they would keep the laws—symbolized by keeping the Sabbath—they would dwell in the land. If they rebelled at God's law, He would throw them out of the land.

"Behold, I set before you today a blessing and a curse: the blessing, if you obey the commandments of the Lord your God which I command you today; and the curse, if you do not obey the commandments of the Lord your God, but turn aside from the way which I command you today, to go after other gods which you have not known" (Deut. 11:26-28).

Moses didn't repeat all the law given in his previous books. The law was divided into three parts. First were the Ten Commandments which expressed God's moral law. Moses repeated the Ten Commandments because these laws transcended time and culture. Second was the civil and criminal laws upon which their national life was based. He repeated some of these laws; the rest were already written for them to read. The third was the ritual law that laid a foundation for their approach to God. The priest could read that to the people, and they could do what God commanded.

Moses repeated the law to a new generation that hadn't heard the law when it was originally given. This last of the five books would be like the last of the Gospels. It repeated what was necessary from the previous books, yet it was independent of them, as it tied them together and brought all four Gospels to a fitting climax.

What would this last book be called? First, Moses called it by its introduction: *These are the Sermons of Moses, eleh hadbarim.* But many Jews would later simply call it *Five* because it was the fifth book. But as more and more people read this book, they gave it a third name—*The Book of Reproofs* because it contained so many warnings. A fourth title was simply *The Reiteration of the Law* because Moses repeated the important laws. In 286 B.C., the Jews translated the Old Testament from Hebrew into Greek and called it *Deuteronomion* which means "Second Law." Our English Bible transliterates the Greek into *Deuteronomy.*

Moses slept hard because preaching was exhausting. Moses didn't just talk to the multitude; he put all his strength into persuading the people to wholeheartedly follow God. While Moses slept and rested, the message he told the leaders was being retold to the clan leaders, and they retold it to the families.

Moses had to rest between his sermons to regain his strength. Then Moses began again on a different topic, rehearsing what happened in the past 40 years. If he could help it, Moses wouldn't let this younger generation make the mistakes of their fathers.

Moses prayed as he prepared his message; then after he finished, he prayed again that his people wouldn't forget what he said.

Unknown to Moses, he would die before this fifth book would be finished. And unknown to us today is the author of the last chapter that tells of Moses' death. Some say Moses wrote it by prophetic utterance—Moses was a prophet (see Deut. 18:15)—God told him what to write. Some think Joshua wrote and added it to this fifth book. Did someone write it that we don't know? No matter what human author penned these words, we know they are Scripture and inspired by God.

These seven sermons by Moses and the events of Deuteronomy cover 37 days.

Why pray this new translation? Because reading usually only goes through our minds. But when you pray the Scriptures, your heart intercedes with God's heart. And if you commit your will to what you know and feel, your whole person has responded to God.

May God touch you through *Praying for a Second Chance* as you reach out to touch Him.

Elmer Towns
Written from my home
at the foot of the Blue Ridge Mountains

THE STORY OF MOSES PREACHING THE BOOK OF DEUTERONOMY

Date: 1451 B.C. ~ Place: East of Jordan

It was a lovely spring morning; new tender grass covered the meadow. The grass bent slightly from a soft breeze. Birds had been chirping since before dawn. The lush meadow was a vast improvement from the desert and its omnipresent howl that irritated everything when the wind blew.

Moses was standing on a large flat rock preaching to the leaders from every tribe and clan. Moses' face was clearly seen; all those standing in the early morning saw the yellow sun reflected off his side profile. He was careful not to face the sun when he spoke—his eyes would squint in the bright morning sun. He was also careful not to stand so his listeners had to peer into the sun as he spoke. The glaring sun would have made it difficult for the listeners to see his facial expressions.

"I want the people to see my sincerity and feel my passion," Moses told those around him.

This was the third sermon by Moses; there would be more to follow. "I have much to tell the people, there is so much they need to know," Moses kept telling those around him. "They must not make the mistakes of their forefathers."

Moses' long, flowing, gray beard bobbed as Moses emphasized important words, His eyes flashed with seriousness. His voice was strong, loud, piercing.

The leaders of the tribes and clans listened carefully, straining to hear every word. As soon as Moses finished speaking, they would walk hurriedly back to their men to repeat every word that Moses spoke. These men would listen as carefully as their leaders, for they would repeat the sermon to every family camping on the edge of the Jordan River.

Moses steadied himself as he came down from the rock; two men reached quickly to keep the old leader from falling. His face was wet with perspiration, his eyes were tired; he had given the last ounce of strength in his sermon.

Moses sat on a nearby rock to regain his strength before returning to his tent to sleep. After splashing some water on his face, his eyes sparkled again.

"Water," he asked, and a leather bottle was handed to him.

Several of his followers complimented Moses on the sermon. They had learned new truths from his message. They were encouraged.

"Why are you repeating yourself?" Eleazer the high priest asked Moses. "You keep saying the same exhortation over and over each time you preach to the people."

"And I will repeat myself again and again," Moses told Eleazar and the others standing by. "I'm not just communicating a message they need to know, I'm warning them against destruction. I'm motivating them to follow God with their whole hearts." Moses explained that it was not enough to hear and know the truth, people must feel the truth...believe the truth...know inwardly the truth...and do the truth.

The men walked with Moses back to his tent. None of the men would sleep till evening, but shortly Moses would be sleeping. "When we hear him snore, we'll know he's all right," one of them commented.

Moses would not preach another sermon the next day; he'd wait to get his full strength back. He'd wait a couple of days.

That afternoon Moses awoke from his midday nap. He ate a meal, and then went to his writing table. "Are you making notes for your next sermon?" his aid asked.

"No, I know what I'm going to say. I'm going to tell the people what the Lord told me. I'm going to remind them what happened to their forefathers."

Moses was sitting at his desk to write down what he had just preached to the multitude. His mind was sharp—he could remember every word. He copied the words carefully.

His aid said to Moses, "You've already written that in your earlier books. Why are you writing it a second time?"

Moses dropped his quill to the table, leaning back to laugh. "If it is important to preach these events and instructions a second time to the people, then it's important to write them a second time." Moses knew that people would read the events and instructions in Exodus, Leviticus, and Numbers. But he wanted them to read it a second time, just as he preached it a second time.

Moses thought quietly to himself, *Line upon line and line upon line; precept upon precept and precept upon precept. I must repeat myself when writing, just as I must repeat myself when preaching.*

Deuteronomy 1

MOSES SPEAKS TO THE PEOPLE OF ISRAEL

These are the sermons that Moses spoke to all the people of Israel when they were in the desert, east of the Jordan River. They were in the Jordan Valley on the plain, opposite Suph, between Paran and the towns of Tophel, Laban, Hazeroth, and Dizahab. It usually takes 11 days (a total of about 100 miles) to travel from Mount Sinai to Kadesh-Barnea, by way of Mount Seir. But now it was 40 years after the Israelites had left Egypt. Their rebellion had prolonged their trip by 38 years. (The following important speech of Moses [see Deut. 1:6–4:40] was delivered about one month before he died.) *Lord, I will learn from the mistakes of others.*

On the first day of the eleventh month, Moses spoke to the people, telling them everything that the Lord had commanded him to tell them, including what happened after the Lord had defeated Sihon, the king of the Amorite people who lived in Heshbon, and Og, the king of Bashan who lived in Ashtaroth in Edrei.

Moses began to explain what God had taught, "Our God spoke to us at Mount Sinai, saying, 'You people have stayed at this mountain long enough. Get ready to travel. Go to the hill country of the Amorites, to all its neighboring places in the Jordan Valley in the hills of the western slopes, in the southern section and along the seashore of Canaan and Lebanon. Go as far as the Great River the Euphrates. Look, I have set this land in front of you. Go in and take possession of it!' The Lord promised to give it to your ancestors—to Abraham, to Isaac, and to Jacob—and to their descendants after them." *Lord, may I always embrace new challenges You give me.*

Leaders Are Appointed by Moses

Moses told the people, "At that time, I spoke to you people saying, 'I
am not able to take care of you all by myself. The Lord your
God has multiplied you. Today there are as many of you as there
are stars in the skies!' I pray that the Lord, the God of your
ancestors, will multiply you 1,000 times more and bless you,
just as He promised. However, I cannot handle the responsibili-
ty of your problems and troubles and arguments all by myself.
Therefore I said, 'Choose for yourselves some men from each
tribe, wise men who have insight and experience. I will appoint
them as your leaders.' And you answered me: 'What you have
spoken is a good thing to do.' So, I took the wise and experienced leaders of your tribes and appointed them as leaders over
you. I appointed commanders over 1,000 people, captains over
100 people, lieutenants over 50 people, and sergeants over 10
people. I made them officials for your tribes.

"At that time, I commanded your judges: 'Listen to the arguments
between your Hebrew brothers. Judge fairly, when it is between
two Israelites or between an Israelite and a foreigner. When
judging, be fair to everyone. Don't act as if one person is more
important than another. Don't be afraid of anyone, because your
decision comes from God. Bring the difficult cases to me.' At
that time, I told you everything you must do." *Lord, just as
Moses delegated to others, may I learn to do what only I can do
and delegate what others can do.*

Twelve Spies Were Sent Out

Moses continued, "Then, as the Lord our God commanded us to travel
from Mount Sinai toward the hill country of the Amorite people,
we went through all that wide, terrible desert which you saw.

Finally we arrived at Kadesh-Barnea on the border of the Promised Land. Then I said to you, 'You have now come to the hill country of the Amorites, which the Lord our God is giving to us. Look, there it is. Go up. Take it. The Lord the God of your ancestors told you to capture it. So, don't be afraid. Don't have any doubts.'" *Lord, give me courage for Your challenges.*

"Then all of you came near me, 'Let's send men ahead of us to spy out the land on our behalf. They could come back and tell us the way we should go. They could tell us about the towns that we will encounter.'" *Lord, make me discerning when I get bad advice.*

"I thought that was a good idea, so I chose 12 of your men—one man for each tribe. They left and went up to the hill country and came to the Valley of Eshcol and explored it. They brought some of the fruit back to us with this report: 'It is a good land that the Lord our God is giving to us!' But you refused to go up to conquer it. You rebelled against the command of the Lord your God. Instead, you grumbled in your tents, saying: 'The Lord hates us. He brought us out of the land of Egypt just to hand us over to the Amorites. They will destroy us. Where can we go now? The spies whom we sent made us afraid. They said, "The people there are bigger and taller than we are. The cities are big, too. They have walls up to the sky. And, we saw the Anakites (a family of giants)."'" *Lord, keep the pessimism of others from ruining my trust in You.*

"Then I said to you, 'Don't be scared. Don't be afraid of those people. The Lord your God is the One who will go ahead of you; He will fight for you just like He did in Egypt. You saw Him do it with your very own eyes. And in the desert, you saw how the Lord your God carried you like a man carrying his son. He has brought you safely all the way to this place.' Nevertheless, you still did not trust in the Lord your God. He went ahead of you in the path as you moved. He found places for you to camp. He led you with fire at night and by a cloud during the daytime. He showed you which way to go." *Lord, may Your past provision in my life contribute to greater faith in You.*

The Lord Punished the People

Moses continued, "When the Lord heard what you said He was angry. He vowed, 'I promised to give the good land to your ancestors, but none of the men of this evil generation will ever see it. Only Caleb, the son of Jephunneh, will see it. And I will give to him and to his descendants the land that he walked on. Why? Because he followed Me completely.' Because of you, the Lord was angry with me also. He said to me, 'You will not enter the land either. But your personal assistant Joshua, the son of Nun, will go there. Encourage Joshua, because he will lead Israel to conquer the land as their own.' The Lord said to us, 'You said your babies would be captured, but they are the ones who will go into the land. Today, they are too young to know right from wrong, so I will give the land to them, and they will take possession of it.'" *Lord, I fear Your punishment.*

"But you must turn yourselves around and travel back to the desert toward the Red Sea. Then you said to Me, 'We have sinned against the Lord. But now we will go up and fight, just as the Lord our God commanded us.' Then each one of you put on his weapons for battle. You thought it would be easy to go up into the hill country. But the Lord said to me, 'Tell them not to go up there. Don't fight, because I will not be with them. Otherwise, their enemies will defeat them.' So I told you, but you wouldn't listen. You rebelled against the Lord's command. Because of your pride, you went on up into the hill country. The Amorites who lived there came out and fought you, and chased you like a swarm of bees. They defeated you from Seir all the way to Hormah." *Lord, may I never face the enemy without Your presence.*

"Then you came back and cried in the presence of the Lord, but He did not pay any attention to you. So, you settled in Kadesh for a long time." *Lord, it's hard to live without Your protective presence.*

Deuteronomy 1

THE STORY OF GOD'S PUNISHMENT

Date: 1451 B.C. ~ Place: East of Jordan

Surely not one of these men of this evil generation shall see that good land of which I swore to give to your fathers.... Moreover your little ones and your children, who you say will be victims, who today have no knowledge of good and evil, they shall go in there; to them I will give it, and they shall possess it (Deuteronomy 1:35,39).

Why does God allow some to live long, but others to die young? Why does anyone have to die? Since God is the original giver of life, and God is all powerful to fix anything, why do we have to die? And for many, why is death so painful?

There is only one word to answer the "death" question. Disobedience! God told Adam and Eve not to eat of one tree. Yet it seems the prohibited tree was the first place Eve went. God had given the penalty, "Thou shalt surely die." Immediately both Adam and Eve died spiritually, and eventually they died physically. You too will die because, "...through one man sin entered the world, and death through sin..." (Rom. 5:12). *Lord, I know I have to die, but I don't want to.*

God told the children of Israel to enter the land He promised them. By miracles He brought them out of Egypt; by a miracle He brought them across the Red Sea. By miracles he fed them and gave them water in the wilderness. Then at Kadesh-Barnea they refused to believe God, and they refused to obey God. So God promised they would die in the desert. Does God mean what He says? Every time! Will God punish when we disobey? Every time! Are you halting in Kadesh-Barnea? Is today a cross-roads? Do you know the consequence of disobedience? *Lord, give me a willing heart to obey You.*

Psalm 90 was written by Moses to reflect on Israel's funeral march in the desert. He comments, "You [God] sweep people away like dreams that disappear..." (Ps. 90:5 NLT). When Israel refused to enter Canaan, God's dream for them died, and so did their dreams of peace. Moses said, "...Grass springs up in the morning...and flourishes, but by evening it is dry and withered" (Ps. 90:5-6 NLT). Then to interpret the metaphor, Moses said, "We wither beneath Your anger...we live our lives beneath Your wrath, ending our years with a groan" (Ps. 90:7,9 NLT). Isn't that a dismal picture of death—it's a groan. That's what will happen if we waste our life. We go out with a groan. *Lord, I want to die easy.*

God didn't kill them immediately for their disobedience. He let them live, but they had to live in the desert they chose. They died in the desert they chose. God will not kill you the moment you disobey (unless it is an unusual circumstance [see Acts 5:1-11]). You choose sin, so God will let you live and die in sin. You choose money, so God will let you live and die chasing the thing you choose. Come to think about it, you can choose where you die. Are you going to die in the desert or in the Promised Land? *Lord, I choose to die in Your will.*

Come back to Psalm 90. When the Israelites were dropping around Moses, what did he ask? "Who can comprehend the power of Your anger? Your wrath is as awesome as the fear You deserve" (Ps. 90:11 NLT). When you see someone die outside the will of God, you ought to fear God, for He could take your life. You ought to worship God for allowing you to live. *Thank You, Lord, for my physical life.*

What should you do when you know you will die? "So teach us to number our days, that we may gain a heart of wisdom" (Ps. 90:12). To number your days is to make the most of the time you have left.

> *Lord, I know I have to die, but I don't want to,*
> *May I have an easy death.*

I know I have Christ as my Savior,
    So I'll go to live with Him at my death.

Teach me to use wisely the time I have left
    So I can glorify You in my life,
    And I'll leave fruit after I'm gone.

Amen.

Deuteronomy 2

THE PEOPLE WANDER IN THE DESERT

Moses continued, "Then we turned around and traveled into the desert
toward the Red Sea, just as the Lord had told me. We went
throughout the hill country of Seir for many days." (About 37
years transpired between Deuteronomy 1 and Deuteronomy 2.
After the adult Israelites rebelled against God, there was nothing
that generation did which was worth reporting.) *Lord, may I live
in Your presence so the events of my life will be worthy.*

"Then the Lord spoke to me: 'You have gone around these hills long
enough. Turn north. This is what you must command the people
to do: "Soon your people will be passing along the borders of
those who live in Seir. They are your relatives, the descendants of
Esau. Though they will be afraid of you, you must be very careful. Do not go to war against them, because I am not giving any
of their land to you—not even a step of a sole of a foot. I have
given the hill country of Seir to Esau as his own. You must pay
them with money for any food that you eat, or water that you
drink. Why? Because the Lord your God has blessed the work of
your hand. Wherever you have traveled throughout this vast
desert, the Lord your God has been with you for these 40 years.
You have never needed anything."'" *Lord, I will obey when You
say "turn around."*

"So, we passed by our relatives who lived in Seir. We turned off the
Jordan Valley road that comes up from the towns of Elath. Then
we turned and went in the direction of the desert of Moab. Then
the Lord said to me, 'Don't bother the people of Moab, nor go
to war against them. Why? Because I am not giving you any of

their land. I have given the whole country to the descendants of Lot as their own.'" (The Emites [or "terrible ones"] previously lived there. They were a large, powerful people. They were very tall, like the Anakites. Before this time, the Horites [cave dwellers] also settled in Seir, but the people of Esau forced them out. They destroyed the Horites and settled in their place. That is the same thing that Israel was doing in the land which the Lord had give them to possess.)

"And the Lord said to me, 'Now go up and cross the Ravine of Zered.' So, we crossed it. It had been 38 years since we left Kadesh-Barnea until we crossed the Ravine of Zered. An entire generation had died during that time, including all the previous fighting men. The Lord had continued to destroy them until they were all gone from the camp." *Lord, I fear You because You keep Your word.*

"Now when the last of those old fighting men had died from among the people, the Lord said to me: 'Today you must go to Ar, on the border of Moab. When you come near the people of Ammon, do not bother them. Do not go to war against them. Why? Because I am not giving you any of their land. I have given that land to the descendants of Lot.'"

That land was also thought to be a land of Rephaites. Those people used to live there, but the Ammonites called them "Zamzummites." They once were a powerful people, and there were many of them. Like the Anakites, they were very tall. Nevertheless, the Lord went ahead of the Ammonites to destroy the Zamzummites. So, the Ammonites forced them out and settled in their place. The Lord did the same thing for the descendents of Esau, when He destroyed the Horites who lived in Seir. The Edomites forced them out and settled in their place; the Edomites live there to this day. The Caphtorite people came out of Crete and destroyed the Avvites. The Avvites had lived in villages as far as Gaza, but the Caphtorites destroyed them and settled in their place. The Lord said, "Get up, cross the Arnon Ravine. Look, I am giving you power to defeat Sihon the Amorite and his land. So, wage war against him; start capturing his land. Today, I will cause all the people of the world to be terrified of you. They will hear about your reputation, and tremble with fear." *Lord, I will fight when You command.*

Israel Defeats Sihon, King of Heshbon

Moses continued, "So, I sent messengers from the desert of Kedmoth to Sihon, the king of Heshbon, offering him peace. I said, 'Let us pass through your country. We will stay on the main road. We will go straight through, not turning right or left. We will pay you in silver for any food that we eat or water that we drink. We only want to travel through your country.'" *Lord, You tell me to live peaceably with all people.*

"'The descendents of Esau who live in Seir permitted us to go through their land. So did the Moabites who live in Ar (Rabbah). We want to cross over the Jordan River into the land which the Lord, our God, has given to us.'"

"But Sihon, the king of Heshbon, would not let us pass through his country. Why? Because the Lord, your God, had made him stubborn. The Lord wanted to hand Sihon over to you. That's the way it is today. Then the Lord said to me, 'Look, I have begun to hand Sihon and his country over to you. Start taking possession of his land to be your own!' Then Sihon and all his army came out to fight us, and we had a battle at Jahaz. But the Lord, our God, handed Sihon over to us. We defeated him, his sons, and all of his army. We captured all of his towns at that time. We completely destroyed every single town—the men, the women, and the children. No human survived. But we did keep for ourselves the animals and the valuable things (the plunder) from the towns.

"We also defeated Aroer, which is on the edge of the Arnon Ravine, and we defeated the town next to the ravine—even as far as Gilead. No town was too strong for us. The Lord, our God, gave all of them to us! However, you did not go near the land of the Ammonites. You did not go near the banks of the Jabbok River, nor did you go near the towns of the hill county. That was everything which the Lord, our God, had commanded." *Lord, teach me where to go, and where I should not go.*

Deuteronomy 3

ISRAEL DEFEATED OG, KING OF BASHAN

Moses continued, "Then we turned and went up the road toward
Bashan. Og, the king of Bashan, and all his army came out to
fight us at Edrei. And the Lord said to me, 'Don't be afraid of
Og, because I have handed him over to you, as well as his entire
army and his land. You must do to him what you did to Sihon,
the king of the Amorites.' So, the Lord our God did deliver Og
and all of his army to us. We defeated them until no one was
left alive. Then we captured all of the towns of Og. There was
not a single town that we did not take from them—60 towns.
We took the whole region of Argob, Og's kingdom in Bashan.
All of them were strong cities. They had high walls and heavy
gates (double-leaved doors) with bars. And we captured many
small towns which had no walls. We completely destroyed them,
just like we had done to the towns of Sihon. We killed all of the
men, women, and children. However, we did keep for ourselves
all the animals and the valuable things (the plunder) from the
towns." *Lord, when I don't understand Your command, help me
trust Your heart.*

"So, at that time, we took control of the land which was east of the
Jordan River. We captured it from those two Amorite kings. That
land stretched from the Arnon Ravine as far as Mount Hermon.
The Sidonian people call Hermon *Sirion* ("glittering"), and the
Amorites call it *Senir* (denoting its shiny qualities because it is
snow-capped year round—9,000 feet high). We captured all the
towns on the high plain and all of Gilead. We took all of
Bashan as far as Salcah and Edrei, towns in Og's kingdom. Og,

the king of Bashan, was the last of the few remaining Rephaites (giants in Trans-Jordania). His bed was made of basalt (an ore with a very high content of iron). That was more than 13 feet long and 6 feet wide, according to standard measurements." (It is still located in the Ammonite city of Rabbah.) *Lord, I pray for modern-day Israel as she struggles to possess the land You promised to her centuries ago.*

The Land Is Divided

Moses continued, "At the time we captured this land, I gave to the Reubenites and the Gadites the territory beginning at Aroer, which is at the edge of the Arnon Ravine, and half the hill country of Gilead, along with its towns. I gave the rest of Gilead to the half-tribe of Manasseh. Also I gave them all of Bashan, the former kingdom of Og. Jair, a descendent of Manasseh, captured the whole region of Argob that extended to the border of the Geshurites and the Maacathites. He named it after himself. So, Bashan is called 'the Towns of Jair' even today. I gave the territory of Gilead to the clan of Machir. I gave the land to the Reubenites and the Gadites the land that begins at Gilead and goes from the Arnon Ravine to the Jabbok River. The Jabbok River is the border of the Ammonites, including the Arabah (the Jordan Valley), along with the Jordan River as the western boundary, from Lake Galilee, as far as the Sea of Arabah, the Dead Sea under the slopes of Mount Pisgah on the east.

"At that time, I gave you this command: 'The Lord your God, has given this land to you as your own. Now all your fighting men must take up their weapons, and cross the Jordan River to conquer the Promised Land. However, your wives, young children, and livestock are allowed to stay here (I know you have much livestock). They are permitted to stay here in the towns which I have given to you. Someday, your Israelite relatives will also have a place to rest. They will occupy the land which the Lord, your God, has given to them on the other side of the Jordan River. After that, each of your soldiers will return to the land which I have given to you." *Lord, teach me to help others in their struggles for victory.*

"Then I commanded Joshua, 'You have seen everything that the Lord your God has done to those two kings (Sihon and Og). The Lord will do the same thing to all the kingdoms where you will be going. Don't be afraid of them! Because the Lord your God will fight for you." *Lord, I will build my future on the past victories You've given me.*

Moses Is Not Allowed to Go Into the Promised Land

Moses continued, "At that time, I begged the Lord, 'O Lord, You have begun to show me, Your servant, how great You really are! You have great strength. No other god in Heaven or earth can do the powerful things that You can do! Please let me cross over the Jordan River. I want to see the beautiful hill country of the Promised Land." *Lord, I understand why Moses prayed this request.*

"However, the Lord was still angry with me because of you people! He would not listen to me. The Lord said to me, 'That's enough! Do not speak to Me anymore about this subject. (God buries His workmen, but His work goes on.) Climb to the top of Mount Pisgah. Look up to the west, to the north, to the south, and to the east. Your eyes can see the land, but you will not cross over this Jordan River!'" *Lord, thank You for glimpses of grace.*

"'Put Joshua in charge. Encourage him to be strong and brave. Because he is the one who will lead these people across the river. And, he will give them the land that they will inherit. But you can only look at it!' (Later, Moses did enter Canaan when he stood with Jesus on the Mount of Transfiguration [see Matt. 17:1-9; Mark 9:2-9; Luke 9:28-31].) So, we stayed in the valley opposite Beth-Peor." *Lord, when You say, "No!" help me see the bigger picture.*

Deuteronomy 4

OBEY GOD'S COMMANDMENTS!

Moses continued, "And now, O Israel, listen to the laws and the rules that I am teaching you people to do, so that you will live. Then you will go in and capture the land which the Lord, the God of your ancestors, is giving you. Do not add to the word that I am commanding you, and do not subtract from it. Obey the commands of the Lord, your God, which I am commanding you." *Lord, I will obey!*

"Your eyes have witnessed what the Lord did at Baal-Peor (see Num. 25:1-9). The Lord, your God, destroyed every single one of you who went after baal. But all who continued to cling to the Lord your God are still alive today. Look, I have taught you the laws and rules which the Lord, my God, commanded me to do. Now you can obey these things within the land which you are about to enter, which will soon belong to you. Obey these instructions very carefully. Because this will show the other nations that you have wisdom and understanding. They will hear about all these laws. And they will certainly say: 'This is a great nation; these people are smart and have insight.' No other nation is as great as we are. The Lord, our God, actually comes near whenever we pray to Him. And no other nation has such fair laws and rules that I am laying out in your presence today." *Lord, You are fair.*

"But, you must be very careful. Watch yourself. Otherwise, you will forget about the things that your eyes have seen. Do not allow them to leave your heart as long as you live. You must continue to teach them to your children and to your grandchildren. On the day when you stood in the presence of the Lord your God, at Mount Sinai, the Lord said to me, 'Bring to Me the people to listen to My words. They need to learn how to revere Me as long as they live in the land. They must teach these things to their children, too.' Then you came closer and stood at the bottom of the mountain, which was ablaze with a fire that reached to the sky. The thick clouds caused it to be very dark. Then the Lord spoke to you from within the fire. You were hearing the sound of words, but you did not see a form. There was only a Voice. The Lord declared His covenant to you, which He commanded you to obey. He gave the Ten Commandments that He wrote on two stone tablets. At that time, the Lord commanded me to teach you the laws and the rules. You must obey them in the land which you will own whenever you cross over the Jordan River. That day, the Lord spoke to you from within the fire at Mount Sinai, but you did not see Him. So, be very careful to watch out for your souls." *Lord, thank You for Your laws, I will obey them.*

"Do not corrupt yourselves by making carved images of any kind of idol, whether they are in the shape of men, or women, or any animals on earth, or birds that fly in the sky, or the shape of anything that crawls on the ground, or of any fish in the water below. Otherwise, when you look up at the sky, you will see the sun, moon, and stars—the whole array of the heavens—you might be drawn away from Me and worship them and serve them. I have given these things for all people everywhere." *Lord, keep me from idols.*

"The Lord has taken you out of Egypt, and brought you out of that furnace for smelting iron, so that you could be a special people who belong to Him." *Lord, thank You for deliverance from the hardness of sin.*

"The Lord was angry with me because of your words. He made a solemn vow that I would not cross over the Jordan River. I cannot go into that beautiful land which the Lord, your God, is giving you to own. Because I will die here in this land, I will not cross over the Jordan River. Instead, you will go across and capture that good land. Watch out for yourselves. Otherwise, you will forget about the covenant of the Lord, your God, which He has made with you. Do not make any idols for yourselves in any form! The Lord, your God, has forbidden that. The Lord, your God, is a jealous God. He is like a fire that burns up things." *Lord, I will be careful about everything, at all times.*

"After you live in the land for a long time, you will have children and grandchildren. Yet you could still do evil things. You might make some kind of idol in some form. Don't do anything which the Lord says is wrong. That would make Him angry. I will ask Heaven and earth to testify against you on that day if you disobey the Lord. Then you will utterly perish from off that land quickly. But you are crossing over the Jordan River to capture the land to live there. If you become evil, you will be completely destroyed. The Lord will scatter you among the nations, and only a few of you will be left alive among those nations where the Lord will send you. There you will worship gods that are made by human beings, made of wood and stone; they cannot see, hear, eat, or smell." *Lord, I hate idolatry, just as You do.*

"But even there you can look for the Lord your God, and you will find Him if you seek Him with all your heart and soul! It will be distressing when all these things happen to you. However, later, you will come back to the Lord your God, and will obey Him. Because the Lord your God, is a merciful God, he will not abandon you or destroy you. He will not forget the covenant that He made with your forefathers which He ratified with a vow.

"Has anything like this ever happened before? No! Look at history, long before you existed, all the way back to the time when God created humankind on the earth. Look from one end of heavens to the other. Nothing like this has ever been heard of. Has an ethnic group ever heard the voice of God speak from within a fire as you have heard, and still lived? No! No other god has ever taken for himself one nation out of another nation. But the Lord your God did this for you in Egypt. He did it right in front of your very own eyes. He did it with plagues, and signs, and miracles, and war, and by awesome sights. He did it by His great power and strength. He showed you things, so that you would know that the Lord is the one true God. Besides Him, there are no other gods. Out of the heavens, God caused you to hear His voice so He could correct you. And, on the earth, He caused you to see His great fire, so you could hear His message. The Lord loved your ancestors. That is why He chose you, their descendents, and brought you out of Egypt, led by His presence and by His great power. He wanted to force pagan nations out of their land ahead of you. These nations are bigger and stronger than you are. Nevertheless, the Lord has brought you to their land to give it to you to own. And, this land is yours today. Therefore, know and be sure that the Lord is God. He is God in heaven above and on the earth below. There is no other God, and you must obey His laws and His commands, which I am commanding you today. Then it will go well for you and your children later. This is how you will live for a long time on the soil, which the Lord, your God, is giving you permanently." *Lord, Your promises are awesome!*

Three Cities of Refuge Established

Then Moses set apart three towns east of the Jordan River as refuges. A person who has killed someone accidentally (unintentionally) may go to any of those towns for safety if he did not previously hate the person he killed. By running to one of those towns, he could save his own life. The towns were: for the Reubenites there was Bezer in the desert. Ramoth-in-Gilead was for the

Gadites. And Golan was for the Manassites; it was in Bashan.
Lord, my safety from sin is in You.

Deuteronomy 5

The Ten Commandments

Moses called to all the people of Israel, and said to them: "Listen Israel to the laws and the rules which I am speaking in your hearing today! Learn them and obey them carefully. The Lord our God, made a covenant with us at Mount Sinai. The Lord did not make this covenant with our ancestors, but with us. He made it with all of us who are still alive here today. The Lord spoke to you face to face from within the fire on the mountain. (At that time, I stood between you and the Lord to declare to you His word because you were afraid of that fire, you would not go up on the mountain.) The Lord said: 'I am the Lord your God. I brought you out of the land of Egypt where you were once slaves.'" *Lord, thank You for speaking in the past, I will listen to You today.*

"'1. You must have no other gods before Me.

2. You must not make for yourself any carved image or the likeness of anything that is in the sky above, on the earth beneath, or in the water that is under the earth. You must not bow yourself down to worship them or serve them. Because, I, the Lord your God, am a jealous God, punishing the children for the sin of their ancestors to the third and to the fourth generations of those who reject Me. However, I am loyal to the thousands who love Me and obey My commands.

3. You must not use the name of Yahweh, your God, irreverently. I will hold such a person responsible who uses My name that way.

4. Guard the Sabbath day, to keep it holy. The Lord, your God, has commanded you to do this. Labor for six days; do all of

your work then. But the seventh day is the Sabbath of the Lord your God. You must not do any work on that day—you, or your son, or your daughter, or your male servant, or your female servant, or your bull, or your donkey, or any of your animals, or your visitor who is within your gates. That way, your male and female servants may rest just like you do. Remember, you were once slaves in the land of Egypt, and the Lord your God brought you out from there by His great power and strength. So, the Lord your God has commanded you to observe the Sabbath day.

5. Honor your father and your mother. The Lord your God has commanded you to do this, then you will live for a long time, so that things will go well for you in the land.

6. You must not commit murder.

7. And you must not commit adultery.

8. And you must not steal.

9. And you must not testify falsely against your neighbor.

10. And you must not covet your neighbor's wife. And you must not covet your neighbor's house, or his land, or his male servant, or his female servant, or his bull, or his donkey, or anything that belongs to your neighbor.'" *Lord, You gave us these commandments to tell us how You expect us to guard ourselves from sin.*

"The Lord gave these commands to your whole congregation on the mountain. He spoke to them with a loud voice from within the fire, speaking to them from the cloud and the deep darkness. He added no more, then He wrote the words on two stone tables, and gave them to me. You heard the Voice from within the darkness; the mountain was ablaze with fire. Then all of your chiefs and tribal leaders—your elders—came closer to me, and said, 'Look, the Lord our God has shown His splendor and majesty to us, and we have heard His voice from within the fire. Today, we realize a person can stay alive, even when God speaks to him. But now, why should we die? This great fire will burn us up. We will die if we hear the Lord our God speak anymore. No human being has ever heard the voice of the living God speaking from within the fire and still lived, but we have. Moses, you go closer and listen to everything that the Lord our God says. Then, you tell us what the Lord our God tells you, and we will listen and obey.'" *Lord, I will listen to Your messengers.*

"The Lord heard what you said to me, and He said to me, 'I have heard what these people said to you. Everything they have said is good. I wish their hearts would always revere Me. I wish that they would always obey all of My commands. Then things would go well for them and their children permanently. Go, tell the people to return to their tents. But you stay here with Me. I will speak to you all the commands, the laws, and the rules. You must teach the people to obey them in the land which I am giving to them to own.'" *Lord, I will teach others your laws.*

"So, be very careful. Do what the Lord your God has commanded you. You must follow the commands exactly. You must live by all the ways that the Lord your God has commanded you. Then you will live and be successful. Then, you will live in the land that you will soon own for a long time." *Lord, I will be careful.*

Deuteronomy 5

THE STORY OF
THE TENTH COMMANDMENT

Date: 1451 B.C. ~ Place: East of Jordan

You shall not covet your neighbor's wife; and you shall not desire your neighbor's house, his field, his male servant, his female servant, his ox, his donkey, or anything that is your neighbor's (Deuteronomy 5:21).

The last commandment summarizes the heart problem that makes a person disobey the previous nine. The word *covet* is used here by God, but it's a word we don't use very often anymore. Actually the word means "desire," or "strong passion." And many wonder why God included this idea of "not coveting" in the tenth commandment. They think that coveting is nothing more than "shopping" for something they plan to get later on.

But coveting is wrong because it's the first step toward stealing a neighbor's possession, or having adultery with a neighbor's wife. Coveting is the beginning of sin.

But people do covet. What does that mean? The more a person covets, the fewer encounters they are having with God. For when you drink deeply of God, no other drink will satisfy fully, satisfy as long, satisfy completely. So, those drinking of God can eliminate their addiction to coveting. *Lord, I drink of You.*

But even people who meet God in daily worship can get sidetracked. Adam and Eve met God each evening to worship Him in the cool of the garden. But that wasn't enough to protect her from evil. What was it about the tree? "…the woman saw that the tree was…desirable" (Gen. 3:6). She coveted something she didn't have.

Sometimes things that are mentioned last on a list are really first in priority. The last commandment dealt with coveting or desiring, yet that was the root priority of the previous sins. We steal because we covet our neighbor's possessions. We commit adultery because we covet sex with another. We lie because we covet the respect of another. And murder is usually connected with coveting. *Lord, I have coveted in the past and will do so in the future. Forgive me and give me victory.*

What part of our body makes us covet the most? The eyes! Our eyes initiate coveting. What we see with our eyes is what we want with our heart. Wait a minute, isn't the heart more involved in coveting than the eyes? Absolutely! The greatest proof is a blind man. He can't see with his eyes, yet his covetous heart lusts after things. *Lord, help me know when I covet.*

Coveting is really a heart problem. Instead of desiring God, we desire something else—possessions, money, positions, or honors. The secret to overcoming a covetous attitude is to guard our hearts. "Keep your heart with all diligence, for out of it spring the issues of life" (Prov. 4:23). *Lord, I give my heart to You again.*

Our satisfaction in life is directly tied to two things. First, you must seek the Lord, and second, you must find God. "The Lord looks down from heaven upon the children of men, to see if there are any who understand, who seek God" (Ps. 14:2). What happens when you search for God with your whole heart? "And you will seek Me and find Me, when you search for Me with all your heart" (Jer. 29:13). *Lord, I'm searching.*

Deuteronomy 6

LOVE THE LORD YOUR GOD

Moses continued, "Now these are the commands, the laws, and the rules
which the Lord your God commanded me to teach you. Obey
them in the land where you are crossing over to take possession.
You, your children, and grandchildren must revere the Lord your
God for as long as you live. Obey all of His laws and His commands which I am commanding you. Then you will live for a
long time. So, listen, Israel, and carefully obey these instructions,
so that all will go well for you and you will multiply in the land
where much food grows. The Lord, the God of your ancestors,
has promised this to you." *Lord, I want to live long and healthy
on this earth.*

The Shema

"Hear O people of Israel! The Lord, our God, is one Lord. You must
love the Lord your God with all your heart, with all your soul,
and with all your strength." *Lord, this is my desire.*

"These words which I am commanding you today will be on your heart.
You must teach them to your children. Talk about them when
you sit in your house, and when you walk on the road, when
you lie down, and when you get up. You must write them down
and tie them to your arms as a sign. And they will be on your
forehead between your eyes to remind you. And you must write
them on the door posts of your houses, and on your gates."
Lord, I will keep Your Word with me and in my heart.

"The Lord your God will bring you into the land which He promised to your ancestors—to Abraham, to Isaac, and to Jacob. God will give it to you. The land has large, beautiful towns that you did not build. The houses there are full of all kinds of good things which you did not supply. They have wells that you did not dig. There are vineyards and olive trees that you did not plant. After you have eaten as much as you want, be sure that you do not forget the Lord. He is the One who brought you out of the land of Egypt where you were once slaves. You must revere the Lord your God. Serve only Him. Make your promises in His name. Do not chase after other gods, the gods of the ethnic groups who are surrounding you, because the Lord your God is a jealous God. He is present with you. If you worship other gods, then the Lord your God will become angry with you and destroy you from off the surface of the earth. You must not test the Lord your God as you did at Massah. Be very careful to obey the commands of the Lord your God. Obey the testimonies and the laws that He has commanded you, and do whatever the Lord sees as good and right, so that things will go well for you. Then, you will go in and capture the good land which the Lord promised to your ancestors." *Lord, I will obey.*

"As you go in, He will force out all of your enemies, just as He has said. In the future, your son will ask you: 'What is the meaning of the testimonies, the laws, and the rules which the Lord our God has commanded us?' Then you will tell your son: 'We were slaves to Pharaoh in Egypt, but the Lord brought us out of Egypt by His great power. The Lord performed great and awesome signs and miracles against Egypt, against Pharaoh, and against his whole family—right in front of our very eyes. Yes, the Lord brought us out of there to bring us here and give us the land which He vowed to our ancestors. Now the Lord has commanded us to obey all of these laws. And, we must always revere the Lord our God for our own good. This has preserved us until the present time.'" *Lord, I willingly testify of Your goodness.*

Deuteronomy 6

THE STORY OF THE LINE BETWEEN GOD AND IDOLS

Date: 1451 B.C. ~ Place: East of Jordan

You shall not go after other gods, the gods of the peoples who are all around you (Deuteronomy 6:14).

God reached down from Heaven to draw a line upon the earth. He drew it across the North African Saharan Desert, through Egypt, straight to one particular mountain. God drew a line at Mount Sinai that separated God-worshipers from idol-worshipers. It was a line that has been repeatedly drawn through the ages. God's people must get on His side of the line; the rest of unbelieving humanity has lined up on the other side with false gods. What is the line? What does it say?

Thou shalt have no other god before Me! God wants His followers to be wholly dedicated to Him—wholly separated from false gods. God originally made all people worshipers, so He wants everyone to only worship Him. But those on the other side of the line bow down to idols. Therefore, God rejects them as they reject Him. He wants us to have no other gods in our life. *Lord, You are my only God.*

So you better quickly get rid of all your idols and images. What? You don't think you have any idols in your home? What do you have that gets priority over God? Anything that gets preeminence before the eternal God is your self-made idol. And when you place anything before God, you might as well be on your knees worshiping it, because that's what you do in your heart. God made you to be a worshiper; so if you don't worship the true God, be careful you're not reacting by worshiping a false god. *Lord, I reject false gods.*

Whether you recognize it or not, the Lord is your God. He has done for all what only God can do. He has given you physical life, created the world in which you live, given you the laws of nature, and protected you until this moment. Are you like many who deny the Lord? Many act as though God is not their God. They go so far as to act as if He isn't a god; they act as if He were not there. That's why God has drawn a line at Sinai. He puts those who worship Him on one side, and those who deny Him on the other side. *Lord, I'm on Your side; I won't try to walk on both sides.*

When God asked Israel to step over to His side of the line, He reminded them of what He had done for them. "I…brought you…out of the house of bondage" (Deut. 5:6). God wanted Israel to remember they were slaves in Egypt. He wanted them to remember the sting of the whip and their backbreaking labor from dawn to dusk. God wanted Israel to remember the cruelty of their human taskmasters. Because He delivered them, now God challenges them to serve Him. *Thou shalt have no other god before Me.* Is that too much to ask, especially since He freed you? If sin was cruel to you, why would you worship an idol instead of God?

Do you understand the word *no?* God said, "No other god." That seems clear to me. When it comes to other gods, the answer is, "No!" God doesn't want you 50 percent of the time, and allow you to worship an idol 50 percent of your time. The same goes for your money and your effort. God doesn't want to be a half-time God. He doesn't even want 90 percent of your time, if you're going to give 10 percent to an idol. As a matter of fact, God doesn't want you 99 percent of the time. He wants all of you—all of your love, all your obedience, and all your worship. That's why God drew the line at Sinai. *Lord, I want to be on Your side, not on the other side.*

Notice the phrase, "No other god before Me." Does the word *before* mean "first"? You have God first, but then you can have your idols after God. That's like going to church on Sunday, but living like you want to all week. No, the word *first* doesn't just mean *first* in time. If that were true, you'd give God your first efforts, your first strength, then serve your idols with what is left. When God is first, nothing else is second. The phrase "before Me" means don't have an idol anywhere around God. Don't bring an idol in the house; don't even bring it on the property. Don't buy an idol or accept it as a gift. The only place for an idol is on the other side of the line from God. *Lord, there are no idols on my side.*

Since you belong to God, He's your life. God is before you, above you, behind you, and He indwells you. God's got you surrounded. Since God said, "No other gods before Me," that means you can't have an idol anywhere in your life. *Lord, I'm on Your side of the line. I've cleaned out all idols.*

What's left? Just you and God. What else do you need? If you know the Creator of the universe, do you need anyone? Anything? The first command negatively told Israel to get rid of idols. It also told the nation positively to make the Lord God the center of their lives. *Lord, I'm here on Your side of the line.*

Deuteronomy 7

THE LORD'S PEOPLE

Moses continued, "The Lord your God will bring you into the land where you are going to take possession of it. God will force out many nations ahead of you: the Hittites, the Girgashites, the Amorites, the Canaanites, the Perizzites, the Hivites, and the Jebusites. These seven nations are bigger and stronger than you. The Lord your God will hand them over to you, and you will defeat them. You must completely destroy them. Do not show them any mercy. Do not marry any of them. Do not give away your daughters to marry their sons. And you must not receive their daughters in marriage for your sons. Because those people would turn your children away from God. Your children would begin serving other gods. The Lord would become angry with you, and He would quickly destroy you." *Lord, I will be separate from other religions.*

"Now, this is what you must do to those people: Tear down their altars. Smash their so-called 'sacred' stone pillars. Cut down their Asherah idols and burn their carved images in the fire. Because you are a holy people to the Lord your God. He has chosen you out of all the ethnic groups on the surface of the earth to be His very own. It was not because you were more numerous than all those other people. You are the smallest nation of all. The Lord chose you because He cares about you and loves you. He kept His vow that He swore to your ancestors. So, the Lord brought you out of Egypt by His great power, redeeming you from the house of slaves, from the control of Pharaoh, the king of Egypt. So, know that the Lord your God is the one true God. He is the faithful God. For 1,000 lifetimes He will keep His covenant and be loyal to those people who love Him, to those who obey His commands. And He will openly pay back those people who hate Him; He will destroy them. He will not be slow to pay back those who hate Him." *Lord, thank You for Your promises of love to me.*

"So, you must be sure that you obey the commands, the laws, and the rules which I am commanding you today. Pay close attention to these rules. Be very careful to obey them. Then the Lord your God will keep the covenant and be loyal to you. He promised your ancestors that He would do so. And He will love you, and bless you, and cause the number of your people to grow. He will bless you with children. And He will bless your fields with good crops. He will give you grain, new wine, and fresh olive oil. He will bless your cows with calves and your flock animals with off-spring in the land which He promised to your ancestors that He would give you. You will be more blessed than any other group of people. Every man and woman will have children. All of your animals will have offspring. And the Lord will take away all sickness from you. He will put none of the terrible diseases upon you which you knew about in Egypt. Instead, He will put them upon your enemies." *Lord, thank You for abundant blessings.*

"You must destroy all the ethnic groups which the Lord your God hands over to you. Don't feel sorry for them. Do not worship their gods. Otherwise they will trap you. You might think to yourselves, 'These nations outnumber us. We cannot force them out.' Don't be afraid of them. Remember what the Lord your God did to Pharaoh and to all of Egypt. You saw for yourselves the great troubles, the signs, and the miracles that God did. You saw how the Lord's great power and strength brought you out of Egypt. The Lord your God will do the same thing to all the ethnic groups that you now fear. In addition, the Lord your God will send hornets among them until those who survive and hide themselves from you are destroyed." *Lord, I remember what You've done for me.*

"You must not dread in front of them, because the Lord your God is among you. He is a great and awesome God. The Lord your God will force those nations out of the land ahead of you, little by little. Don't destroy them all at once, otherwise, the wild animals would become too numerous for you. But the Lord your God will hand those ethnic groups over to you. He will throw them into such a state of confusion that they will be exterminated. And the Lord will hand over their kings into your hands. You must destroy them; people won't even know that they ever existed. No one will be able to stop you; destroy them all. Burn up the idols of their gods in fire. Do not desire the silver and gold which is on them. Do not take it for yourself, or you might be ensnared by it. It is a disgusting thing to the Lord your God. Do not bring any of those disgusting things into your house. If you do, you will be completely destroyed along with it. Utterly hate and reject those things. They must be completely destroyed!" *Lord, my house will be clean.*

Deuteronomy 8

ALWAYS REMEMBER THE LORD

Moses continued, "You must carefully obey every command that I command you today. Then you will live and increase in number. Go in and take possession of the land which the Lord has vowed to your ancestors. Remember the whole journey that the Lord your God has led you in the desert for these past 40 years. God wanted to take away your pride and humble you. He tested you to discover what was in your heart. He wanted to know whether you would obey His commands or not." *Lord, when You find sin in my life, cleanse me by the blood of Christ.*

"And God did take away your pride. He let you get hungry, then He fed you with manna. Manna was something which neither you nor your ancestors had ever experienced. This was to teach you that humankind does not live on food alone. Instead, we live on every word which comes out of the mouth of the Lord. During these past 40 years, your clothes did not wear out, and your feet did not swell up. And in your heart you have known that the Lord your God does correct you. He corrects you just as a father corrects his son. Now, you must obey the commands of the Lord your God by living as He has commanded you and revering Him, because the Lord your God is bringing you into a good land. The land has streams, wells, and springs flowing in the valleys and in the hills. It is a land of wheat, barley, grapevines, fig trees, pomegranates, olive oil, and honey. It is a land where you will have plenty of food, you will have everything you need there. The stones are made of iron, so you can dig copper out of its hills. You will have all you want to eat, then you will praise the Lord your God because He has indeed given you a good land." *Lord, thank You for all Your provisions to me.*

"Watch yourselves. Then you won't forget about the Lord your God, so that you start disobeying His commands, His rules, and His laws, which I am commanding you today. When you obey, you will eat all you want, and you will build nice houses and live in them. And your herds and flocks will get bigger and bigger. And your money will grow, and you will have more and more of everything. Beware lest your heart becomes proud and you forget about the Lord your God. He brought you out of the land of Egypt, where you were slaves. God led you through the vast and terrible desert. There was no water, poisonous snakes, and stinging insects. But God brought water out of solid rock. God fed you manna in the desert, something which your ancestors had never experienced. God wanted to humble you to take away your pride and to test you. He did it so you would prosper, otherwise you might think to yourself: 'I am rich because of my own strength and power.' So, remember the Lord your God. It is *He* who gives you the power to become rich. He confirms His covenant which He promised to your ancestors. So it is today. But if you truly forget about the Lord your God and you follow other gods and worship them, and bow down to those gods, then I testify against you today, that you will be utterly destroyed. The Lord will destroy the other nations ahead of you, and you will be destroyed in the same way if you do not obey the Lord your God." *Lord, I will not forget.*

Deuteronomy 9

THE ISRAELITES DID NOT OBEY

Moses continued, "Listen, O Israel. You will cross over the Jordan River soon (about one month). You will go in to force out nations that are bigger and stronger than you. They have great cities with walls up to the skies. The people are Anakites (the sons of Anakim, a family of giants). They are big and tall. You know about them. You have heard it said: 'No one can stop the Anakites!' But today know that the Lord your God is going in ahead of you. He will destroy them like a fire that burns everything up. He will defeat them and humble them ahead of you, and you will force them out. You will destroy them quickly, just as the Lord has told you. The Lord your God will force them out ahead of you. After that, do not think to yourself, *The Lord brought me here, and I own this land because I am so good.* No! It is because these nations are evil, that is why the Lord will force them out ahead of you." *Lord, keep me humble when You use me.*

"You are going in to take possession of the land. But it is not because you are so good and honest. It is because these nations are evil. That is why the Lord your God will force them out ahead of you. The Lord will confirm the word which He promised to your ancestors—to Abraham, to Isaac, and to Jacob. The Lord your God is indeed giving you this good land to own. But know this, it is not because you are good. No, you are a stubborn people. Remember this and do not forget it. You made the Lord your God angry in the desert. Since the day you left the land of Egypt until you arrived here, you have been rebellious against the

Lord. Even at Mount Sinai, you made the Lord angry and He was angry enough to destroy you." *Lord, forgive every sin of mine.*

"I went up on the mountain to receive the stone tablets which were the covenant that the Lord had made with you. I stayed on the mountain for 40 days and 40 nights. I did not eat food or drink water. The Lord gave me two stone tablets. God had written on them with His own finger all the words which He spoke on the mountain from within the fire." *Lord, I receive and believe in your Word.*

"So, at the end of the 40 days and 40 nights, the Lord gave the two stone tablets of the covenant to me. Then the Lord told me, 'Get up, go down quickly from here, because your people whom you have brought out of Egypt are ruining themselves. They have quickly turned away from the path that I commanded and have made a metal idol for themselves.' And the Lord spoke to me, 'I have watched these people, they are very stubborn. Leave Me alone, so that I can destroy them. I will make the whole world forget who they ever were. Then I will make another nation from you, stronger and greater than they are.'" *Lord, help me learn from the sin and judgment of others.*

"So, I turned and went down the mountain that was burning with fire. And the two stone tablets of the covenant were in both of my hands. When I looked, I saw that you had sinned against the Lord your God. You had made for yourselves a metal idol in the shape of a calf. You had quickly turned away from the path which the Lord had commanded you. So, I grabbed the two stone tablets, and threw them down right in front of you, breaking them in pieces." *Lord, give me righteous indignation against sin, just as Moses had.*

"Then, just as before, I bowed myself face down on the ground in the presence of the Lord. I did this for 40 days and 40 nights. I did not eat food or drink water, because of all the sins you had committed. You did evil in the sight of the Lord, making Him angry. I was so afraid of the Lord's anger and rage because He was angry enough to destroy you. But the Lord listened to me at the time. He also was angry at Aaron so that He wanted to destroy Aaron, too. But then I prayed for Aaron also. Then I took that sinful calf-idol which you had made and burned it in the fire. I crushed it into a powder as fine as dust, and I dumped that gold dust into a stream that flowed down from the mountain." *Lord, I will be quick to repent of sin.*

"Also, at Taberah at Massah, and at Kibroth-Hattaavah, you made the Lord angry. The Lord said at Kadesh-Barnea, 'Go up and take possession of the land which I have given to you.' But you rebelled against the command of the Lord your God. You did not trust Him or obey Him. You have been rebels against the Lord as long as I have known you." *Lord, forgive my past sins, and keep me from sin in the future.*

"The Lord had said that He was going to destroy you, but I bowed down humbly in His presence for those 40 days and 40 nights. I prayed to the Lord saying, 'O Lord God, do not destroy Your people. They are Your very own people. In Your greatness, You redeemed them and brought them out of Egypt by Your powerful hand. Remember Your servants—Abraham, Isaac, and Jacob. Do not look at how stubborn these people are. Do not look at their sin or their evil ways. Otherwise, Egypt will say, "The Lord was not able to take His people into the land which He promised to them." They will say, "The Lord hated them, that's why He brought them out. He wanted to kill them in the desert." O Lord, they are Your very own people. You brought them out of

Egypt with Your great power and strength.'" *Lord, I will be an intercessor for Your people, just like Moses.*

Deuteronomy 10

THE SECOND SET OF STONE TABLETS

Moses continued, "At that time, the Lord said to me, 'Chisel two stone tablets like the first ones. Then, come up to Me on the mountain. Also make a wooden chest. I will write on the tablets the same words which were on the first tablets, which you broke. And you must put the new tablets inside that chest.'"

"So, the chest was made out of acacia wood. And I chiseled out the two stone tablets like the first ones. Then I went up on the mountain. I had the two tablets in my hand. And the Lord wrote the same things on these tablets that He had written before. The Lord wrote the Ten Commandments, which He had spoken to you on the mountain from within the fire on the day of the assembly. Then the Lord gave them to me." *Lord, thank You for grace and mercy.*

"Then I turned and went down the mountain. And I put the tablets inside the chest that was made. That is what the Lord had commanded. The tablets are still there in the Ark of the Covenant."

"The people of Israel traveled from the wells of the Jaakanites to Moserah. Aaron died there, and he was buried. Aaron's son, Eleazar, became high priest in Aaron's place. From Moserah they traveled to Gudgodah. And from Gudgodah, they traveled to Jotbathah, a place with streams of water. At that time, the Lord selected the tribe of Levi to carry the Ark of the Covenant of the Lord. They were to serve the Lord. They were to bless the people in the name of the Lord—they still do this today. That is why the Levites did not receive any land to own, along with their

Hebrew brothers. Instead, they received the Lord Himself as their inheritance. This is what the Lord your God told them." *Lord, the greatest inheritance of all is You, Yourself.*

Moses continued, "I stayed on the mountain for 40 days and 40 nights, just like the first time. The Lord listened to me this time; it was not His will to destroy you. And the Lord said, 'Get up. Go cause the people to advance, so that they may go in and take possession of the land which I vowed to their ancestors.'" *Lord, I will obey when You say "go."*

What God Expects From His People

Moses continued, "And now, O Israel, this is what the Lord asks of you: Revere the Lord your God. Do what He has told you to do. Love Him, serve the Lord your God with your whole heart and with all your soul. Obey the Lord's commands and His laws which I am commanding you today for your own good. The Lord owns the whole world and everything in it. Everything belongs to Him. Yet the Lord delighted in and loved your ancestors. And, He chose you, their descendants, above all the other ethnic groups. Give yourselves completely to serving the Lord. Don't be stubborn anymore. Because the Lord your God, He is the God of all gods, and the Lord of all lords. He is the great God. He is powerful and awesome. He does not take sides. And He will not be talked into doing evil. He is fair to the orphans and the widows. He loves foreigners. He gives them food and clothing. So, you ought to love foreigners too, because you were once foreigners in the land of Egypt. You must revere the Lord your God and serve Him. Cling to Him, and make your vows in His Name. You should praise Him, He is your God. He has done great and wonderful things for you. You have seen them with your own eyes." *Lord, I revere and worship You.*

"There were only 70 persons of your ancestors when they went down to Egypt. And now, the Lord your God has made you as numerous as the stars in the sky!" *Lord, I bless You for prospering Your people.*

Deuteronomy 11

THE IMPORTANCE OF OBEDIENCE

"But you will soon cross over the Jordan River to capture that land. It is a land of hills and valleys that drinks rain from the skies. It is a land which the Lord, your God, loves and His eyes are constantly upon it. He watches over it from the beginning of the year to the end of the year.

"If you carefully obey My commands which I am commanding you today, if you love the Lord your God and serve Him with your whole being, then He will send rain upon your land at the proper time, in the fall (the early rain) and the spring (the latter rain), so that you will be able to harvest your grain, your new wine, and your olive oil. And God will put grass in the fields for your animals, and you will have plenty to eat." *Lord, I'm overwhelmed by Your promises.*

"Watch yourselves. Don't be fooled, nor turn away and serve other gods. Do not worship them. If you do such things, then the Lord will become angry with you, and His anger will burn against you. He will shut the skies so that it will not rain, and the soil will not grow crops. And you will soon die in the good land which the Lord is giving to you." *Lord, Your warnings are accurate.*

"Remember these words in your hearts and minds. Write them down and tie them to your forearms as a sign. Tie them on your foreheads to remind you to do God's will. And you must teach them to your children. Talk about them when you sit at home, and when you walk along the road. Talk about them when you lie down, and after you get up. Write them on the door frames of your house, and on your gates. Then both you and your children will live a long time in the land which the Lord vowed to give your ancestors, for as long as the skies are above the earth." *Lord, I will keep Your Word in front of me at all times.*

"If you are very careful to obey every command that I give you, and if you will love the Lord your God, and if you will do what He has told you to do, and if you will cling to Him, then the Lord will force out all those nations from the land ahead of you. Then you will take possession of the land from the nations that are bigger and stronger than you. Everywhere you step will belong to you. Your land will extend from the desert to Lebanon. And it will go all the way from the Euphrates River to the Mediterranean Sea. No one will be able to stop you. The Lord your God will do what He promised; everywhere you go, He will cause the people to be afraid." *Lord, I say "amen" to Your promises.*

"Today, I am letting you choose either a blessing or a curse. You will be blessed if you obey the commands of the Lord your God, which I am commanding you today." *Lord, I say "yes."*

"But you will be cursed if you disobey the commands of the Lord your God. So, do not turn aside from the path that I am commanding you today. Do not worship other gods that you have not known. When the Lord your God brings you into the land that you will soon possess, then you must announce the blessings on Mount Gerizim, and announce the curses on Mount Ebal. (These two peaks in central Palestine were about 3,000 feet in elevation. They were close to one another with a small valley between them.) These mountains are on the other side of the Jordan River. They are west, toward the sunset, near the great trees of Moreh. They are in the land of the Canaanites who live in the Jordan Valley opposite Gilgal. Soon you will cross over the Jordan River to go in and take possession of the land that the Lord your God is giving to you. You will capture it and settle there. Then you must be very careful to obey all the laws and rules that I am laying out in front of you today." *Lord, when You bless me, I will say "amen."*

Deuteronomy 11

THE STORY OF A CONTRAST BETWEEN EGYPT AND CANAAN

Date: 1451 B.C. ~ Place: East of Jordan

For the land which you go to possess is not like the land of Egypt from which you have come, where you sowed your seed and watered it by foot, as a vegetable garden; but the land which you cross over to possess is a land of hills and valleys, which drinks water from the rain of heaven, a land for which the Lord your God cares; the eyes of the Lord your God are always on it, from the beginning of the year to the very end of the year (Deuteronomy 11:10-12).

The picture of Israel coming out of Egypt is a picture of the believer's deliverance from the slavery of sin. Moses reminds his listeners of the difference between their former slavery and their promised inheritance in Canaan. He also reminds them of the harshness of Egypt compared to God's natural blessing in the Promised Land. And finally he tells them, "The eyes of the Lord your God are always on it (the Promised Land), from the beginning of the year to the very end of the year." Why? Because it is a land that the Lord their God cares for.

The land of Egypt did not have an abundant natural rainfall, nor did it have springs of water from the heart of the earth. All Egypt had was the Nile River, that mighty river running through the heart of the land. It overflowed every spring to give them an abundance of water. They captured the excess water in large lake-like reservoirs. Then they dug trenches to channel water to the fields. When Moses reminded Israel they "watered it with their foot," it meant they pumped water by a foot-powered treadmill. Each slave lifted the water only one or two feet, since Egypt is flat land and the flat Nile River basin was watered by foot power.

But the Promised Land of Canaan was watered by rain from Heaven. It was not flat like Egypt, so Moses reminded them, "A land of hills and valleys that drank the water from heaven and gave forth its abundance."

The Promised Land is symbolic of God's care and provision of His own. And how do we know God will care for His children in the Promised Land? First, His eyes are upon that unique spot on the earth because He cares for it. And second, God cares for it from the beginning of the year until the end of the year.

My Time to Pray

Lord, since You cared so much for the land of promise,
And it was just dirt, rocks, and trees,
How much more do You care for me.

The land of promise was just a place You loved,
But I am Your redeemed born-again child.

I love You and serve You with all my heart.
I worship You for Your greatness of care
That You extend to someone lowly as me.

Amen.

Deuteronomy 12

THE ONE PLACE FOR WORSHIP

Moses continued, "These are the laws and rules which you must carefully obey in the land which the Lord, the God of your ancestors, is giving to you to take possession for as long as you live on the earth. You will be forcing out these nations. You must completely destroy all the places where they worshiped their gods. These places are on tall mountains and hills, and under every green tree. Tear down their altars. Smash their so-called 'sacred' stone pillars. Burn up their Asherah idols. Cut down the carved images of their gods, and destroy their names from those places." *Lord, I will get rid of all traces of idolatry.*

"Don't worship the Lord your God that way. Instead, look for the place which the Lord your God will choose to put His name to dwell there. There God will manifest His glory (Shekinah)—His presence. God's place will be somewhere among your tribes. (It was in Jerusalem.) Go there to worship Him." *Lord, today I go to worship You, to Your place—the church.*

"Bring your whole burnt offerings and sacrifices to that place. Bring 10 percent of what you gain and bring your special gifts. Bring what you have vowed and your voluntary gifts. Also bring the firstborn animals of your herds and flocks. You will meet there with the Lord, your God. You and your families will eat in God's presence, and enjoy all the good things for which you have worked, because the Lord your God, has blessed you." *Lord, I will tithe to You.*

"You will not be able to behave as we do now, with everybody worshiping wherever he thinks is right. As yet, you have not arrived at the resting place. But the Lord your God will give you the inheritance soon." *Lord, I will go to meet You in my church.*

"You will cross over the Jordan River, and settle in the land that the Lord your God is causing you to inherit. There, He will give you rest from all your enemies, and you will live in peace. Then the Lord your God will choose the place where He wants to be worshiped. To that place, you must bring everything I command you: your whole burnt-offerings, your sacrifices, your offerings of 10 percent, your special gifts, and all the best things which you have vowed to the Lord. And you will rejoice there in the presence of the Lord your God, you, your sons and your daughters, your male and female servants, and the Levites from within your towns who have no land of their own. Watch out. Otherwise, you would offer your whole burnt offerings wherever you please. This is wrong. Offer your whole burnt offerings only in the special place where the Lord will choose within the territory of one of your tribes. You must do everything I am commanding you there!

"Nevertheless, you may kill your animals within any of your towns. And you may eat as much of their meat as you want. Eat it as if it were a deer or a gazelle. This is the blessing which the Lord, your God, is giving to you. You may eat any clean or unclean meat. But do not eat the blood. You must pour it out on the ground like water. Now, inside your towns you must not eat what belongs to the Lord, the 10 percent of your grain, of your new wine, or your olive oil, or the firstborn animals of your herds and flocks, or whatever you have vowed to donate of the special gifts you want to give to the Lord. If you eat these things when you are together in the presence of the Lord, you must eat them in the place where the Lord your God chooses to be worshiped. Everyone must do this, you, your sons and your daughters, your male and female servants, and the Levites from within your towns. You will rejoice in the presence of the Lord in everything that you undertake." *Lord, I commit myself to worship in Your special place.*

"Watch yourselves. Don't neglect the Levites (the Israelites still had a standing obligation to support the Levites) as long as you live on the land.

"When the Lord your God enlarges your borders, as He has promised you, your appetite will crave some meat. You will think: 'I am going to eat as much meat as I want.' Be careful. The Lord your God will indeed choose the place where He is to be worshiped. However, it may be too far away from you to take the animals there. If it is, you may kill animals from your herds and your flocks, which the Lord has given to you. As I have commanded you, within your towns, you may eat as much of them as you desire. Eat them as you would eat wild gazelle or deer meat. Both clean and unclean people may eat of this meat. Be sure you do not eat the blood, because the blood is the life. So, you must not eat the life along with the meat. You must not eat blood. Pour it out on the ground like water. Because you don't eat blood, then things will go well for you and your children. You will be doing what the Lord sees as right. Take your consecrated things and the things which you have vowed to give to God, and go to the holy place where the Lord's presence is found. Then you can present your whole burnt offerings on the altar of the Lord your God. Offer both the meat and the blood. The blood of your sacrifices should be poured out beside the altar of the Lord your God. However, you may eat the meat." *Lord, I offer myself in worship to You.*

"Be careful and obey all these words that I am commanding you. Then things will always go well for you and your children after you.

You will be doing what the Lord your God sees as good and right. You will enter the land and take it away from the nations there. The Lord your God will destroy those people ahead of you. Force them out and settle in their land. They will be destroyed ahead of you. Watch yourselves; otherwise, you will get trapped into following them. You might start asking about their gods: 'How did these nations worship their gods? Could we ourselves worship them too?' Don't try to worship the Lord your God that way. The Lord hates those disgusting things which they have done for their gods. They even burn up their sons and daughters in the fire as sacrifices to their gods!" *Lord, I separate myself from false worship of false gods.*

"Be sure to do everything that I have commanded you. Do not add anything to it, and do not take anything away from it!" *Lord, I will obey.*

The qualification for the place where God wanted worship in the *Old Testament* involves: (1) Where His presence dwelt, (2) Where the symbols of worship were located (the Ark of the Covenant, the Brazen Altar and furniture of the Tabernacle), (3) Where the Levites ministered. The qualifications for *New Testament* worship involve: (1) The church, which is the Body of Christ in His New Testament presence, "Where two or three are gathered together in My name, I am there in the midst of them" (Matt. 18:20), (2) Where the symbols of redemption are located—baptism and the Lord's table, (3) Where the pastor (shepherd) ministers spiritual gifts.

Deuteronomy 13

WORSHIP THE ONE TRUE GOD

Moses continued, "Suppose somebody appears among you who claims
to be a prophet, or someone who says that he can predict the
future by using dreams. He might say that he will show you a
miracle or a proof that he is from God. And suppose the miracle
or the sign which he foretold happens. Then he might say: 'Let
us follow after other gods (gods that you have not known), and
let us worship or serve them.' You must not listen to the words
of that so-called prophet or that dreamer of 'dreams.' The Lord
your God is testing you. He is discovering if you love Him with
your heart and with all your soul. Follow only the Lord your
God. Reverence Him. Keep His commands and obey Him. Serve
Him, and cling to Him. That so-called 'prophet' or dreamer of
'dreams' must be executed. Why? Because He told you to turn
away from the Lord your God. It was the I AM who brought
you out of the land of Egypt. It was He who redeemed you from
the house of slavery. That deceiver is trying to drive you away
from the path which the Lord your God has commanded you to
take. You must remove any evil that is among you." *Lord, I will
reject anyone who pulls me away from You.*

"Some relative may try to entice you to serve or worship other gods. It
might be your brother by blood, your son, your daughter, or the
wife whom you love dearly, or it might be a close friend. He
might say in secret, 'Let us go and worship other gods.' (Now
these are gods that neither you nor your ancestors have known.)
They are the gods of the nations around you. Some are nearby,
and some are far away from you. False gods are located from

one end of the land to the other. You must not give in to him. Don't listen to him. Don't feel sorry for him. Do not spare him or hide him from punishment. You must surely put him to death. Your very own hand must be the first to begin executing him. Then everyone else must join in, throwing stones at him until he dies. Why? Because he tried to pull you away from the Lord your God. The Lord has brought you out of the land of Egypt where you were once slaves." *Lord, I reject all manmade gods.*

"When everyone in Israel hears about this, they will be afraid. Then no one among you will ever try such an evil thing again. The Lord your God is giving you some towns in which to settle. There you might hear something about one of them, when someone might say, 'Some evil men have come in among you and are leading those who live in that town away from God. They are saying: "Let us go and worship other gods that you have not known."' Then you must investigate it. Look into the matter and check it out thoroughly. Listen, it might be true. If it is proved that such an abominable thing has indeed happened among you, then you must surely kill everyone who lives in that town with swords, completely destroying even the animals and everything in it by the edge of the sword. Gather up everything that those people owned and put it in the middle of the town square. Then you must totally burn up the town and everything that they had owned for the Lord your God. That town must never be rebuilt. It will lie in perpetual ruins. Do not keep any of the cursed things found in that town for yourselves. Then the Lord will not be angry anymore. He will give you mercy, and will feel sorry for you. Then He will make your nation grow larger, just as He vowed to your ancestors. You will have obeyed the Lord your God, keeping all of His commands, which I am commanding you to do today." *Lord, I put to death all evil lust within my life: I will not tolerate anything that You hate.*

Deuteronomy 14

Clean and Unclean Foods

Moses continued, "You people are the children of the Lord your God. When someone dies, do not cut yourselves or shave your heads to show your sadness. You are a holy people. You belong to the Lord your God. He has selected you out of all the nations on the surface of earth to be His very own people, a special treasure." *Lord, thank You for choosing me.*

"You must not eat anything that the Lord thinks of as disgusting. These are the animals which you may eat: cattle, sheep, goats, harts, gazelles, roe deer, wild goats, ibexes, antelopes, and wild sheep. You may eat any animal that has a split hoof and chews the cud.

"But you may not eat these animals: camels, rabbits, or rock-badgers. Though these animals chew the cud, their feet are not divided, so they are 'unclean' for you. Pigs are also 'unclean' for you. They have split hoofs, but they do not chew the cud. Do not eat their meat or touch their dead bodies. There are many things that live in the water that you may eat—anything that has fins and scales. But do not eat anything that does not have fins and scales. It is 'unclean' for you. You may eat any clean bird. But you must not eat these birds: eagles, vultures, black vultures, red kites, falcons, any kind of kite, any kind of raven, horned owls, screech owls, seagulls, any kind of hawk, little owls, great owls, white owls, desert owls, ospreys, cormorants, storks, any kind of heron, the hoopoe, or bats. All insects with wings are 'unclean' for you. Do not eat them. Other things with wings are 'clean.' You may eat them.

"Do not eat anything you find that is already dead. You may give it to a foreigner who lives in your town; he may eat it. Or you may sell it to a foreigner. But, you are a holy people, you belong to the Lord your God.

"Do not cook a baby goat in its mother's milk.

"Be sure to save 10 percent of all your crops each year. Take it to the place where the Lord your God will choose where He is to be worshiped. There you may eat the tenth of your grain, your new wine, and your olive oil, and there you may eat the firstborn animals of your herds and your flocks. Then you will learn to always reverence the Lord your God." *Lord, I will fellowship with You at Your designated place.*

"But if the place where the Lord will choose to be worshiped is too far away, and He has blessed you so much that you cannot carry the tenth; exchange your one-tenth for silver. Then take the silver with you to the place where the Lord, your God, will choose. Use that silver to buy anything you wish—cattle, sheep, goats, wine, or anything you want. Then you and your family will eat and celebrate there in the presence of the Lord your God. Do not neglect the Levites who are living in your towns. They have no land of their own among you to grow and produce crops." *Lord, I will give to You.*

"At the end of every third year, you must bring 10 percent of that year's crop to store in your towns. This will go to the Levites, so that they may eat and be satisfied. It is also for foreigners, orphans, and widows who live in your towns. All of them should eat and be satisfied, too. Then the Lord your God will bless you and the labor of your hands." *Lord, I will give to others who are needy.*

Deuteronomy 15

FORGIVE DEBTORS EVERY SEVEN YEARS

Moses continued, "At the end of every seven years (the sabbatical year), you must forget about collecting what people owe you. This is how you are to do it: everyone who has loaned money must cancel the obligation. He must not force his Hebrew neighbor and his brother to pay it back. Why? Because for the sake of the Lord, the cancellation of debts must be proclaimed. You may make a foreigner pay what he owes you, but you must not collect what your Hebrew brother owes you. There should be no needy people among you. The Lord your God will richly bless you in the land that He is giving to you. The Lord your God will bless you if you will only obey Him completely. But you must be very careful to obey each command that I am commanding you today. The Lord your God will bless you, just as He promised. You will lend to men of other nations, but you will not need to borrow from them. Instead, you will rule over many nations by your financial prosperity, but they will not rule over you." *Lord, I will use my money and resources for Your influence.*

"There might be a poor man among you, one of your Hebrew brothers who is living in one of the towns in your land, which the Lord your God is giving to you. Do not be selfish or be greedy toward him. But give freely to him, and freely lend to him whenever he needs. Beware of evil thoughts within yourself, thinking, The seventh year to forgive what people owe is near. You might show ill-will toward your needy brother by not giving him anything. Then he might complain to the Lord about you, and the Lord would find you guilty of sin. You must give freely to the poor person, not wishing that you didn't have anything to give. Why? Because the Lord your God will bless your work and everything that you touch. There will always be poor people within the land, so give freely to your Hebrew brothers, contributing to poor and needy people in your country." *Lord, I will give.*

How to Treat Your Slaves

Moses continued, "If your Hebrew relative, whether it is a man or a woman, is sold to you as a servant, that person will serve you for six years. But in the seventh year you must set that individual free. And when you let him go free from you, don't send him away empty-handed. Reward him with some of your flock animals, your grain, and your wine. Give to him as the Lord your God has blessed you. Remember that you were also once slaves in the land of Egypt, but the Lord your God saved you. That is why I am giving this command to you today.

"But your servant might say to you, 'I don't want to leave you!' He might love you and your family because you have been so good to him. If he says this, then stick an awl through his ear into the door post. Then he will be your servant for life. You may also do this for your female servant. Do not think of it as a harsh thing when you let your servant go free. After all, he served you for six years. You paid him only half of what a hired person would have cost. The Lord your God will bless you in everything you do." *Lord, I want to be Your servant, I never want to leave You. I'll be Your servant forever.*

The Firstborn Animals

Moses continued, "Consecrate all the firstborn, male animals of your herds and your flocks, they belong to the Lord your God. Do not put the firstborn calves of your cattle to work. And don't shear the wool from the firstborn lamb of your flock of sheep. Each year you and your family are to eat these firstborn animals in the presence of the Lord your God. Eat them in the place that He will choose to be worshiped. An animal might have a physical defect. It might be lame or blind or have some other serious defect. Do not sacrifice that animal to the Lord your God. However, you may eat that animal in your own town. Both 'clean' and 'unclean' people may eat it. It would be like eating a gazelle or a deer. But do not eat its blood! Pour it out on the ground like water." *Lord, I will consecrate.*

Deuteronomy 16

THREE FESTIVALS EACH YEAR

Moses continued, "Celebrate the month of Abib (*first fruits*) and keep
the Passover for the Lord your God. It was during Abib that the
Lord God brought you out of Egypt at night. And you must
offer a Passover sacrifice to the Lord your God; it should be an
animal from the flock or from the herd. Offer it at the place
which the Lord will choose as a dwelling place for His name.
Do not eat it with bread that has been made with yeast. Instead,
for seven days eat bread made without yeast. This is the bread of
suffering, because you left the land of Egypt in a hurry. So, all
during your life you must remember the time when you left the
land of Egypt. There must be no yeast anywhere within your
country for seven days. Offer the sacrifice on the evening of the
first day. And eat all the meat before morning." *Lord, may I
never forget my suffering that brought me to this hour.*

"Do not offer the Passover sacrifice in just any town which the Lord
your God gives you. Offer it only at the place where He will
choose as a dwelling place for His name. Offer it in the evening
as the sun is going down. That was when you left Egypt. Roast
the meat, then eat it at the place which the Lord your God will
choose for Himself. Then the next morning turn back and go to
your home. Eat bread made without yeast for six days; on the
seventh day have a special meeting for the Lord your God. Do
not work on that day." *Lord, I will celebrate.*

"Count off seven weeks from the time you begin to harvest the stalks of
grain. (The counting began on a Saturday, and it ended on a
Saturday. The next day—Pentecost—would be a Sunday.) Then

celebrate Pentecost (which means 50, also called the Feast of Weeks or Feast of Harvest) for the Lord your God. Bring Him an offering as your special gift to Him. Give to the Lord your God as He has blessed you. Rejoice before the Lord your God. Rejoice at the place that the Lord your God will choose as a dwelling place for His name. Everyone should rejoice: you, your sons and daughters, your male and female servants, the Levites in your town, the foreigners, the orphans, and the widows who live among you. Remember, you were once slaves in Egypt, so be very careful to obey all these laws." *Lord, thank you for Pentecost when the Holy Spirit came.*

"Celebrate the Feast of Tabernacles for seven days (in the present month of October). Do it after you have gathered in your harvest from the threshing floor, and your wine press. Everybody should rejoice at your feast: you, your sons and daughters, your male and female servants, the Levites, the foreigners, the orphans, and the widows in your towns. Celebrate the feast to the Lord your God for seven days. Celebrate it at the place where the Lord will choose, and He will bless all of your harvest. He will bless all the work that you do, and you will be very happy." *Lord, thank You for Your harvest in my life.*

"All your males must come into the presence of the Lord your God three times a year. They must come to the place where He will choose. They must come at these times: the Feast of Unleavened Bread (Passover), the Feast of Pentecost, and the Feast of Tabernacles. However, no man should come before the Lord without a gift. Each of you must bring a gift in his hand in proportion to the way that the Lord your God has blessed you." *Lord, it's a great privilege to give to You.*

The Legal System

Moses continued, "Appoint judges and supervisors for yourselves. Appoint them in every town, tribe by tribe, which the Lord your God is giving to you. And, they must truly judge the people with fairness. Do not twist justice or take sides. Do not let people bribe you to make wrong decisions. That kind of so-called 'reward' makes wise people seem blind, and it corrupts the words of good people. Always do what is right, then you will live and possess the land that the Lord your God is giving to you." *Lord, I will always do right.*

"Do not set up for yourselves a wooden Asherah idol next to the altar of the Lord your God which you will build for yourselves. And do not set up for yourselves so-called 'sacred' stone pillars. The Lord your God hates those things!" *Lord, I will love You only and worship You only.*

Deuteronomy 17

JUDGMENT OF EVIL AND RULES FOR THE KING

"Do not offer cattle or sheep that have physical defects as a sacrifice to the Lord your God. That is an abominable thing to the Lord your God.

"Suppose a man or a woman is found among you doing something evil in the sight of the Lord your God in one of the towns which the Lord your God is giving you. That man or that woman is breaking His covenant. That person might have served other gods. He might have bowed down to them, or to the sun, or to the moon, or to the stars of the sky. I have forbidden this kind of idolatry. Should someone tell you about this, you must investigate this matter very carefully. It might be true. Such a disgusting thing may have happened in Israel. If so, then you must take that man or that woman who has done this evil thing to the town gate (there was a place near the city gate where judicial proceedings took place). Throw stones at that person until he or she dies! There must be two or three witnesses who say that they saw him or her actually do it. Then that person should be put to death. But if there is only one witness who testifies, then the accused person should not be put to death. The witnesses must be the first ones to throw stones at the person. Then everyone else will follow their lead. You must get rid of evil among you." *Lord, I will be harsh with sin in my life because You do not tolerate evil of any kind.*

"Some cases that come before you may be too difficult to judge. It may
be a case of murder, quarreling, or attack. Take these cases and
go up to the place where the Lord your God will choose (the
supreme council of the Jews). Go to the Levitical priests, to the
judge who is on duty at that time. Ask them about the case, and
they will declare the decision to you. You must accept the decision that they declare to you. They will be in the place of the
Lord your God. Be very careful to do everything they tell you,
following the instructions that they give to you. Do whatever
they decide. The person who does not show respect for the
judge or the priest who is on duty must die. They are there serving the Lord your God. You must get rid of evil from Israel. Then
all the people will hear about this and they will be afraid. They
will not show disrespect anymore." *Lord, I worship Your holiness.*

Rules for the King

Moses continued, "You will enter the land which the Lord your God is
giving you. You will soon take it as your own and settle in it.
Then you will say, 'Let us appoint a king over us like the other
nations all around us' (See 1 Samuel 8:4-7. The people were not
commanded to appoint a king, but the prophet Moses predicted
that they would desire to do so later). Be sure to appoint the
king over you who the Lord your God chooses. He must be one
of your people. Do not appoint a foreigner as your king. He
would not be a fellow Israelite. And the king must not collect
too many horses for himself, nor send people to Egypt to get
more and more horses. The Lord has told you, 'Do not go back
that way again.' And, the king must not take many wives for
himself. If he does so, then his heart will be led away from God.
Also he must not accumulate too much silver and gold. When
he becomes king, he should have a copy of the teachings of this
law written on a scroll by himself. He should make his copy

from the Levitical priests. (The priests were official custodians of the written Law of Moses.) And the king should keep it with him at all times. He should read from it every day of his life, then he will learn to reverence the Lord his God. Then he will carefully obey all the words of these teachings and these laws. He should never think that he is better than his Hebrew brothers. He must not stop obeying the commands of God in any way. Then he and his descendants will rule over his kingdom in the midst of Israel for a long time." *Lord, I will hold the Scriptures in my heart and obey them constantly.*

Deuteronomy 18

A SHARE GIVEN TO THE PRIESTS AND LEVITES

Moses continued, "The priests are from the tribe of Levi, and the whole tribe of Levi will not receive a share of the land with Israel. That tribe will eat the offerings made to the Lord by fire—that is their share (or inheritance). They will not inherit any of the land like their Hebrew brothers. They will inherit the Lord Himself; this is what He promised them." *Lord, I choose You over money or things.*

"When you offer a bull or a sheep as a sacrifice, you must share it with the priests. Give them the shoulder, the two jowls, and the internal organs. You must give to them the best of your grain, and your new wine, and your olive oil. Also give them the first wool that you shear from your sheep. Why? Because the Lord your God has chosen the priests and their descendants out of all your tribes to stand and serve His name always." *Lord, thank You for ministers today.*

"Now suppose a Levite moves from one of your towns somewhere in Israel where he was living and comes to the place which the Lord will choose. He may serve in the Name of the Lord his God, and be treated like all his fellow Levites who serve in the presence of the Lord. They will all have an equal share of the food. This is separate from what he has received from the sale of his family possessions." *Lord, I will take care of Your servants.*

Forbidden Pagan Practices

Moses continued, "You will enter the land which the Lord your God is giving to you. But you must not learn or follow the abominable customs that those other nations do. There should be none among you who offers his son or his daughter as a sacrifice in the fire. Do not let anyone practice divination or do sorcery (witchcraft). No one should be a fortune-teller or one who casts so-called 'spells' on people. Do not let anyone try to control others using so-called 'charms.' Don't let them be mediums or spiritists or those who try to communicate with the spirits of dead people (through séances). Because anyone who does any of these things is disgusting to the Lord. That is why the Lord your God will expel such disgusting practices out of the land ahead of you. You must be innocent; have integrity with respect to the Lord your God, because these nations whom you will force out already listen to people who use sorcery and divination. But the Lord your God will not permit you to do such things." *Lord, I will flee all dark, evil practices.*

"The Lord your God will raise up a Prophet for you like me. He will come from among your own brothers. Listen to Him.

"This is all that you asked the Lord your God to do when you were gathered at Mount Sinai. You said, 'Don't make us listen to the voice of the Lord our God again. Don't make us look at this terrible fire anymore. Otherwise, we will die.'

"So the Lord said to me, 'What they have said is good. So, I will raise up a Prophet for them like you. He will come from among their own brothers. I will put My words in His mouth, and He will tell them everything I order Him to do. That Man (Jesus Christ) will speak for Me. Anyone who won't listen when He speaks will have to answer to Me." *Lord, thank You for the prediction that*

Jesus would come into the world. The fulfillment of that prediction gives me assurance of my faith.

"A so-called 'prophet' might say something that I did not tell him to say. He might say that he is speaking a word for Me. Or a so-called 'prophet' might be speaking in the name of other gods. That prophet must be killed. You might be thinking, 'How can we know for sure whether a message is from the Lord or not?' A so-called 'prophet' may say in the name of the Lord that something is certainly going to happen. If that prediction does not happen or come true, then it is not the Lord's message! That prophet was merely speaking his own ideas. Don't be afraid of him." *Lord, I will believe only those who speak for You if they speak exactly what the Scriptures say.*

Deuteronomy 19

THE CITIES OF REFUGE

Moses continued, "The Lord your God is giving to you the land of the other nations. He will destroy them, and force them out and settle you in their towns and in their houses. Set aside three cities in the middle of the land which the Lord your God is giving to you to possess as a city of refuge. Then, divide the land which the Lord your God is giving to you into three areas and designate a city of refuge in each one. Build roads. Then someone who accidentally kills another person may run to those cities (a city of refuge).

"This is the case for someone who kills another person. He may run to one of those cities to save his life. However, he might have killed his neighbor without intending to kill him. He did not hate that neighbor previously. Suppose when a man goes into the forest with his neighbor to cut wood, he swings his ax to cut down a tree. But the ax-head flies off the handle and hits his neighbor and kills him. The man who killed him may run to one of those cities of refuge to save his own life. Otherwise, the dead man's relative who has the duty of punishing a murderer would be angry and chase him. If that city were too far away, the relative would catch him. The relative would kill that man; however, that man should not be killed because he did not previously hate his neighbor. That is why I command you to choose those three cities which you must set aside for yourselves." *Lord, I have a city of refuge for when I sin, it is Jesus Christ.*

"You must carefully obey all these commands which I am commanding you today. Love the Lord your God, always do what He wants you to do. If you do so, then the Lord your God will enlarge your land, just as He promised your ancestors. Then He will give you the entire land which He promised. After that, choose three additional cities of refuge (for safety). This is so innocent people will not be killed within your land, which the Lord your God is giving to you to own. By doing this, you will not be guilty of murder.

"But suppose a person does hate his neighbor. And suppose he hides and waits for him, then attacks and kills him, and then runs to one of those cities of refuge. Then the elders of his own town must send someone for him; they should bring the murderer back from the city of refuge. They should hand the murderer over to the relative who has the duty of taking revenge on him. That relative can kill the murderer. Show him no mercy. You must remove guilt from Israel that comes from murdering innocent people. Then things will go well for you." *Lord, I know You hate murder. You even hate it when we get so angry we want to murder someone.*

"Do not move the stone that marks the border of your neighbor's land. People set them in place long ago. They mark what you will inherit in the land which the Lord your God is giving to you to possess."

Witnesses

Moses continued, "One witness is not enough to convict a man of a crime or a sin that he committed against God. The testimony of two or three witnesses is true. If a witness tells a vicious lie while accusing a person of a crime, then the two parties who are arguing must stand in the presence of the Lord. (Judges were acting as representatives of God, lying to them was equivalent to lying to God.) They must stand in front of the priests and the judges who are on duty at that time. The judges must investigate the matter very carefully, because the witness might be a liar. He might be telling lies about his fellow Israelite. If so, you should punish him with the same punishment that he wanted for his fellow Israelite. You must get rid of the evil from among you. The rest of the people will hear about this and be afraid. No one among you would ever try doing such an evil thing again. Show no mercy to that liar! A life must be paid for a life—an eye for an eye, a tooth for a tooth, a hand for a hand, or a foot for a foot!" *Lord You judge sin. I'm glad Jesus took my punishment for my sin.*

Deuteronomy 20

HOW TO MAKE WAR

Moses continued, "When you go out to war against your enemies, you might see some horses and chariots. And their army might be larger than yours. But don't be afraid of them, because the Lord your God will be with you. He brought you up out of the land of Egypt. Before you go into battle, the priest must come near and speak to the army. He should say to them: 'Listen, O Israel. Today you are going into battle against your enemies. Don't lose your courage or be afraid. Don't panic or be terrified at their presence, because the Lord your God is going with you. He will fight for you against your enemies. He will give you a military victory.'" *Lord, thank You for my spiritual victory in Christ.*

"The officers should say to the army, 'Has anyone built a new house but not yet dedicated it to God? Let him go back home; he might die in battle, then someone else would dedicate his new house. Has anyone planted a vineyard and not yet begun to enjoy it? Let him go back home; he might die in battle, then someone else would enjoy his vineyard. Is any man engaged (betrothed) to a woman and not yet married to her? Let him go back home. He might die in battle, then someone else would marry her.'

"Then the officers should also say to the army, 'Is anyone here afraid? Has anyone lost his courage? Let him go back home, then he will not cause others to lose their courage, too.' When the officers have finished speaking to the army, they should appoint army chiefs to lead the army. When you will march up to attack a town, first make them an offer of peace (a chance to surrender). They might accept your offer of peace and open their gates to you. If that happens, all the people of that town will become your slaves. They will work for you. But suppose the people of that town do not want to surrender to you. They might want to fight you in battle. Then you must surround that town (lay siege to it). The Lord your God will hand over that town to you. Then you must kill all the males with your swords. You may seize everything else within the town for yourselves. Capture the women and the children and the animals. You may use these things which the Lord your God gives you from your enemies (plunder) for yourselves. Thus you must do to all the towns that are far away from you. However, they must not be the nearby nations. But, in the towns of these groups which are close by, you must not let anything that breathes stay alive. This is the land which the Lord your God is giving to you to possess. Completely destroy these people—the Hittites, the Amorites, the Canaanites, the Perizzites, the Hivites, and the Jebusites—just as the Lord your God has commanded you." *Lord, this is a picture of the spiritual victory You want for us over sin.*

"They must not teach you what they do for their gods. And, if you do those abominable things, then you will eventually sin against the Lord your God. You might surround a town for a long time, and attack a town, trying to capture it. If so, do not destroy its trees with axes to build a siege-works against them. You may eat the fruit from the trees, but do not cut them down. The trees in the field are not soldiers. There is no need to make war on the trees. However, you may cut down the trees which you know are not trees that supply food. You may use those trees to build siege-works to attack a city as you wage war against the enemy. You may cut down trees until that town is captured." *Lord, teach me Your view of conservation.*

Deuteronomy 21

UNSOLVED MURDERS

Moses continued, "Suppose some victim is murdered. He might be lying in a field in the land which the Lord your God is giving to you to possess. And no one knows who killed him. Your elders and judges should go out to the spot of the murder, and measure how far it is to the surrounding towns. The elders of the town which is nearest to the victim are responsible. They must take a young cow of the herd that has never been worked or worn a yoke, and lead that heifer down to a valley, which has never been plowed or planted. That field must have a stream flowing through it. And there in the valley, they must break the animal's neck. (The killing of this heifer was not a sacrifice. Its blood was not drained; its meat was not to be eaten. This ceremony was meant only to be symbolic.) Then the priests should come forward and give blessings in the name of the Lord.

"The priests are to conduct hearings of all the disputes and any assault case. Then all the elders of the town which are nearest to the murder victim should wash their hands. They should do this over the heifer whose neck was broken, next to the stream. And they should declare, 'We did not kill this person, nor did we observe the murder. O Lord, please remove this sin of Your people, Israel. You have redeemed them. Do not blame Your people and don't hold us responsible for this innocent man's murder.' And so, the murderer's guilt will be atoned. Then you will have removed from your midst the guilt of the murder of an innocent person. You will be doing what the Lord sees as right." *Lord, may I live a blameless life.*

Female Prisoners of War

Moses continued, "You will be going to war against your enemies. The Lord will help you to defeat them. You will surely capture them. You might see a beautiful woman among the captives, and you might be attracted to her. If so, you may take her as your wife, and bring her into your home. First, she must shave her head and trim her fingernails. She must change out of the clothes that she was wearing when she was captured. She must live in your house and mourn over the loss of her parents for one full month. After that, you may marry her and have sex with her. She will become your wife. But suppose you are not pleased with her. If that happens, then let her go wherever she wants. However, you are not allowed to sell her for money. You must not treat her as a slave, because you have taken away her honor."

The Rights of the Firstborn Son

Moses continued, "If a man had been married twice, he might have loved one wife but not the other. And suppose both wives gave birth to sons for him. However, his firstborn son might be the son of the wife whom he did not love. Someday that man must bequeath his property to his sons. That man must not show partiality to the younger son of his favorite wife. The firstborn son is the son of the wife that the man had not loved. He must agree to give the firstborn son two shares according to the right of primogeniture of everything he owns. The firstborn son is from the wife that he did not love. That son was the first to prove that his father could have children. So, he has the rights that belong to the firstborn son."

The Rebellious Son

Moses continued, "Suppose a man has a son who is stubborn and turns against his father and mother and won't obey them. He doesn't listen when they correct him. Both his parents must take him to his town's elders at the gate. And they will say to the elders of his town: 'This son of ours is stubborn and rebellious. He won't obey us. He eats too much, or he is always drunk.' Then, all the men of his town must throw stones at him until he dies! Get rid of evil among you. All the people of Israel will hear about this and be afraid."

Various Laws

Moses continued, "Suppose a man is guilty of a sin that deserves the death penalty. Then you must put him to death and later display his corpse on a tree. But you are not allowed to leave his dead body hanging on the tree all night. Be sure to bury him that same day. Anyone whose corpse is hanging on a tree is condemned by God. You must not desecrate the land that the Lord your God is giving to you to possess." *Lord, Jesus became guilty of all the sins of Israel, if not all the sins of the world. He was hanged on a tree (cross) for me. Thank You for forgiveness.*

Deuteronomy 22

MISCELLANEOUS INSTRUCTIONS

Moses continued, "You might see your fellowman's bull or his sheep running loose. Do not ignore them. You must surely take them back to your brother. The owner may not live very close to you. Or you may not know who he is. If so, then take the animal home with you. Keep it until its owner comes looking for it. Then you must give it back to him. Do the same thing if you happen to find his donkey or his coat or anything that he may have lost. Don't just ignore it. You might see your fellowman's donkey or his bull fallen down on the road. Don't ignore them. You must surely help that animal get up on its feet." *Lord, I will love my neighbor as myself.*

"A woman must not wear men's clothes. And a man must not wear women's clothes. Anyone who does such things as this is doing an abominable thing as far as the Lord your God is concerned." *Lord, I'm proud of my gender and I will dress accordingly.*

"If there happens to be a bird's nest in front of you beside the road, or in any tree, or on the ground, and the mother bird is sitting on the young birds or the eggs, do not take the mother along with the young birds. You may take the young birds, but you must surely let the mother bird go free. Then things will go well for you. And you will live a long time. (God was teaching them through Moses that all life depends upon an ecological balance.)

"When you build a new house, build a guard rail (banister) around the edge of your roof. Then you will not be guilty of accidental death if someone were to fall off the roof." *Lord, I will look out for others.*

"Don't plant two different kinds of seeds in your vineyard. Otherwise, both crops will be ruined.

"Don't plow with a bull and a donkey tied together.

"Don't wear clothes made of wool and linen woven together.

"Make tassels for yourself and put them on the four corners of your robe."

My Time to Pray

Lord, You expect us to have "common sense."
Help me learn as much as I can,
About living practically and wisely.

Lord, You gave me a good mind at birth
Help me live wisely and practically.

Lord, there are so many ways to get hurt,
Or lose something or suffer an accident.
Help me look out for myself and others.

Amen.

Laws Concerning Sexual Matters

Moses continued, "Suppose a man marries a girl and has sex with her. But later he decides that he does not love her anymore. So, he tells lies about her and gives her a bad name. He might say: 'I married this woman, but when I had sex with her, I did not find that she was a virgin.' Then the girl's parents must bring proof that she was a virgin. (The blood-stained wedding sheet at consummation proved that the girl was previously a virgin before her marriage. Apparently, the bride's parents retained possession of this cloth.) They must bring it to the elders at the town gate. The girl's father will say to the elders, 'I gave my daughter to this man to be his wife. But now he does not want her. Listen, this man has told lies about my daughter. He has said, "I did not find your daughter to be a virgin!" But here is the proof that my daughter was a virgin.' Then her parents are to show the sheet in front of the elders of the town. Then the elders of the town will take the man and punish him. They must make him pay about 2½ pounds of silver and give it to the girl's father, because the man had given a virgin of Israel a bad name. So, she will continue to be the man's wife, and he will never be allowed to divorce her for as long as she lives.

"However, suppose the things that the husband said about his wife are true. And the signs of virginity were not found in the girl. If so, the girl must be brought out to the door of her father's house. Then the men of the town must put her to death by throwing stones at her. She has done a disgraceful thing in Israel. She had sex before she was married. You must get rid of evil among you. If a man gets caught having sex with another man's wife, then both of them—the woman and the man who had sex with her— must die. Get rid of this evil from Israel.

"If a man meets a virgin in a town and has sex with her, but she is engaged to marry another man, then you must take both of them out to the town gate. Put them both to death by throwing stones at them. Kill the girl because she was inside a town and did not scream for help. And kill the man for having sex with another man's wife. You must get rid of evil among you.

"However, a man might seize a girl out in the countryside, and force her to have sex with him even though she is engaged to another man. If that is the case, then only the man who had sex with her must die. Don't do anything to the girl. She has not committed a sin worthy of death. This case is like the person who attacks his neighbor and murders him. Why? Because the man caught the engaged girl in the countryside and no one was there to save her when she screamed. If a man seizes a virgin who is not engaged to be married, and he forces her to have sex with him, and people find out about it, then the attacker must pay the girl's father a bride-price of 1¼ pounds of silver. And, he must also marry the girl, because he has dishonored her. And he can never divorce her for as long as he lives.

"A man must not marry his father's wife. He must not dishonor his father in this way."

My Time to Pray

Lord, there are many laws about having sex,
I know You have commanded us
To have sex only within marriage.

Lord, I commit myself to be sexually pure,
And I pray for all my friends and relatives,
That they will make that same commitment.

Amen.

Deuteronomy 23

BANNED PEOPLE

Moses continued, "No man who has been emasculated by crushing or cutting (castration) may come into the congregation of the Lord.

"No one born out of wedlock may come into the assembly of the Lord. His descendents may not come in for ten generations.

"No Ammonite or Moabite male may come into the congregation of the Lord. And none of their descendants may ever come in for ten generations. Why? Because the Ammonites and Moabites would not give you food and water on the road when you came out of Egypt. Instead, they hired Balaam to put a curse upon you. He was the son of Beor from Pethor in northwest Mesopotamia. But the Lord your God would not listen to Balaam. The Lord your God turned the curse into a blessing for you, because the Lord your God loves you. Do not wish for peace with them or good relations with them, as long as you live.

"Don't hate Edomites, because they are your relatives. Don't hate Egyptians, because you were foreigners in their country. The great-grandchildren of these two ethnic groups may come into the congregation of the Lord.

"When you are camped in war time, keep yourselves away from all 'unclean' things. Suppose a man becomes 'unclean' because of an 'accident' during the night. If this happens, then he must go outside the camp and not come back in until he is 'clean.' But when the evening comes, he must take a bath in water, and at sunset, he may come back into the camp.

"Choose a place outside the camp where people may go to relieve themselves. Take a little shovel with you. When you relieve yourself
out there, you must dig a hole with the shovel and turn around
and cover up your waste. The Lord your God moves around
throughout the camp. He will protect you. He will help you to
defeat your enemies ahead of you. Therefore, the camp must be
holy. The Lord doesn't want to see anything 'unclean' among
you. If so, He would turn away from you."

God's Preventative Protection

God protects His people in preventative and curative ways. By refrain-
ing from food that might carry germs or bacteria, God was giving health preventatively. A dead body is filled with maggots,
infectious poisonous disease, bacteria, germs, etc. The unclean
animals that they couldn't eat were scavengers that lived on
garbage or dead animals. When a person ate a scavenger animal, bird, fish, etc., he was taking into his system the potential
disease in the scavenger's body. By not eating them, God was
preventing disease among His people.

The feces and urine of a person or animal contains the poison and bacteria flushed out of the body. By lying on the ground it could be
tracked into their tents or get on their clothing or bodies, expos-
ing them to disease.

When many soldiers were camped together—or people in wilderness
areas—there was always the potential of being exposed to disease. God was preventing disease by instructing soldiers to use a
shovel to cover their waste.

The dreaded black plague that devastated many European towns during
the Dark Ages was probably caused when feces and urine in
congested towns were not properly disposed. Rats that fed on

feces spread the disease. Proper sewage in civilized towns adequately prevents this disease.

But God knows it's impossible to keep germs and other infectious things out of our system. Therefore God created a human body that includes a liver and kidneys to strain out dangerous threats to the body.

More Laws

Moses continued, "A runaway slave might come to your nation for help. Do not hand him over to his pagan master. Let the slave live among you anywhere he chooses, in any of your towns that he likes. Do not mistreat him.

"No Israelite man or woman must ever become a pagan temple prostitute. Do not bring the earnings of a female or a male prostitute to the house of the Lord your God to pay for what you have vowed to the Lord. The Lord your God hates prostitution.

"You may loan your fellow Israelite money or food or anything else. But don't make him pay back more than what you loaned him. You may charge a foreigner, but not a fellow Israelite. Then the Lord your God will bless everything you put your hand to. He will bless you in the land which you are entering to take as your own.

"You might make a vow to give something to the Lord your God. Do not be slow to pay it. The Lord your God will surely demand it of you. Do not be guilty of sin. But if you do not make the vow, then you will not be guilty. You must actually do whatever you say you will do. You were the one who voluntarily chose to make the vow to the Lord your God—what you have promised with your own mouth.

"When you go into your neighbor's vineyard, you may eat as many grapes as you wish, but do not fill your basket with his grapes. When you go into your neighbor's standing grain stalks, you may pick the heads of grain with your hands, but you must not cut down his standing grain with your sickle."

My Time to Pray

Lord, these practical instructions are based
On the instruction of our Lord:

"Do unto others as you would have them
Do unto you."

Lord, help me live wisely and practically
In all ways.

Amen.

Deuteronomy 24

DIVORCE AND OTHER THINGS

Moses continued, "Suppose a man marries a woman, then decides that she does not please him. He has found something indecent in her. So, he writes out divorce papers for her. Then he puts them in her hand and sends her out of his house. And suppose after she leaves his house, she goes and marries another man. But suppose her second husband does not like her either. So, he writes out divorce papers for her. He gives them to her and sends her out of his house. Or maybe the second husband dies. In either case, her first husband who divorced her is not allowed to marry her again. She has become 'unclean' to him. That would be a disgusting thing in the presence of the Lord. Do not bring sin upon the land which the Lord your God is giving you to possess.

"A man who has just married must not be sent to war, and he must not have any other duty laid upon him. He should be free to stay at home for one year to make his new wife happy.

"Suppose a man owes you something. Do not take his pair of millstones for grinding grain, not even the upper one, in place of what he owes. This is how he makes his living. He would be taking away his family's means of preparing food in order to stay alive.

"Suppose a man kidnaps a person—an Israelite—to make him a slave or sell him. That kidnapper must be executed. You must get rid of evil among you.

"Be careful when someone has leprosy. Do exactly what the Levitical
   priests teach you. Be very careful to do what I have commanded
   them. Remember what the Lord your God did to Miriam on
   your way out of Egypt.

"You might make a loan of some kind to your neighbor. But don't go
   into his house to get something in place of it. Stay outside. Let
   the man himself go in and get what he promised to you.
   Suppose a poor man gives you his coat to show that he will pay
   the loan back. Don't keep his coat overnight. You must surely
   give his coat back to him at sunset. He really needs his coat to
   sleep in. He will bless you. And the Lord your God will see that
   you have done a good thing.

"Do not cheat a hired servant who is poor and needy. He might be a
   fellow Israelite. Or he might be a foreigner who lives in one of
   your towns in your land. Each day, pay him his money for that
   day's work before sunset. He is poor and really needs the
   money. Otherwise he may complain to the Lord about you, and
   you would be guilty of sin.

"A father must not be put to death when his children do wrong. And
   children must not be put to death when their fathers do wrong.
   Each person must die for his own sin. Do not be unfair to a foreigner or an orphan. Do not take a widow's coat in place of a
   loan. Remember that you were once slaves in Egypt. And the
   Lord your God saved you from there. That is why I am commanding you to do this.

"As you gather your harvest in the field, and you leave a bundle of
   grain, don't go back to get it later. Leave it there for the foreigners, orphans, and widows. Then the Lord your God can bless
   everything you do. You may beat your olive trees to knock the
   olives off the branches, but don't shake the branches a second
   time. Leave what is left on the trees for the foreigners, the

orphans, and widows. You may harvest the grapes in your vineyard, but don't pick over the vines a second time. Leave what is left on the vines for the foreigners, the orphans, and widows. Remember that you were once slaves in the land of Egypt. That is why I am commanding you to do this."

My Time to Pray

Lord, teach me the "sympathy side" of Your law.
I want to treat everyone fairly.

Lord, I want to obey Your law accurately.
But I have a sinful nature that distorts
The way things really are.

Lord, I will be gracious to other needy people,
So someone will be gracious to me.

Amen.

Deuteronomy 25

ADDITIONAL LAWS

Moses continued, "Suppose two men have an argument, and they go to court. And, the judges decide the case, declaring one man to be right and the other man wrong. The wrong-doer might have to be punished with a beating. If so, then one of the judges must make him lie face down. And they will whip him in front of that judge. The number of lashes should match the crime. However, do not hit him more than 40 times. If he is beaten more than that, it would disgrace your brother in your sight.

"Don't cover the bull's mouth while it is walking around on the straw."

Levirate Marriage

Moses continued, "Suppose two brothers are staying together and one of them dies without leaving a child. His widow must not marry someone else outside her husband's family. Her husband's brother must go to bed with her, taking her as his wife. As the brother-in-law, this is his duty to her. The firstborn son that she has must be named after the dead brother. Then the dead brother's name will not be forgotten from Israel.

"But suppose a man does not want to marry his brother's widow. Then she should go up to the elders at the town gate and say, 'My husband's brother refuses to continue his brother's name in Israel. He is not willing to do his duty to me.' Then the elders of his town must summon that brother-in-law and talk to him. But suppose he is still stubborn and says, 'I do not want to marry her.' If this happens, then the widow may come up to him in front of the elders and she may pull off one of her brother-in-law's sandals from his foot (symbolically removing his lordship). Then she may spit in his face and say, 'This is being done to the man who will not build up his brother's family.' Then that man's family will be known in Israel as 'the family of the unsandaled one.'"

Further Laws

Moses continued, "Two men might be fighting with each other, and suppose the wife of one of them comes to rescue her husband from his attacker. If she reaches out and grabs the attacked by his genitals, then you must cut off her hand. Show her no mercy.

"Do not carry two different sets of weights with you, one heavy and one light. Do not have two different sets of measures in your house, one large and one small. You must have accurate and honest weights and measures. Then you will live for a long time in the land which the Lord your God is giving to you. It is a disgusting thing to the Lord your God when anyone is doing such practices."

Destroy Amalek

Moses continued, "Remember what the Amalekites did to you along the way when you came out of Egypt. You were tired and worn out when they attacked you from the rear. They killed all those who were lagging behind. They had no fear of God. The Lord your God will give you rest from all your enemies who will surround you in the land which He is giving you to possess. You must destroy any memory of the Amalekites on the earth. You must not forget."

My Time to Pray

Lord, thank You for telling us how to interpret
The laws You've given to us.

The way Moses interpreted these laws,
Are a pattern how to interpret them all.

Lord, I want to keep all Your laws
As best I can.

Give me strength and wisdom to always do right,
Give me mercy and grace when I fail.

Amen.

Deuteronomy 26

GIVE GOD YOUR BEST

Moses continued, "Soon you will enter the land which the Lord your
God is giving you to own. You will capture and settle in it. Then,
you will take some of the first harvest of crops from your land
which the Lord your God is giving to you, and you will put the
food in a basket and go to the place where the Lord your God
will choose to be worshiped. Go to the priest who is on duty at
that time and say to him, 'Today I declare this to the Lord my
God, I have come into the land which the Lord promised to my
ancestors to give us.' The priest will receive your basket of food
from your hand, and will place it in front of the altar of the Lord
your God. Then you will announce in the presence of the Lord
your God, 'My forefather was a wandering Aramean. He went
down to Egypt, and though few in number, he and his family
stayed there. But they became a great, powerful, and numerous
nation there. But the Egyptians were cruel to us. They enslaved
us, and made us work very hard. So we cried out to the Lord the
God of our ancestors. And He heard our voices and saw our mis-
ery, our toiling, and our oppression. The Lord brought us out of
Egypt with His great power and strength. He used awesome terror, signs, and miracles. Then He brought us to this place and
gave us this land where much food grows. Now I bring You part
of the first harvest from this land to You, Who Is Always Present.
You have given me this land.' Then place the basket in the presence of the Lord your God and bow yourself down before the
Lord your God. Then you and the Levites and the foreigners who
are among you should rejoice in all the good things which the
Lord your God has given to you and your family." *Lord, I was a*

sinner lost in my sin. Jesus died for me to forgive every charge against me. Jesus brought me into a new transformed life. Now I give to You, Lord, a portion of what You have allowed me to earn.

"Bring 10 percent of all your harvest on the third year. This is the year to give 10 percent of your harvest. Give it to the Levites, the foreigners, the orphans, and the widows. Then they may eat in your towns and be satisfied. Then say to the Lord your God, 'I have removed from my house the sacred portion of my harvest. And I have given it to the Levites, the foreigners, the orphans, and the widows. I have done everything that You commanded me, I have not broken Your commands. I have not forgotten.'" *Lord, I will not keep back the tithe that belongs to You.*

"'And I have not eaten any of the sacred tithe while I was in sorrow. I have not removed any of it while I was "unclean." I have not offered it for corpses (no part of the tithe could be used to buy a coffin or burial clothes for the dead). I have obeyed You, O Lord, Who Is Always Present, my God. I have done everything You commanded me. So, look down from Heaven, Your holy home. Bless Your people, Israel, and bless the land that You have given to us. You vowed it to our ancestors. It is a land where much food grows.'" *Lord, I give back to You what belongs to You.*

"Today the Lord our God commands you to obey all these laws and rules. Be very careful to do them with your whole being. Today you have said that the Lord is your God. And you have promised to do what He wants you to do. You have promised to keep His laws, His commands, and His rules. You have promised that you will obey Him. So, today the Lord has declared that you are His very own people, a special treasure, just as He has promised to you. But you must obey all of His commands. The Lord will make you greater than all the other nations that He has made. He will give you praise, fame, and honor, and you will be a holy people to the Lord your God just as He promised." *Lord, I promise.*

Deuteronomy 27

THE ALTAR AT MOUNT EBAL

Moses and the elders of Israel commanded the people, saying, "Keep all the commands which I command you today. Soon you will cross over the Jordan River entering the land which the Lord your God is giving to you. On that day set up some large stones. Cover them with plaster (a permanent whitewashing to render them all the more conspicuous). As you cross over, write all the words of these teachings on them. (The lengthy inscription on the rock face at Behistun is nearly three times longer than the entire Book of Deuteronomy.) Then you may enter the land which the Lord your God is giving you. It is a land where much food grows. It is just as the Lord, the God of your ancestors, promised. After you have crossed over the Jordan River, set up these stones on Mount Ebal as I command you today, and cover them with plaster. Build an altar there to the Lord your God, but do not use any iron tool to cut the stones. (In God's eyes, man's chisel would have polluted the stones.) Build the altar of the Lord your God with uncut stones (their natural unpolished state). Offer whole burnt offerings on it to the Lord your God. And offer peace offerings there also. Eat them and rejoice in the presence of the Lord your God. Then write very clearly all the words of these teachings on the stones." *Lord, I have written Your words (memorized them) in my heart.*

Then Moses and the Levitical priests spoke to all Israel saying, "Be quiet, O Israel. Listen. Today you have become the people of the Lord your God. So, obey the Lord your God. Keep His

commands and His laws that I am commanding you today."
Lord, I hear and obey.

The Curses at Mount Ebal

On that same day, Moses also charged the people: "You will cross over
the Jordan River. Then these tribes must stand on Mount
Gerizim to bless the people: Simeon, Levi, Judah, Issachar,
Joseph, and Benjamin. (This set of six was all the descendants of
Leah and Rachel, except for Reuben and Zebulun.) And these
tribes must stand on Mount Ebal to announce the curses:
Reuben, Gad, Asher, Zebulun, Dan, and Naphtali. (The descendants of Zilpah and Bilhah—Reuben had lost his favored, firstborn status. Zebulun was Leah's youngest son.) (The twin peaks
of Gerizim and Ebal are about 800 feet higher than the valley
which separated them. It was a lush, well-watered valley that
was about 500 yards wide. It was a natural amphitheater aided
by the favorable contour of the two mountains. Mount Ebal was
on the north, and Mount Gerizim was on the south. This location was about 40 miles north of Jerusalem and 20 miles west
of the Jordan River.)

"The Levites will answer and recite to all the people of Israel in a loud
voice (12 regulations, one for each of the 12 tribes, symbolic of
all of the laws of God).

"Then the Levites will say, 'God's curse is upon anyone who makes an
idol and secretly worships it. Manmade idols are an abomina-
tion to the Lord.'

"Then all the people will answer, 'Amen.'

"The Levites will say, 'God's curse is upon anyone who dishonors his
father or his mother.'

"Then all the people will say, 'Amen.'

"The Levites will say, 'God's curse is upon anyone who moves the stone that marks his neighbor's border.'

"Then all the people will say, 'Amen.'

"The Levites will say, 'God's curse is upon anyone who leads a blind person away from the road.'

"Then all the people will say, 'Amen.'

"The Levites will say, 'God's curse is upon anyone who is unfair to foreigners, orphans, or widows.'

"Then all the people will say, 'Amen.'

"The Levites will say, 'God's curse is upon a man who has sex with his father's wife. It is a dishonor to his father!'

"Then all the people will say, 'Amen.'

"The Levites will say, 'God's curse is upon anyone who has sex with an animal!'

"Then all the people will say, 'Amen.'

"The Levites will say, 'God's curse is upon a man who has sex with his sister.'

"Then all the people will say, 'Amen.'

"The Levites will say, 'God's curse is upon a man who has sex with his mother-in-law.'

"Then all the people will say, 'Amen.'

"The Levites will say, 'God's curse is upon anyone who killed his neighbor secretly.'

"Then all the people will say, 'Amen.'

"The Levites will say, 'God's curse is upon anyone who accepts money to murder an innocent person.'

"Then all the people will say, 'Amen.'

"The Levites will say, 'God's curse is upon anyone who does not agree with the words of these teachings and does not obey them.'

"Then all the people will say, 'Amen.'"

My Time to Pray

Lord, it does me good to repeat Your prohibitions,
Because I will never forget them,
Or carelessly do them.

Lord, keep me from outward sin against You,
And keep me from secret sin.

Amen.

Deuteronomy 28

THE BLESSINGS FOR BEING OBEDIENT

Moses continued, "If you truly obey the Lord your God then you will carefully follow all of His commands which I am commanding you today. Then the Lord your God will set you high above all the other nations on earth. If you obey the Lord your God, then all these blessings will overtake you:

"You will be blessed in the town, and you will be blessed in the country-side.

"Your children will be blessed. Your crops will be blessed. Your animals will be blessed with offspring too. Your cattle will be blessed with calves, and your sheep with lambs.

"Your basket and your kitchen will be blessed.

"You will be blessed when you come in and when you go out.

"The Lord will let you defeat your enemies who come to fight you. They will attack you from one direction, but they will run away from you in seven directions.

"The Lord will order blessings upon you with barns that are full. He will bless everything you do. He will bless you in the land which the Lord your God is giving to you.

"The Lord will uphold you as His holy people, just as He vowed to you, if you keep the commands of the Lord your God, and if you do what He wants you to do. Then everyone on earth will see that you are the Lord's people. And they will be afraid of you.

"The Lord will cause you to prosper. You will have many children. Your animals will reproduce. Your soil will yield good crops in the land which the Lord promised to your ancestors that He would give to you.

"The Lord will open up to you His storehouse. The skies will send rain upon your land at the proper season, and He will bless everything you do. You will lend money to many nations, but you will not need to borrow from them.

"The Lord will make you like the head and not like the tail. You will be on top, not on the bottom, if you listen to the commands of the Lord your God that I am commanding you today. Be careful to keep them. Do not disobey anything I command you today. Don't follow other gods or serve them."

My Time to Pray

Lord, thank You for the happiness You send,
To those who keep Your law.

Lord, I will strive with all my might
To honestly keep all Your laws.

Amen.

The Curses for Being Disobedient

Moses continued, "But suppose you don't want to obey the Lord your God, and you would not carefully follow all of His commands and laws which I am commanding you today. Then all of these curses will come upon you and catch up with you:

"You will be cursed in the town, and you will be cursed in the country-side.

"Your basket and your kitchen will be cursed.

"Your children will be cursed. Your crops will be cursed. The calves of your cattle will be cursed. And the lambs of your sheep will be cursed.

"You will be cursed when you go in and cursed when you go out.

"The Lord will send upon you confusion and punishment in everything you do until you are destroyed. You will be ruined overnight. If you abandon God you will do wrong.

"The Lord will cause the plague to cling to you until He has destroyed you off the land where you are headed to take possession.

"The Lord will strike you with infectious diseases, with fever, with inflammation, with extreme heart, with plant diseases, and with mildew. These things will pursue you until you perish.

"The sky above your head will become like bronze (no rain), and the earth below you will be like iron (destroying your crops with an extended drought).

"The Lord will turn the rain of your land into dust and ashes that will come down on you until you are destroyed.

"The Lord will hand you over to your enemies; they will strike you down. You will attack them from one direction, but you will run away from them in seven directions. And you will become a thing of horror to all the kingdoms of the earth. Your dead bodies will become food for all the birds of the air and the animals of the earth. There will be no one to scare them off!

"The Lord will punish you with the boils of Egypt, you will get hemorrhoids, scabs, and itches that cannot be cured.

"The Lord will hit you with insanity, with blindness (perhaps this was spiritual blindness), and with a confused mind. You will feel around in the broad daylight like a blind man in the dark. You will fail in everything you do. People will always oppress you, and they will steal from you every day. There will be no one to save you. You will be engaged to a woman, but another man will force her to have sex with him. You will build a house, but never live in it. You will plant a vineyard, but you will not enjoy its grapes. Your bull will be killed in front of your very eyes, but you will not eat any of its meat. Your donkey will be confiscated right in front of you, and it will not be brought back. Your flock will be given away to your enemies, and there will be no deliverer for you. Your sons will grow tired watching for them every day. But there'll be nothing you can do. People whom you do not know will eat the crops which you have worked so hard to grow. You will always be mistreated and abused all of your lives. The things that your eyes will see will cause you to lose your mind.

"The Lord will hit you with terrible, incurable boils all over your knees and legs. In fact, they will extend from the soles of your feet to the top of your heads.

"The Lord will send you away, as well as the king whom you will have set up over you, to a nation that you will not have known. Your ancestors didn't know that nation either. There you will serve other gods made of wood and stone. You will become a thing of horror among all the ethnic groups where the Lord will drive you. They will laugh at you and make fun of you.

"You will plant plenty of seed in your field, but your harvest will be small. Locusts will eat the crop. You will plant vineyards and cultivate them, but you will not pick the grapes or drink the wine, and worms will eat them. You will have olive trees in all of your territory, but you will not anoint yourself with any olive oil. No, the olives will drop off the trees. You will have sons and daughters, but you will not be able to keep them; they will go into captivity. Swarms of locusts will take over all of your trees and crops.

"The foreigners who live among you will get stronger and stronger, and you will gradually get weaker and weaker. Foreigners will lend money to you, but you will not be able to lend to them. They will be like the head, but you will be like the tail.

"All these curses will come upon you. They will chase you and catch you, until you are destroyed. Why? Because you did not obey the Lord your God. You did not keep His commands and laws which He commanded you. The curses will be signs and miracles to you and to your descendants permanently. You had plenty of everything, but you did not serve the Lord your God with joy and a glad heart. Therefore, you will serve your enemies whom the Lord sends against you. You will be hungry, thirsty, naked, and destitute. The Lord will put an iron yoke on your neck, until He has destroyed you. The Lord will raise up a nation against you from far away, from the end of the earth. That nation will swoop down like an eagle. You won't understand their language. They will be a nation with mean faces. They will show no respect to old people; they won't favor the young, either. They will eat your young animals and the harvest of your fields, until you are wiped out. They will leave you no grain, no new wine, and no olive oil. They will not leave you any calves from your herds or lambs from your flocks. You will be ruined. Though you trust in your high, fenced walls, they will fall down. That nation will surround all of your towns everywhere throughout your country, which the Lord your God has given to you.

"You enemy will surround you. Those people will make you starve. You will eat your own babies, the flesh of your sons and daughters whom the Lord gave to you. Even the most gentle and kind man among you will become mean. He will be so cruel to his brother, to his wife whom he loves, and to his children who are still alive. He will not even share with them some of the flesh of his children that he is eating. He has nothing left. Your enemies will surround you; they will cause every single town to starve. The most gentle and kind woman among you will become mean, too. She was so gentle and kind that she would hardly even walk on the ground. Nevertheless, she will be cruel to her husband whom she once loved, and she will become cruel to her own son and her own daughter. She will give birth to a baby, but she will plan to eat the baby and whatever comes after the birth itself. She will eat them while the enemy surrounds the town. Those people will make you starve in all your towns.

"Be very careful to obey the words of this teaching. They are written in this book. You must revere the glorious and wonderful name of the Lord your God.

"The Lord will cause incurable diseases and horrible epidemics that can never be stopped. These things will happen to you and to your descendants. You will have long and serious diseases. You will also have long-lasting, miserable sicknesses. And the Lord will bring upon you all the diseases of Egypt that you dread. And the diseases will stay with you. The Lord will also give you every disease and sickness which is not written in this Book of the Teachings—until you are destroyed!

"You people may have outnumbered the stars, but only a few of you will be left. You will not have obeyed the Lord your God. The Lord was once happy because of you. He gave you good things. He multiplied you. But now, the Lord will be happy to ruin and destroy you. You will be plucked up from the land where you are entering to take possession.

"Then the Lord will scatter you among all the nations from one end of the earth to the other. There you will serve other gods of wood and stone. They are gods that neither you nor your ancestors ever knew. You will have no rest among those nations; there will be no rest for the sole of your foot. Instead, the Lord will give you a trembling heart, and failing eyesight, and sorrow of soul. You life will always be in danger. You will be filled with terror day and night. You will not even be certain that you will survive. In the morning you will say, 'I wish it were evening,' and in the evening you will say, 'I wish it were morning,' because of the dread which your heart will feel, because of the things you have seen.

"The Lord will send you back to Egypt in ships. (Josephus reported that multitudes of Jews were transported in ships to Egypt and sold as slaves. Though the Israelites had crossed the Red Sea with a high hand, many of them would return to bondage in Egypt in slave ships to work in the mines.) I, Moses, told you that you would never go back to Egypt. But you will try to sell yourselves there as male and female slaves to your enemies. However, no one will buy you."

My Time to Pray

Lord, I tremble at the curses You promised
To Your people, Israel.

Lord, You kept these promises when You sent
Nebuchadnezzar to destroy the Promised Land
And take Israel captive to Babylon.

Lord, You did it again when Your people rejected
Jesus as their Messiah.

Lord, it is a terrible fate, but You warned
The Jews to worship You only.

Lord, one day "all Israel will be saved," and
Your people will return to their Land,
To live happily with You.

Lord, may I learn from Israel's disobedience,
And always obey and worship only You.

Amen.

Deuteronomy 29

THE COVENANT RENEWAL

The Lord commanded Moses to give a covenant to the Israelites in the
land of Moab. (This was a new generation, therefore it was necessary for Moses to rehearse the privileges and obligations of
this covenant. The people needed to know the conditions of the
covenant so they could comply.) This agreement was in addition
to the agreement that He had made with them at Mount Sinai.

Moses summoned all the Israelites together, and said, "You have seen
everything that the Lord did to Pharaoh, his officers, and his
whole country in your sight in the land of Egypt. With your own
eyes, you witnessed the great plagues and miracles. But to this
very day, the Lord has not given you a mind that understands.
You don't really understand what you see with your eyes, or
what you hear with your ears. I have led you in the desert for 40
years. During that time, neither your clothes nor your sandals
wore out. You ate manna, not bread, and you drank no wine or
strong drink. This was so you would understand that He is the I
AM, your God.

"As you came to this place, Sihon the king of Heshbon and Og the king
of Bashan came out to fight us. But we defeated them. We captured their land, and gave it as a possession to the Reubenites,
the Gadites, and the eastern half-tribe of Manasseh.

"So, you must carefully obey every word of this covenant. Then you will
be successful in everything you do. Today you are standing in the
presence of the Lord your God. Here are the leaders of your
tribes, your elders, your officers, and every man of Israel. Here

are your wives, your little children, and the foreigners who live among you, who chop your wood and carry your water. You are all here to enter into a covenant and an oath with the Lord your God. He is making this covenant with you today. This will confirm you as the Lord's very own people. He Himself will be your God, just as He told you. He vowed it to your ancestors—to Abraham, to Isaac, and to Jacob.

"But the Lord is not making this covenant and oath with you alone. No, He is also making the covenant with those who are not here today, those who are not yet born. You are standing here in the presence of the Lord your God. You know how we once lived in the land of Egypt and you know how we passed through the countries when we came here. And you saw their hated idols made of wood, stone, silver, and gold. Make sure that the heart of no man, woman, clan, or tribe among you turns away from the Lord our God. Don't let them go and serve the gods of those nations. Otherwise, that would be like a root that becomes a bitter or a poisonous plant. Such a person might hear the words of these curses, and instead of paying attention, he invokes a blessing on himself. Therefore, he thinks, *I will be safe from God's judgment even though I plan stubbornly to continue doing whatever I want to do.* That person could bring disaster upon your entire country—everything. The Lord would never be willing to forgive such a person. His anger would be like a burning fire against that man. All the curses written in this book would rest upon him. And the Lord would destroy any memory of him on the earth. The Lord would single him out from all the tribes of Israel for punishment. All the curses of the covenant would happen to him that are written in this Book of the Teachings (Torah)." *Lord, take away any spiritual blindness that would deceive me.*

"Your children coming after you would see this, as well as foreigners from faraway lands. They would see the disasters that come to this land, the diseases that the Lord sends upon it, and they would say, 'The whole land is nothing but burning sulphur and salt; nothing is planted, nothing grows, and nothing blooms. It will be like the downfall of Sodom and Gomorrah, and Admah and Zeboyim. The Lord destroyed them because He was angry.' Yes, all the other nations will ask, 'Why has the Lord done this to this land? Why is He so angry?'" *Lord, the Promised Land was desolate for centuries, proving this prediction correct. Help me believe all your predictions.*

"And the answer will be, it is because His people broke the covenant the Lord the God of their ancestors made with them when He brought them out of the land of Egypt. They went and served other gods. They bowed down to gods that they had not known. The Lord did not allow that. So, the Lord became very angry at the land so that He brought all the curses that are written in this book upon the land. The Lord became angry and furious with them, that He uprooted them from their land and threw them into another land.

"There are some things which the Lord our God has kept secret, but the things that He has revealed to us and to our children are so that we will obey all the words of these teachings." *Lord, I will do all You show me.*

Deuteronomy 30

GOD'S PROMISE REMAINS CONSTANT

Moses continued, "All these blessings and curses which I have laid out before you will happen to you. The Lord your God will send you away to all the nations. There you will think about these things. Then you and your children will return to the Lord your God, and you will obey Him.

"You must obey everything I am commanding you today. Then the Lord your God will restore you from your exile. He will feel sorry for you, and will collect you again from the ethnic groups where He scattered you. Even though He may send you to the ends of the skies, He will collect you from there, and bring you back from there. The Lord your God will bring you back to the land that belonged to your ancestors. It will be yours, and He will give you success, and multiply you more than your ancestors. And the Lord your God will circumcise your hearts and the hearts of your descendants. Then you will love the Lord your God with your whole being." *Lord, I believe You will keep this promise to Israel in the future. You will give them the land you promised to Abraham, Isaac, and Jacob.*

"Then the Lord your God will turn all of these curses against your enemies, who hate you and are cruel to you. Then you will obey the Lord again, and you will keep all of His commands which I am commanding you today. The Lord your God will make you successful in everything you do. You will have many children. Your animals will have many young ones. Your fields will produce good crops. And the Lord will be happy with you again, just as He was with your ancestors. Why? Because you will heed the

Lord your God. You will obey His commands and His laws which are written in the Book of this Teaching. You will return to the Lord your God with your whole being." *Lord, I love You with my whole being.*

"This command that I command you today is not too hard for you. It is not beyond what you can do. It is not up in Heaven so that you have to ask, 'Who will go up to Heaven and get it for us? Then we can obey it.' It is not on the other side of the ocean so that you have to ask, 'Who will go across the sea and get it for us? Who will tell it to us so we can obey it?' No, the word is very near you—in your own mouth and in your own heart, so you can obey it. (It is not the lack of information regarding God's will, but the lack of commitment to do God's will.)" *Lord, I commit myself to Your will.*

"Look, today I offer you life and success, or, death and evil. Today, I am commanding you to love the Lord your God. Do what He wants you to do. Keep His commands, His laws, and His rules. Then you will live and grow and multiply. Then the Lord your God will bless you in the land you are going to take as your own." *Lord, I want Your blessings.*

"But suppose you turn away your hearts from the Lord and you won't obey Him? Suppose you bow down and serve other gods? I tell you today that you will surely be destroyed. And you will not live very long in the land which you are crossing over the Jordan River to enter and possess." *Lord, bring me home before I ever deny You.*

"Today I call Heaven and earth to be witnesses against you. I have laid out before you life or death—blessings or curses. Therefore, choose life. Then you and your children will live. Love the Lord your God. Obey Him. Cling to Him, because He is your life. And He will allow you to stay on the land for as long as you live. This is the land that the Lord vowed to give to your ancestors—to Abraham, to Isaac, and to Jacob." *Lord, I choose life.*

Deuteronomy 31

JOSHUA BECOMES THE NEW LEADER

Then Moses went and spoke these words to all the Israelites telling them, "I am now 120 years old (40 years had passed in the desert since Moses was 80). I cannot lead you anymore. The Lord has told me, 'You will not cross over this Jordan River.' The Lord your God is the One who will cross over ahead of you. He will destroy those nations in front of you. You will capture their land. And Joshua is the one who will cross over ahead of you (Joshua was 78 years old; he died 32 years later at 110 [see Josh. 24:29]), just as the Lord has said. The Lord will do the same thing to those nations that He did to Sihon and to Og and to their land. The Lord destroyed them. The Lord will hand them over to you. Do to them exactly as I have commanded you. Be strong and brave. Don't be afraid of them. Don't be scared. It is YAHWEH your God who will go with you, He will not fail you or abandon you." *Lord, thank You for Your promises to me.*

Then Moses summoned Joshua and spoke to him in front of all the Israelite people saying, "Be strong and brave. Lead these people into the land which the Lord vowed to give to their ancestors. Help the people take what belongs to them. The Lord is the One who will go ahead of you. He will be with you. He will not fail you or abandon you. Don't be afraid. Don't worry." *Lord, thank You for leaders like Joshua.*

So, Moses wrote down these teachings. He gave the entire book to the priests and to all the elders of Israel. They carried the Holy Ark of the Covenant of the Lord.

Then Moses commanded them: "Read these teachings aloud for all
Israel to hear. Do it at the end of every seven years—the Year of
Jubilee (the year of releasing people from their debts). Do it during the Feast of Tabernacles. All the Israelites will come to
appear before the Lord your God. They will stand at the place
which the Lord will choose. Gather all the people—the men, the
women, the children, and the foreigners living within your
towns. Then they can listen and learn to fear the Lord your God.
Then they can carefully obey all the words of these teachings.
Their children do not know this law. They must hear it, and
learn to fear the Lord your God for as long as they live on the
land to which you are crossing over the Jordan River to possess."
Lord, I will teach Your commandments to children.

The Lord said to Moses, "Look, soon you will die. Get Joshua and present yourselves to Me at the Tabernacle. I will put him in charge."
So, Moses and Joshua went to present themselves to God at the
Tabernacle. The Lord appeared at the Tent in a cloudy pillar and
stood over the entrance of the Tabernacle. Then the Lord said to
Moses, "Look, you will soon die. Then these people will not be
loyal to Me. They will worship the foreign gods of the land
where they are entering. They will abandon Me, and break My
covenant with them. At that time, I will become very angry at
them. I will abandon them and turn away from them. They will
be destroyed. Many terrible things will happen to them. Then at
that time, someone will say, 'Our God is not with us. That is
why these terrible things are happening to us.' I will turn completely away from them because they have done wrong by turning to other gods." *Lord, I fear Your absence from my life.*

"Now write down this song for yourselves, and teach it to the Israelites.
Then have them sing it because it will stand as evidence against
them. I will bring them into the land which I vowed to their
ancestors. It is a land that flows with milk and honey. They will

have all the food that they want, and they will live comfortably. But then they will turn to other gods and serve them. They will reject Me and break My covenant. Then many troubles and terrible things will happen to them. And this song will testify against them. The song will not be forgotten by their descendants. I know what they plan to do today, even before I take them into the land which I promised to them." *Lord, You know my future. Protect me spiritually.*

So that day, Moses wrote down this song and taught it to the Israelites. Then the Lord gave this command to Joshua, the son of Nun: "Be strong and brave. Bring the people of Israel into the land which I vowed to give them, and I Myself will be with you." *Lord, be with me as You were with Moses and Joshua.*

Moses Speaks to the Levites

Moses finished writing all the words of these teachings in a book. Then he commanded the Levites who carried the Holy Ark of the Covenant of the Lord, "Take this Book of the Teachings, and put it inside the Holy Ark of the Covenant of the Lord. It must stay there as a witness against you.

"I know how stubborn and disobedient you are. Look, you have disobeyed the Lord while I am still alive and with you. You will be even more rebellious after I am dead. Gather all the elders of your tribes and your officers. I will say these things for them to hear. And I will ask Heaven and earth to testify against them. Why? Because I know that after I die, you will utterly corrupt yourselves. You will turn away from the commands that I have given to you. Then terrible things will happen to you in the future. You will do what the Lord sees as wrong. You will make

Him angry with the idols that you will make with your hands."
Lord, keep me from any manmade idols.

Deuteronomy 32

MOSES' SONG

And Moses spoke this whole song for the entire congregation of the
people of Israel to hear:

"Hear, O heavens, and I will speak;
    Listen, O earth, to what I say.

My teaching will fall like rain,
    My speech will drop like dew.

It will be like a light shower on fresh grass,
    Like the rain on young plants.

Because I will proclaim the name of the Lord,
    Exalt our God, the Rock, perfect is His work.

Because He is always just
    He is a dependable God who never does wrong.
    He is righteous and fair.

Israel has acted corruptly toward Him;
    It's not God's fault that His children are defective,
    They are a perverse and crooked generation.

People, is that any way to repay the Lord? No!
    You are not wise; you're foolish.

He is your Father and Your Maker, isn't He?
    He paid for you; He has stabilized you.

Remember the old days.
    Think about the years of many generations.

Ask your father, he will tell you,
    Ask your elders, they will inform you.

The Most High God gave land to the nations;
    He divided up the human race.

He set up boundaries for the ethnic groups;
    He counted the Israelites. Why?

Because the Lord's share is Jacob, His people;
    They were His very own.

He found them in a desert land;
    It was a windy, empty land.

He surrounded them with love and took care of them;
    He protected them as something very precious.

As an eagle building its nest flutters over its young,
    It spreads out its wings to catch them,
    It carries them on its feathers.

The Lord alone led them;
    There were no foreign gods among them.

The Lord caused them to ride on the high places of the earth;
    They ate from the fruits of the fields.

He gave them honey from the rocks,
    Olive oil from the solid rock.

There was butter from the cows
    And milk from the sheep,

With the fat of lambs and rams,
    The best rams of Bashan and male goats.

They had the best part of the wheat;
    You drank grape juice.

But Israel got fat, and kicked;
    He became fat, grew heavy and stubborn.

He abandoned the God who made him;
    He rejected the Rock who saved him.

He made God angry with disgusting idols;
    They made sacrifices to demons, not the one true God.

They were gods which they had never known;
    New gods that your ancestors did not dread.

You deserted the Rock, who fathered you;
    You forgot the God who gave birth to you.

The Lord saw this and rejected Israel;
    God's sons and daughters had provoked Him.

He said, 'I will turn away from them;
    I will see what will happen to them.

They are evil people;
    They are children who are not faithful.

They used things that are not gods
    To make Me jealous;
    They used worthless idols to make Me angry.

So, I will use those who are pagans
    To make them jealous.

And I will use a dumb nation
    To make them angry.

My anger has started a fire.
>It burns down to the lowest Sheol.

It will burn up the ground and its crops.
>And it will scorch the foundations of the mountains.

I will heap troubles on them.
>I will use up My arrows at them.

They will be worn out by hunger and consumed by burning
heat;
>They will be destroyed by terrible diseases.

I will send vicious animals upon them,
>And vipers gliding through the dust.

Out in the streets, the sword will kill;
>Inside their homes there will be terror.

Both young men and virgins will die,
>So will little babies and gray-haired men.

I have said, "I will scatter them far away
>And no one will remember them."

But I didn't want their enemies to brag;
>Their foes might misunderstand.

They might say: "We have won!
>The Lord has not done any of this.'"

Israel has no sense;
>They do not understand.

I wish they were wise and could understand;
>I wish they could see what is going to happen to them.

One person cannot chase 1,000 people,
  And two people cannot defeat 10,000.

No, this only happens if their Rock has abandoned them;
  The Lord would have to shut them up.

Their rock is not like our God;
  Even our enemies would agree with that.

Their vine comes from the vine of Sodom,
  From the fields of Gomorrah.

Their grapes are poisonous grapes.
  Their clusters of grapes are bitter.

Their wine is like the venom of vipers,
  Like the deadly poison of cobras.

'I have been reserving this;
  I have locked it away in My storehouses.

Revenge belongs to Me—
  I will repay.'

Their foot will slip in due time;
  The day of their disaster is near.

And their punishment will come quickly;
  The Lord will defend His people.

He will have compassion on His servants;
  He will see that their strength is gone.

He will see that no one remains,
  Neither the slaves nor the free ones.

Then He will say, 'Where are their gods?
  Where is the rock in which they trusted?

Who ate the fat from their sacrifices?
> Who drank the wine of their drink-offerings?

Let those gods rise up to help you;
> Let them protect you.

Now you will see that I AM, the one God, am He;
> There is no god but Me.

I can kill, or I can preserve life;
> I can hurt, or I can heal.

There is no one who can deliver you from My hand;
> I can lift My hand to the heavens and declare this:

"As surely as I live forever,
> I will sharpen My flashing sword.

And I will take it in My hand to punish;
> I will get revenge on My enemies.

I will pay back those who hate Me;
> My arrows will be covered with their blood.

My sword will eat their flesh;
> The blood will flow from those who are killed
> And from the captives,

From the long-haired heads of the enemy,
> Be happy, O you nations, along with His people.'"

He will repay for the blood of His servants;
> He will punish His enemies.

And He will make atonement for His land and His people."

Moses came with Joshua, the son of Nun. And together they spoke all the words of this song for the people to hear. When Moses finished reciting all these words to all Israel, he said to them: "Pay attention to all the words that I have solemnly declared to you today. Command your children to carefully obey everything in these teachings. These words should not be unimportant words for you—they are your life. By these words, you will live a long time on the land that you are crossing over the Jordan River to possess." *Lord, my heart's desire, "Sing them over again to me, wonderful words of life."*

Moses Is Prepared for His Death

The Lord spoke to Moses again on that same day saying, "Go up into these Abarim Mountains. Go to Mount Nebo (Pisgah is merely an older name for Nebo) in the country of Moab. It is directly across from Jericho. Look at the land of Canaan I am giving to the Israelites to possess. You will die on that mountain which you climb. That was how your brother Aaron died on Mount Hor. You both sinned against Me among the Israelites at the waters of Meribah-Kadesh in the desert of Zin. You did not honor Me as being holy among them. Nevertheless, you will look at the land only from a distance. But you will not enter the land which I am giving to the people of Israel." *Lord, Your judgment is eternal. Have mercy on me for Jesus' sake.*

Deuteronomy 32

THE STORY BEHIND
THE PREDICTION OF MOSES' DEATH

Date: 1451 B.C. ~ Place: East of Jordan

Go to Moab, to the mountains east of the river, and climb Mount Nebo, which is across from Jericho. Look out across the land of Canaan, the land I am giving to the people of Israel as their own special possession. Then you will die there on the mountain. You will join your ancestors, just as Aaron, your brother, died on Mount Hor and joined his ancestors (Deuteronomy 32:49-50 NLT).

None of us wants to die, but we all will if Jesus doesn't come first. So if we must die, let's do it the way Moses died. Let's die well. Moses apparently didn't die of disease, accident, or any other cause. He just quit living, and the Lord buried him on Mount Nebo.

Incidentally, that's a wonderful place to be buried. From the top of Nebo you can see the whole Promised Land from Mount Hermon in the north, to the desert in the south. You can see all the way to the Mediterranean Sea. The place where Moses died is the place from which you can see all the Promised Land. Isn't that grace?

Moses climbed to the top of Nebo when he was 120 years old. That's quite a trip for an old man. I rode up to the top in a tour bus, but would have difficulty walking it now at age 75. God must have helped him, and it took more than a day to make the trip. *Lord, help me when I can't help myself.*

As Moses was walking the gentle slopes of Nebo, he must have known this was his last trip. If you knew this was your last day, what would you be thinking? *Lord, keep my thoughts on You.*

When Moses got to the top, he was not thinking about the past, or his failures, or his achievements. He thought about the future. God showed him the land where the children of Israel would live. Even though Moses was old, he still had good eyesight (see Deut. 34:7). And if he had trouble with distance, God helped him, "...I have caused you to see it with your eyes..." (Deut. 34:4). Wouldn't you like God for a tour guide of Israel? Since God reminded Moses this was the land promised to Abraham and his seed, I think God was showing Moses the future. I think Moses saw the land fully inhabited with Israel. *Open my eyes to see.*

If I had been the Lord, at the last minute I would have reversed the judgment and let Moses go over into the Promised Land. It must have been an emotional moment, Moses and the Lord surveying the Promised Land together. I'd have let Moses enter, but God will always be true to His promise. He cannot deny Himself; He will be true to His word. Moses did not enter the land, but was buried on Mount Nebo.

Since God keeps His word in judgment, He'll keep His promise of blessing. He will receive all who come to Him through Jesus (see John 6:37). He will hear the request of all who pray through Jesus' name (see John 14:14-15). He will give eternal life to all believers in Jesus (see John 14:1-4). *Lord, I have confidence in You.*

That must have been quite a worship service at the top of the mountain— Moses having fellowship with God about the past promises to Abraham. Do you worship when you read in Scripture about what God has done in the past? *Lord, help me learn from my past.*

Then God and Moses could have turned back to look in another direction to see the children of Israel massed together at the bottom of Nebo, ready to cross the Jordan. They were outside the Promised Land. The Shekinah-glory cloud had led them out of Egypt. They had spent 40 years wandering in the desert. Now Israel was poised to cross Jordan and enter the Land. God and Moses could have rejoiced over getting Israel to that point in time. That was a good time to worship God.

God buried Moses. We don't know how He did it. Actually, it doesn't matter, because if God did it, Moses was buried right. Also we don't know where God did it. If any went looking for the place, they couldn't find it because, "…no one knows his grave to this day" (Deut. 34:6). Perhaps, that is because God planned to bring Moses back to the Mount of Transfiguration during the time of Christ (see Matt. 17:3). Also, God didn't want people worshiping the place where a great man died. People should worship the Lord who worked great things through the man who gave himself to God. *Lord, help me learn the lessons Moses learned.*

Then Moses died well on the top of Mount Nebo. God approved and buried him. His was a life well-lived and his death was well-received by God. *Lord, may I die well.*

My Time to Pray

Lord, I want to die very simply in Your presence
Just as Moses died with You.

Lord, in the flesh I resist my physical death,
But in my spirit I seek You.

Amen.

Deuteronomy 33

MOSES BLESSES ISRAEL

Moses, the man of God, pronounced this blessing to the Israelites
before he died saying,

"The Lord came from Mount Sinai,

He rose up like the sun from Seir.

He shined forth from Mount Paran,

He came as King with thousands and thousands of angels.

He came with a flaming fire at His right hand;

Yes, the Lord truly loves His people.

He takes care of all those who belong to Him,

They all sit down at His feet

And they receive instruction from Him.

Moses gave us the teachings;

They belong to the congregation of Jacob.

The Lord became King over Israel;

The leaders of the people gathered together;

The tribes of Israel assembled."

Moses said this about the people of Reuben:

"Let the people of Reuben live and not die

But let his men be few in number."

Moses said this about the people of Judah:

"O our Lord, listen to Judah's prayer;

Bring them back to their people.

God's hands defend them;

God helps them against their enemies."

Moses said this about the people of Levi:

"O Lord, Your Thummim and Your Urim belong to Levi whom You love;

O Lord, You tested him at Massah

You argued with him at the waters of Meribah.

He said about his father and mother:

'I don't care about them.'

He did not acknowledge his brothers,

He did not even know his own children.

But he protected Your word,

He observed Your covenant.

He teaches Your precepts to the people of Jacob

And Your teachings to the people of Israel.

He offers incense before You,

And, he presents whole burnt offerings on Your altar.

O Lord, bless all of his skills,

    Be pleased with the work they do.

Defeat those who attack them,

    Don't let their enemies rise up again."

Moses said this about the people of Benjamin:

    "The Lord's loved ones will lie down in safety beside Him,

    The Lord protects them all day long;

The one whom the Lord loves rests close to Him."

Moses said this about the people of Joseph:

"May the Lord bless their land

    With the precious dew from Heaven above,

    And with the deep water from the springs that lie below.

Let the sun produce the best fruits,

    Let each month bring its finest produce,

    Let the ancient mountains yield the choicest crops,

And let the everlasting hills give the best fruits,

    Let the earth and its fullness give the best fruits;

    Let the Lord who dwelt in the burning bush

    Be pleased.

May these blessings rest upon the head of Joseph;

    May they rest upon the forehead of the one

Who was consecrated above his brothers.

Joseph has the majesty of a firstborn bull;

He is as strong as a wild ox.

He will gore the other nations,

Even those nations that are far away.

These are the ten thousands of Ephraim,

Such are the thousands of Manasseh."

Moses said this about the people of Zebulun:

"Be happy when you go out, O Zebulun,

And be happy in your tents O Issachar.

They will summon the ethnic groups to the mountain

And there they will offer righteous sacrifices.

They will feast upon the abundance of the oceans

From the treasures hidden in the sand."

Moses said this about the people of Gad:

"Praise God who gives Gad more land;

Gad lives there like a lioness,

He tears off arms and heads.

They chose the best land for themselves;

They received a prime share

Like what is given to an officer.

When the leaders of the people gathered,

The people of Gad did what the Lord said was right

And they judged Israel fairly."

Moses said this about the people of Dan:

"Dan is like a lion's cub

That jumps out of Bashan."

Moses said this about the people of Naphtali:

"Naphtali enjoys the Lord's special favor;

They are full of His blessings;

Take possession of the west and the south."

Moses said this about the people of Asher:

"Asher is the most blessed of the sons;

Let him be favored by his brothers.

Let him dip his feet in olive oil;

Your feet will walk on iron and bronze.

As your days, so shall your strength be."

Conclusion for All 12 Sons

"There is no one like the God of Israel;

He rides on the skies to help you,

On the clouds in His majesty.

The eternal God is your place of safety,

His arms will always support you.

He will force out the enemy ahead of you;

He will say: 'Destroy him.'

So the people of Israel will lie down in safety,

Jacob's spring is secure

In a land of grain and new wine.

There the skies will drop their dew;

O Israel, you are blessed!

There is no other nation like you;

You are a people saved by the Lord.

He is the Shield of your help;

He is your glorious Sword.

Your enemies will be afraid of you;

You will trample their high places."

My Time to Pray

Lord, You have blessed Israel abundantly,
Bless me also with Your blessing.

Lord, each son had a different blessing,
Bless me differently from others,
With the blessing You've designed for me.

Amen.

Deuteronomy 33

THE STORY OF BLESSING THE TRIBE OF ASHER

Date: 1451 B.C. ~ Place: East of Jordan

And of Asher he said: "Asher is most blessed of sons; let him be favored by his brothers, and let him dip his foot in oil. Your sandals shall be iron and bronze; as your days, so shall your strength be" (Deuteronomy 33:24-25).

Feet? Who would bless the feet of someone? Don't we bless their head to learn to think magnificent thoughts? Or we bless their hands to make money or to do other exploits. Then again, the heart is blessed to love deeply, or extend mercy, or to be a gracious host or hostess. But feet—why did Moses bless the feet of Asher?

Obviously, every Israelite wanted to be blessed with children, so Moses blessed Asher, "Let Asher be blessed with children."

Obviously, every Israelite wanted good relations with his brothers, so Moses blessed Asher, "Let him be acceptable to his brethren."

But then Moses said, "Let him dip his foot in oil." What did that mean?

Oil is a symbol of the Holy Spirit, so if we are to "walk in the Spirit" (Gal. 5:25) then our feet must be anointed by God's Spirit—we must dip our feet in the oil of the Holy Spirit. This is a picture of God blessing Asher so they would follow the Lord.

Anyone used of God knows they must have the Holy Spirit anointing so that the Spirit touches their mouth to speak, or He touches their hands to serve, or He touches their eyes to see spiritual things in the Scriptures that others don't see. As I study the Bible to preach or teach, I ask for the Holy Spirit to anoint my mind and spiritual eyes to see deep truths in Scripture. That's what Moses asked for Asher.

Lord, anoint me to learn Your lesson for my study
Of Moses' writings in the Book of Deuteronomy.

Take away my blindness to spiritual truth,
Teach me by Your Holy Spirit.

Amen.

Then Moses said another thing, "Your sandals shall be iron and brass." Wouldn't iron shoes be uncomfortable and refuse to bend with your feet, as a leather shoe or sandal would bend? Why did Moses bless Asher with "iron and brass shoes"?

One Bible version translates this phrase, "That you may walk on the ground that contains iron and brass." Moses was blessing Asher with material prosperity that he could dig iron from the earth. A farmer without iron or brass would have a difficult time plowing the earth. All his instruments would be crude and antiquated. But a farmer with iron and brass tools would be more prosperous; he could do more and do it faster. Moses was blessing Asher so he would discover the iron under his feet. Moses wanted Asher to live in the Iron Age, not the Stone Age.

The last part of this verse promises, "As your days, so shall your strength be." Moses was promising Asher if he has difficult days, God will give him strength equal to his challenge. If work is difficult, "So shall your strength be." If health fails and sickness rages, "So shall your strength be." If difficulties attack, "So shall your strength be."

Notice the promise was not for one day, but "days." When problems last a long time, "So shall your strength be." Just as God supplied manna to feed them for 40 years, now the promise was to Asher, "So shall your strength be."

God doesn't give strength before we need it, but "as your days" demand. Just as Israel had enough manna to eat whether they gathered plenty or little, so God will measure strength to help us face the need of each day. An Israelite couldn't gather manna to last his family two or three days, so God doesn't give you strength for next week's needs. No! He gives daily strength for daily needs. And when He gives continually, it means, "As your days, so shall your strength be."

My Time to Pray

Lord, teach me to live for today,
  And trust You for strength for today.

I'm not responsible for a day I haven't lived
  And You won't give me strength till I need it.

Lord, I'll fill each day with work and faithfulness,
  Knowing You'll give strength for that day.

I'll not worry about tomorrow till it gets here,
  Teach me to live for You day by day.

Amen.

Deuteronomy 33

THE STORY OF MOSES CHALLENGING ISRAEL TO CONQUER THE PROMISED LAND

Date: 1451 B.C. ~ Place: East of Jordan

"There is no one like the God of Jeshurun, who rides the heavens to help you, and in His excellency on the clouds. The eternal God is your refuge, and underneath are the everlasting arms; He will thrust out the enemy from before you, and will say, 'Destroy!' Then Israel shall dwell in safety, the fountain of Jacob alone, in a land of grain and new wine; his heavens shall also drop dew. Happy are you, O Israel! Who is like you, a people saved by the LORD, the shield of your help and the sword of your majesty! Your enemies shall submit to you, and you shall tread down their high places" (Deuteronomy 33:26-29).

Many Christians think that Moses' challenge to cross Jordan is a picture or type of death. Some sing, "I won't have to cross Jordan alone," meaning Jesus will meet them in death to see them safely to the other side—Heaven.

But Jordan is not a picture of death, and the Promised Land is not a picture of Heaven. When Israel crossed Jordan, they had to fight enemies and conquer them before inhabiting the land of milk and honey. The land was filled with all types of foes—the giants of Anakim, the treacherous Canaanites, and the deceptive Gibeonites. The cities had high walls that needed patience to breech.

No, conquering Canaan is not a picture of going to Heaven; it is a type of the victorious Christian life. Yes, God will supernaturally open up the Jordan River. Yes, God will flatten the walls of Jericho.

But a greedy Achan will steal money, just as our old greedy sinful nature will steal God's blessings and defeat us in our next battle. Just as the victorious Christian life needs daily victories over sin, so Israel faced one battle after another to conquer the land.

Even though God had promised them the land, they had to plan and fight to get it. When God was with them, they won. Just so, we must face temptations and trails daily, and when God is with us, we can be victorious.

Just as they had to defeat one foe at a time, fight one battle at a time, so we must constantly—and daily—fight each battle.

When you say the *victorious* Christian life, you suggest a defeat is possible. You suggest some may run from the battle. You suggest some don't want to fight; they'd rather give in and give up.

Just as "nothing ventured—nothing gained," so no cross, no crown. Those who don't pick up their cross and follow Christ won't hear Him say, "Well done, good and faithful servant..." (Matt. 25:21).

My Time to Pray

Lord, thank You for the challenge of victorious living,
    I'd rather fight on Your side
    Than battle the world alone.

Lord, I pray for continuous victory
    Over the world, the flesh, and the devil.

I will gladly fight the battle of faith,
    Knowing You have promised my victory
    And a home in Heaven with You.

      Amen.

Deuteronomy 34

THE DEATH OF MOSES

Then Moses climbed Mount Nebo. He went up from the plains of
Moab to the top of Mount Pisgah. It is across from Jericho.
From there, the Lord showed him the entire land of Canaan. He
could see from Gilead to Dan. He could see all of the territory
of Naphtali and the land of Ephraim and Manasseh. He could
see all the land of Judah—as far as the Mediterranean Sea. He
could see the southern desert and the whole Valley of Jericho up
to Zoar. (Jericho is called the City of Palm Trees.)

Then the Lord said to Moses, "This is the land which I vowed to
Abraham, to Isaac, and to Jacob. I said to them, 'I will give this
land to your descendants.' I have permitted you only to look at
it, Moses, but you will not cross over there!"

Then Moses, the servant of the Lord died there in the land of Moab,
according to the command of the Lord. The Lord buried Moses
in the land of Moab, in the valley (ravine) which is opposite
Beth-Peor. However, even today no one knows where the grave
of Moses is located.

Moses was 120 years old when he died, yet his eyes were not weak, and
he was still strong. (Moses was in full possession of his faculties
and strength.) The Israelites cried for Moses for 30 days. They
stayed in the plains of Moab until the time of mourning was
over.

Joshua the son of Nun was then filled with wisdom, because Moses had commissioned Joshua. So, the Israelites listened to Joshua, and they obeyed what the Lord had commanded Moses.

In Israel, there has never arisen another prophet like Moses. The Lord knew Moses face to face. The Lord sent Moses to do all the signs and miracles in the land of Egypt. He did them to Pharaoh and his officers, and his entire country. Moses had great power. He did awesome deeds for all the Israelites to see. Amen.

Deuteronomy 34

THE STORY OF THE DEATH OF MOSES

Date: 1451 B.C. ~ Place: Mount Nebo

Wh`*`hat word best describes the death of Moses? *Alone.*

Moses climbed Mount Nebo without Joshua, knowing he would die alone on the top of the mountain. It would be good to die on top of the mountain alone. Death wouldn't come in his tent with loving priests and elders in attendance.

His foot wearily sought safe places to step; Moses arrived on the top of Nebo alone. (I, Elmer, have been to this spot.) From there, Moses could see Mount Hermon over a hundred miles to the northern border of the land promised to Israel, and he could look over the Jordanian Mountains to see the Mediterranean Sea. But most importantly, he could see the rich grass of the eastern plains of Jordan, and with his naked eye, he could see waving golden grain and the forest at the heart of the Promised Land—grapevines, olive bushes, and fertile pastures where cattle grazed. But Moses saw it alone. Momentarily, he would lie down to die—alone.

The Bible tells of the life of its heroes. It tells of their lonely dreams and their ignominious defeats. It tells of their exploits...their sufferings...their expectations and how God intervened for them. But little is said of the death of most, because the Bible is about life, so we can learn to live.

The only death that is fully detailed is that of Christ. His passion and suffering is described minutely and endlessly; the crown of thorns, the scourging, the nails, the spears, all the gory instruments of pain tell of imminent death. Yet Moses' death is described simplistically brief.

If we could gather a wildflower growing over his grave, would it tell how God Himself dug the hole in the ground, or was the body of Moses laid in a cave-tomb? Did God recite the words of Job: "Though worms shall destroy this body, yet in my flesh will I see God" (Job 19:26, *expanded*)? Did God offer a prayer as He committed Moses' body to the ground?

As Moses lays down in death on top of Nebo, we see the great lesson of God's forgiveness and sin's consequences. In an outburst of temper at the waters of Meribah and in impetuous rebellion to God's command to "speak to the rock," Moses, in public mutiny before the multitude, smote the rock. It was then Moses felt the hurricane of God's wrath against sin, "You shall not enter the Promised Land."

God forgave Moses, but the consequences remained. He didn't enter the Promised Land. The thief on the cross was pardoned, but he still felt the sting of death. The Lord forgave David's sin with Bathsheba, but his child died. So we should never think lightly of iniquity, nor think that a casual sin doesn't have long-term loss and sorrow. Haven't we all lost the benefit that we could have enjoyed—but sin? One act of rebellious pride laid Moses in a grave outside the land of milk and honey. Even though Moses was called "friend" by God, even though Moses was the law giver, even though Moses saved the entire nation, look what sin did for him. He died alone outside the land.

There's an old tale that the angels sought to be the ones who transported Moses in death into the presence of God. Which angel would God choose?

Since angels escort a dead saint into God's presence, the angel who had been his instructor on Mount Sinai asked for the privilege to instruct Moses in the joys of eternal life. But he was not chosen.

The angel that stood between Israel and the charging Egyptian army on the other side of the Red Sea (see Exod. 14:19) came to ask permission to protect Moses in death. He was not chosen.

The angel who had led Israel through the wilderness (see Num. 20:16) asked if he might lead Moses into the promise of Heaven itself. But he was not chosen.

Then the angel of death, the one who visited the homes of the Egyptians to take the firstborn, was ready to take the life of Moses. But he was stopped.

God Himself would do this job. The Bible explains, "So Moses the servant of the Lord died there in the land of Moab, according to the word of the Lord. And He [God] buried him in a valley in the land of Moab, opposite Beth Peor; but no one knows his grave to this day" (Deut. 34:5-6).

The Almighty would not delegate the internment to angels. He would not let Moses' body rot out in the open under the siege of the elements and ever-present bacteria. Animals would not scavenge his body. No. No inferior hand or force would touch this aged body—this decayed tabernacle—God Himself buried His servant and friend.

Then to add divine insult to those who went looking for Moses' remains, "no one knows his grave to this day" (Deut. 34:6). Then it was as if God wrote an epitaph over his grave, "Moses was one hundred and twenty years old when he died. His eyes were not dim nor his natural vigor diminished" (Deut. 34:7).

While some think Moses wrote the 34th chapter prophetically, other scholars think Joshua wrote it after Moses died. Joshua probably wrote it because he says no one knows the location of Moses' grave "to this day." This is a familiar phrase used by Joshua throughout his book (see Josh. 5:9; 6:25; 7:26; 9:27; 10:27; 14:14; 15:63; 22:3; 23:8).

EPILOGUE

My Time to Pray

*Lord, Moses wrote down Your words and actions to guide
    Your people,*

Of the future for their life and service to You.

If Moses had not written these things down,

*We wouldn't know about spiritual warfare and victory
    today*

As Israel battled the force of evil in its day.

*You provided an accurate record of all that hap-
    pened*

Between Egypt and the Promised Land.

*You included a record when Your people sinned against
    You, and refused*

To obey Your commandments and follow Your direction.

*If You had not told the story of their murmuring
    and rebellion,*

I might think it strange when I have yearnings to doubt or

Disobey Your commands.

My heart might get me so discouraged that I would give up,

Just as Your people in the wilderness gave up and disobeyed You.

Lord, when I read of their doubts and murmurings,
It makes me realize I am not unique.

These records challenge me to faithfulness and victory.
Just as You

Led your people to victory in the wilderness,

You can lead me to victory in the wilderness where I live.

Lord, this book challenges me to live constantly for You,

I promise to follow You explicitly.

Amen.

ABOUT THE AUTHOR

DR. ELMER TOWNS is an author of popular and scholarly works, a seminar lecturer, and dedicated worker in Sunday school. He has written over 125 books, including several best sellers. He won the coveted Gold Medallion Book Award for *The Names of the Holy Spirit*.

Dr. Elmer Towns also cofounded Liberty University with Jerry Falwell in 1971 and now serves as Dean of the B.R. Lakin School of Religion and as professor of Theology and New Testament.

Liberty University is the fastest growing Christian university in America. Located in Lynchburg, Virginia, Liberty University is a private, coeducational, undergraduate and graduate institution offering 38 undergraduate and 15 graduate programs serving over 39,000 resident and external students (11,300 on campus). Individuals from all 50 states and more than 70 nations comprise the diverse student body. While the faculty and students vary greatly, the common denominator and driving force of Liberty University since its conception is love for Jesus Christ and the desire to make Him known to the entire world.

For more information about Liberty University, contact:

Liberty University
1971 University Boulevard
Lynchburg, VA 24502
Telephone: 434-582-2000
Website: www.Liberty.edu